The Guardian Third World Review

THE GUARDIAN
THIRD WORLD
REVIEW

Voices from the South

Editors
Victoria Brittain
and
Michael Simmons

HODDER AND STOUGHTON
LONDON SYDNEY AUCKLAND TORONTO

British Library Cataloguing in Publication Data

The Guardian Third World review: voices
   from the South.
   1. Developing countries
   I. Brittain, Victoria   II. Simmons, Michael
   III. The Guardian
   909'.097240828   HC59.7

ISBN 0 340 40134 6

First published 1987

Photoset by Rowland Phototypesetting Ltd,
Bury St Edmunds, Suffolk.

Printed in Great Britain
for Hodder and Stoughton Educational
a division of Hodder and Stoughton Ltd, Mill Road,
Dunton Green, Sevenoaks, Kent by Richard Clay Ltd,
Bungay, Suffolk.

Contents

2   ASIA

3   LATIN AMERICA AND THE CARIBBEAN

All the articles in this publication should be considered in the context of the time in which they were written. In a number of cases the circumstances as well as some of the salient facts may have changed. But that immediacy is the strength as well as the weakness of the daily newspaper . . .

Acknowledgments

Our special thanks to Peter Preston, Editor of *The Guardian*, and to Ian Wright, for the autonomy and independence we enjoy in editing these pages—the sort of independence which is one of the real pleasures of working for a newspaper like ours. Thanks, too, to Altaf Gauhar who cooperated so closely when the original idea was being nursed into life.

The editors and publishers would also like to thank the following for permission to reproduce illustrations in this book: John Pridmore (page 10); Quartet Books (page 21); Robin Laurance (page 24); E. Hamilton-West (pages 32, 55 and 251); Werner Gartung (page 43); UN/John Isaac (page 65); Sophie Baker (pages 72 and 241); USED/Guardian (page 111); George Caudley (page 158); Universal Pictorial Press and Agency Ltd (page 162); UPI (pages 179 and 215); Martin Argles (pages 169 and 198); Frank Martin (page 211); Press Association (page 215); Philip Wolmuth (page 178).

Cover photograph by Tom Learmonth.

Foreword

On 27 November, 1947, the Caracas newspaper, *El Nacional*, carried an article by the Chilean poet, Pablo Neruda, which led the President of Chile to file a petition before the Supreme Court requesting his impeachment. Neruda's article, 'The Crisis of Democracy in Chile is a Dramatic Warning for our Continent', is the finest example of what *Third World Review* tries to do—from another continent, in another language, in another era.

Neruda opened his article with these words: 'I want to inform all my friends on our continent of the disastrous events which have taken place in Chile. I am aware that a large number of persons will be confused and surprised, since the North American news monopolies will no doubt (in this matter as in others) have produced the same result as everywhere else: to falsify truth and distort reality.'

A poet like Neruda can be thirty years ahead of other people's perceptions, but by the mid-1970s a dissatisfaction with the general treatment of Third World reality in First World newspapers was a growing phenomenon, not only among those written about, but also by those doing the writing or editing.

When the *Third World Review* started in March 1978, it was unique and experimental. Newspapers in Britain and elsewhere devoted almost no space to Third World issues and Third World writers, as a consequence, had almost no platform. Today consciousness of Third World issues is at an all-time high and Third World writers – as our daily correspondence shows – have a platform. Imitators of the Review, and direct repercussions from it, are many and varied. The experiment has more than paid off.

In 1978, the so-called North/South dialogue was in its infancy, Herr Willy Brandt had not yet 'reported', and awareness of such clamant problems as Third World debt, the (already) long-standing Sahelian famine, the predatory nature of the multinationals, the ruthless character of certain hitherto 'acceptable' regimes – for instance – was confined to specialists. In our columns discussion of precisely such problems, as well as the many issues that spring from them, has become routine – and newsworthy. Governments as well as other newspapers have reacted to what has appeared in our pages.

The experiment by its very nature was in some senses a tentative affair to begin with. It was an editorial decision that it should run for an agreed trial period and, it has to be admitted, the pages' contents were more often well-meaning rather than stimulating, let alone controversial. Readership response, however, was such that the tentativeness was soon thrown out of the window and for those editing the pages, it very quickly became clear that reporting the Third World aroused strong feelings, deep convictions—and controversy.

Inevitably, we are constantly plied by the well-meaning, whether in government, the universities or even in the occasional altruistic local community, to carry bland articles. Some, despite the limited amount of available space, we are able to publish. But the pages have now gone beyond that. We like to think a lot more people have become well-meaning, in the best sense of the word, as a result of reading our pages.

The Third World – a term about which we feel very ambivalent – has become for many the *first* world, too important in many cases to be left to national or international policy-makers and far too important for the journalism of casual visitors giving the cursory once-over. It is an area whose myriad specialists are those who live there, usually unheard outside.

The extracts in this book are heavily slanted towards Africa. Over the last two or three years the gathering crisis on that continent has been more fully exposed and explored than in the previous decade or more. The distinguished African contributors to the *Review*, such as Ngugi, Soyinka, Museveni, Mamdani and Khalif tell the truths about their own countries with the unmistakable clarity which Neruda's voice carried back in Chile in the 1940s. Like him, all of them have paid high prices for refusing the cosy role of state intellectuals.

The Argentinian novelist Ernesto Sabato, who led the Argentine National Commission of Disappeared People after the military dictatorship from 1976–83, wrote in his introduction to its horrifying report: 'Only democracy can save a people from horror on this scale; only democracy can keep and safeguard the sacred essential rights of man.' Newspapers are an essential component of that democracy and much of the writing that has appeared in *Third World Review* has contributed to the possibility of more debate within and about Third World societies.

The need for a New Information Order is widely acknowledged even though Unesco's attempt to start putting one into practice fell foul of a US Administration passing into history

as the most ideological ever. In a modest way the editors of
Third World Review have been allowed, and in fact encouraged,
to create a weekly page of South/North dialogue led from the
South.

Victoria Brittain
Michael Simmons
1987

1 AFRICA

The settlers under the skin

Ngugi wa Thiong'o   *Published 19 November 1982*

In 1977 the editors and publishers of *The Kenya Historical Review* released a special issue on the Mau Mau movement. The cover is a picture of British forces and their African collaborators hunting down Mau Mau freedom fighters in the forests of Nyandarwa and Mount Kenya. Inset in the bottom right corner of the cover is a tiny frame of a pathetic face of a dead Mau Mau guerrilla made even more pathetic by the sickly yellowish background against the luxurious green of the British Forces. The editors and the publishers were Kenyan. But the issue in the choice of contributions and cover illustration, and in the arrangement of the content was clearly a scholarly attempt at the ideological burial of Mau Mau as a credible anti-imperialist nationalist movement, a kind of intellectual rationale to cut it out of the central stream of more than eighty years of Kenya's history of struggle.

But squeezed somewhere in the middle of the special issue was a well argued contribution by a brilliant committed scholar, Maina-wa-Kinyatti, in which he took issue with the entire anti-Mau Mau intellectual establishment and described 'Mau Mau as the peak of African nationalism in Kenya.'

In 1980, Maina-wa-Kinyatti followed up that call for committed scholarship by editing and publishing Mau Mau songs under the title: *Thunder From The Mountains – Mau Mau Patriotic Songs.* Kinyatti spent many days and nights in the homes of former Mau Mau guerrillas, peasants and workers, recording their voices as they sang, and he clearly wanted Kenyans to share with him the elation he himself had felt when listening to the guerrilla lyrics.

But his main objective is clearly to fight against the reactionary interpretation of Mau Mau in historical scholarship. Put concretely, the question is this: if you deny Mau Mau its national character, if you, by an intellectual magic wand, were to wave it away from the central stream of Kenya's history of struggle, to whom have you left the stage?

The struggle on the interpretation of Kenya's history was clearly more than an academic debate: it was an intellectual reflection of the warring, antagonistic positions in Kenyan society since 20 October, 1952, when Kenyatta and Kau leaders were led to prisons and detention camps and Kimathi led the youth into the forests and mountains to wage an armed struggle for independence from the British, the first of its kind against any colonial power in Africa. The opposed positions on the place of Mau Mau history reflect the direction Kenyan society had taken in the Fifties and Sixties, and now in the Seventies and Eighties.

With the publication of *Thunder from the Mountains* two years ago Maina-wa-Kinyatti had clearly angered more than just the academic and intellectual establishment. He had frightened the men at the top whose views the academic and intellectual establishment merely reflect. They who in the Fifties had feared the possible consequences of the British colonialists leaving the country, had found a new more powerful neo-colonial master in the United States of America. Were they perhaps disturbed by the vision of a Mau Mau coming back even though only in books and lecture halls?

At any rate, on 2 June, 1982, Maina-wa-Kinyatti was arrested. The police raided his home in his absence. The result of four-and-a-half months of police custody was that he had to be hospitalised in chains for an eye operation. He was then formally tried for being in possession of a 'seditious' publication: Moi's *Divisive Tactics Exposed*.

Among the documents produced in court as evidence of sedition and subversion was the last chapter of his almost completed monumental history of Kenya: *The Current History of Kenya 1979–80*. The man who had been digging up the truth about Kenyan people's struggles had to go. History had to be jailed.

The ruling authorities were trying to stage an impossible drama; they were putting Kenyan history on trial for being subversive of the existing order. That order is one of repression, and exploitation of Kenyans by neo-colonial forces headed by the USA and aided by colonial homeguards and empire loyalists. They would like to bury that history and to silence for ever those who wanted to unveil it for Kenya and the world.

So on 18 October, 1982, two days before the 30th anniversary of Mau Mau Freedom Fighters' Day, Maina-wa-Kinyatti was himself jailed for six years.

The drama was farcical, though obviously punitive and vengeful in its intention. Beneath the farce is a cruel historical irony. This: those who are presiding over Kenyan affairs –

driving Kenyan patriots into prisons and detention – are the same people who in the Fifties were actively opposing the Mau Mau struggle for independence.

I need go no further than Daniel Arap Moi (Kanu President and Head of State); Charles Njonjo (Minister for Constitutional Affairs, and the man who steered Kenya into a Kanu one-party state); and Jeremiah Kiereini, Chief Secretary and the executive head of the entire administration.

At the height of the British colonial terror campaign against Mau Mau freedom fighters and the Kenyan people, 1954–1955, Daniel Toroitich Arap Moi was a colonial government appointee in the then settler-run Kenya Legislative Council. The Colonial administration had hand-picked him for the job. Later Moi, the good African, became a leader of the KADU party, a Muzorewa type of black front for settler interests, whose main plank was *majimboism*, thus weakening an independent Kenya by splitting it into regional fiefdoms.

Charles Mugane Njonjo has a parallel record in colonial service. From 1954–60 he was an Assistant Registrar-General in the Registrar-General's department. He rose to Crown Counsel, Senior Crown Counsel and to Deputy Public Prosecutor at the time of Independence. Thus in 1955 and five years after, he was administering the State of Emergency laws which saw thousands of Kenyans hounded into prisons and detention camps.

Jeremiah Kiereini who has been signing some of the recent detention orders, was in the colonial rehabilitation programme.

Both Moi and Njonjo have at various times praised the last colonial governor, Malcolm MacDonald, for his contribution to bringing independence to Kenya. These survivors from the colonial service are of course only representatives of a social stratum, the comprador bourgeois ruling class. Absurd as it might seem or sound, this class perceives its role as effectively that of colonial restoration with themselves as both the representatives of the West and the modern landlords or white settlers in black skins.

Let me illustrate: The arrest of Maina-wa-Kinyatti on 2 June, 1982, was preceded and followed by intensified cultural repression with plays being stopped and an open air theatre, built by peasants and workers at Kamiriithu, razed to the ground.

The plays stopped were either those depicting the historical emergence of neo-colonies as in Joe de Graft's *Muntu*; those exposing the brutality of colonial labour conditions as in *Maitu Njugira (Mother Sing For Me)*; and those glorifying the resistance to colonialism as in Al Amin Mazrui's *Kilio Cha Haki (The Cry For Justice)*. It is quite telling that Al Amin

Mazrui was himself detained without trial exactly two weeks after his play *Kilio Cha Haki* was performed at the University.

In the same period, and in contrast to this censorship of any cultural expression that exposed colonialism, was the state patronage of Western shows and pro-colonial culture. Thus for instance almost the entire establishment (ministers, civil servants, top businessmen) headed by Charles Njonjo as the guest of honour, trooped to the Kenya National Theatre to see a ballet version of *Alice in Wonderland*. Even more telling was the government purchase of the television version of Elspeth Huxley's glorification of colonialism, *The Flame Trees of Thika*, which they gave prime time on national television in April and May. Obviously the top men in authority identify, not with the menial servitude of the Kenyan worker or his resistance to such servitude, but with the heroic deeds of the colonial adventurers among Kenyan natives smitten dumb and wide-eyed in servile gratitude for charitable deeds and kindly light amidst the encircling gloom.

Lead kindly light; it is not an accident that the missionary is held in great esteem as the educational mentor of this class. Powerful men in today's Kenya virtually grovel at the feet of the missionary remnants as if still seeking approval and praise. Well they might show gratitude: like their colonial counterparts they have learnt the value of religion in its search for love, peace, unity and non-violence between the oppressor and the oppressed. Thus church building and church going are now national pastimes.

The leisure time of many of this class, when they are not at church, is divided between collecting money from poor peasants at Harambee weekend extravaganzas; golfing and playing a little squash and tennis; relaxing in sauna baths and massage parlours; gracing shaggy dog and flower shows; visiting casinos for a little gambling and ogling at dancing nudes from Las Vegas and Stockholm.

A caricature? Yes, but it accurately describes the infantile imitative mentality, the crass world outlook which like borrowed robes, sits uneasily on them, and the total lack of any originality in the Kenyan neo-colonial ruling class. Their vision of society be it economic, political or cultural is derived from the only experience they know and care to know – the colonial, economic, political and cultural order. Their image of authority, of progress, of prosperity, of managing the affairs of the nation is derived from colonialism.

Hence in industry and finance they see themselves as no more than an attachement of the Western bourgeoisie, and their mission, to quote Fanon, being 'the transmission line' between the nation and imperialism. They are happy, content really, to be only the agents for international tractors, motor vehicles, pharmaceuticals, textiles, boots, tinned foods and fruits, videos, television sets, bottled water, every little thing manufactured abroad.

In agriculture, it has been the same story. After independence, there was the rush to Africanise the inequalities of the colonial era. The state bought out the settlers. Many of the huge farms were then handed over to a few private hands. A few European settlers and multinationals still own huge coffee, fruit, and sugar plantations. Land hunger, the very basis of the Mau Mau struggle, haunts the vast majority of Kenyans. The situation was not compensated for by increased productivity. On the contrary! For unlike their settler white counterparts who farmed full-time and reinvested in 'their' lands, the new owners did so on the telephone for they had full-time jobs as government ministers, MPs, civil servants, or managers of other businesses.

The regime then falls back on the favourite time-worn solution: begging. In 1979–80 we Kenyans had the humiliating spectacle of the leader accompanied by nearly all his cabinet flying from one Western capital to another begging for food. Begging and its corollary, charity, have become the central themes in an elaborate system of dependency. On this occasion the USA bailed out the regime with tons of yellow maize.

In return the regime immediately gave America military bases on Kenyan soil, our soil, without any debate or any form of consultation with parliament or with the seventeen million Kenyans whose lives would now be part of American war games.

The failure to break new grounds, the whole philosophy of economic and political *Nyaoism* has led to mass poverty and the alienation of the regime from the people, and it is this increased alienation which more immediately explains the turn events are taking. Over the years, the regime has responded to this alienation by increasingly becoming distrustful of the people.

If you have no faith in the people, then you cannot trust them with democracy, can you? They will spoil the game. You cannot allow them to organise anything on their own: what might they not whisper together? For years opposition has been hounded to jail and detentions, or harassed into uneasy silence. The party over the years became a bureaucratic skeleton manipulable by one, two or three people. In the end, this skeleton legalised itself into the only Party. Even welfare-type organisations like Gema, Luo Union, Akamba People's Union, Mijikando Union, were outlawed by a presidential decree. Strikes are banned. And workers' organisations, even such bodies as the University

Staff Union, Kenyan Civil Servants Union, are banned, again through a presidential decree. Any organisation such as drama societies that might bring ordinary people together are banned. In Kenya it is illegal for more than five people to meet without a police licence.

You rule by fear and you become ruled by fear. Both the Kenyatta and the Moi regimes were actually afraid of their own army and police force. They relied instead on secret military and defence pacts with foreign powers. Kenyatta started it in 1964 with a military pact with Britain which allowed a British military presence in Kenya. Moi completed it, on a grand scale, by giving military bases to the US, and even having US pilots to fly Kenyan Air Force planes.

Over the years, the comprador bourgeoisie in Kenya have gradually come to look at the country and its people through the eyes of an outsider almost as if they had come to see themselves as foreigners. How else explain the extreme distrust of any genuine Kenyan initiative?

The result is that what is happening in Kenya today, October, 1982, is almost a word for word, act for act, character for character, replay of the events of October, 1952, when the British declared a State of Emergency, suspended any pretence of democracy and the rule of law, mounted cultural repression on a mass scale, killed thousands of Kenyans, and hounded others to detention, prison, or exile. A colonial restoration in other words.

There is a difference, of a kind, I suppose. The theatre then was colonial, the local director was the British settler regime acting on behalf of the real masters in London. Today the theatre is neo-colonial, the local director is the Kenya comprador bourgeois regime acting on behalf of the real masters in London and Washington. But there are unbroken links, economic, political, cultural, and even character, between the colonial and the neo-colonial theatre and these are concretely illustrated in the arrest, trial and gaoling of Maina-wa-Kinyatti and the detention without trial of all the other patriots.

But even more dramatic symbolism of this continuity is provided by the regime's systematic attempt at the humiliation of Oginga Odinga. He was one of the founders of Kanu when it was still a nationalist party in 1960. Now, for telling the world that Mau Mau was a glorious struggle Odinga was excluded from power by the British and deprived of his passport several times. Today those who were opposing Kanu then are denying him any participation in the political life of Kenya by excluding him from the party he founded. Again he has been deprived of his passport and now he is even restricted to the town of Kisumu.

Maina-wa-Kinyatti was only 10 years old when the British

declared a State of Emergency all over Kenya on 20 October, 1952, arrested the Kau and Mau Mau leadership, and unleashed a reign of terror which was to last for ten years. Kinyatti's father and elder brother, like thousands of other Kenyans, were imprisoned. He himself, though only a boy, was forced to go into hiding.

He returned to Kenya from studies in America in 1973 and joined the history department, Kenyatta University College, where his lectures and seminars started attracting a wide circle of students because in him they saw a new, fresh interpretation of history, an approach that made sense of their past and did not alienate them from Kenya. Through his eyes they were able to look at Kenya, Africa, and the Third World as men and women of that environment and not outsiders or foreigners. Of course he asked awkward questions: the masses were the makers of history, but how come they always lost out? What were the historical roots of the post-independence betrayal of the people? It was these questions and the fact that he put Kenya first and did not steal or buy farms or run extra businesses that have led to six years in prison.

The fact that he put Kenya first is what links him with the others arrested after him and detained without trial. Willy Muntunga, for instance, was a brilliant law lecturer in the faculty of law at Nairobi University. As Secretary-General of the University Staff Union (banned by Moi in 1980) he had worked tirelessly to make it into a strong organisation. But perhaps his greatest crime was giving free legal advice to poor people. This was unheard of in Kenya: a lawyer giving his services free?

Kamoji Wachira, lecturer in geography, has made the only comprehensive study of Kenyan indigenous trees. He is a respected ecological consultant. What? Study Kenyan trees? Suspiciously entering forests and bushes and coming out with mere twigs and seeds? Detain this man!

Al Amin Mazrui is a brilliant linguist and writes plays in Kiswahili, about the struggle of ordinary Kenyans. He is asthmatic, has a weak heart, but works incessantly. In a society where working hard for your daily bread is despised – that's for peasants and workers! – an educated person who taxes his health draws suspicions. It is worse when such a person is taxing his health, not to amass some ill-gotten wealth, but to write in praise of the struggle of Mau Mau patriots or of peasants and workers. Why should he write a play called *The Cry for Justice* and in the language of the people?

The two politicians, George Anyona and Koigi wa-Wamwere, both detained by Kenyatta and now by Moi, were conspicuous not only as consistent critics of corruption who never amassed wealth but also for their hard work and attention to detail. As for Khaminwa, lawyer and advocate of the high court, he had the audacity to be faithful to his professional ethic and to take up the cases of even those at loggerheads with the President – Anyona and Odinga for instance.

The fact is that at the University of Nairobi and Kenyatta College there had, over the years, developed a new breed of young scholars – bright, confident, original, honest – whose simple life-style was a stunning contrast to the dominant imported culture of borrowed plumes.

In the mentality of the Kenyan ruling class, to put Kenya first; to love Kenya; to have faith in the capacity of Kenyan people to change their lives; to insist that people are the subjects and not just the passive objects of development; to insist on certain minimum professional ethics and democratic principles; to reveal that ordinary peasants and workers struggled for liberation; to sing praises to the Mau Mau movement; to write positively about the anti-imperialist heroes of Kenya history, Katilili, Koitalel, Waiyaki, Nyanjiru, Kimathi, etc; to reject foreign bases; to reject a society based on corruption; to reject the rule of fear; to oppose imperialism and its local Kenyan allies, is *a crime*. Above all to reject the philosophy of merely following in Moi's footsteps is treason.

For such crimes, many Kenyans are now incarcerated in the very prisons and detention camps that used to hold Mau Mau freedom fighters. Maina-wa-Kinyatti for instance was in the very prison cell where his father and his elder brother were held by the British.

What then is the significance of 20 October, 1952, in Kenya today? The extreme and well organised repressive measures of the British imposed State of Emergency called forth in Kenyan people organised resistance on a scale that later forced British colonialism to concede independence. Organised repressive terror was met by organised revolutionary resistance! That's the lesson of Kenyan history.

After Maina-wa-Kinyatti was sentenced to six years in prison, the crowd of peasants and workers, some of whom had come from more than fifty miles away, burst into defiant liberation songs. The police charged at them. But they went on singing their defiance. The lesson of that gesture, two days before 20 October, the thirtieth anniversary of the Mau Mau armed struggle, was not lost on Kenyans.

This new mood in Kenya has been exemplified by the astonishing composure of the dozens of young students who, without lawyers, in court on sedition charges which bring ten years in jail, bravely call for power to the people as they are led away in chains.

That for me is the revolutionary significance of October, 1952, in Kenya today: repression by the powerful met by indomitable resistance from those they thought powerless. And, as Mau Mau was a precursor of liberation struggles against colonialism across the world from Asia to Africa, so is today's struggle in Kenya against US neo-colonialism part of a battle that straddles the Third World.

This speech was delivered in London on the thirtieth anniversary of the start of the Mau Mau struggle for independence from the British.

Legacy of a murdered luminary

Basil Davidson   *Published 18 February 1983*

The archipelago of Cape Verde is not, at any rate as yet, a country widely known or even heard of. South of the Canaries, it consists of 10 volcanic islands off the mid-Atlantic coast of western Africa; its Republic came into being in 1975, when its 320,000 people seized independence from Portugal.

Success has come against the odds. Independence coincided with a 10-year drought, which seemed to doom the islands to irreversible poverty.

Yet Cape Verde today is an optimistic country and at peace with itself. Gloom and doom make no part of the daily scene.

The reasons are that the Cape Verdians have managed to produce a leadership of extraordinary talent and integrity, and, in 1975, the foundations of a political system that has proved increasingly efficient.

Democracy begins 'at the base' with forms of local autonomy and decision-making launched even in the most remote of the islands. These forms of 'public participation' are the sinews of a society which has at last begun to take destiny into its own hands, and has already found the experience a good one.

All this is the legacy, in particular, of one of the most remark-able political thinkers and constructive men of action that any part of the Third World has produced for many decades. This was Amilcar Cabral, born of Cape Verdian parents in 1924 at Bafata on the neighbouring mainland of Guinea-Bissau.

Cabral was founder and leader of a long campaign and eventually a long war for independence from Portugal that began in Guinea-Bissau in 1963 and ended in complete success on the mainland in 1974, and in the archipelago in 1975.

Tragically, he was murdered by agents of the then Portuguese dictatorship in January, 1973.

By that time Cabral had won a worldwide fame and admiration among all those who thought that dictatorship was deplorable and colonialism no different, and therefore no better. Manifestly much more than a bout of 'radical chic' or a passing fashion in the 'politics of contestation' this admiration for Cabral has more than survived the 10 years since his death.

Amilcar Cabral: worldwide admiration

Cape Verde's capital, Praia, has just produced a striking demonstration of the staunchness and extension of Cabral's reputation and influence. In a characteristically modest but well designed place of assembly, built two years ago, a gathering of some 50 political scientists, writers, commentators, and assorted specialists of considerable distinction met recently to discuss Cabral's importance for the world as well as for Africa, and marked with homage the tenth anniversary of his death.

Respected historians from New York and California sat alongside others from the Soviet Union; while joining these 'extremes', as it were, a broad range of academic talent added one political opinion or another from about 30 European, Asian, and African countries.

Invited by surviving comrades of Cabral, notably President Aristides Periera and Prime Minister Pedro Pires, the aim was to review Cabral's contributions to the theory and practice of anti-colonial and post-colonial transformation. They centred round two aspects of Cabral's effectiveness that proved decisive in his life and work, and have steered the Cape Verdians since his death.

These characteristics were an intense capacity for experiencing and analysing situations within their own reality, and, secondly, a practice of reacting to them with an always stubborn independence of mind and political posture.

Inheriting these characteristics, the Cape Verde Republic offers clear evidence of the influence of both. For the curious and unusual fact is that although the country is extremely weak in its economy, and greatly dependent on outside aid, its Government has achieved a status of unconditional political independence that appears to be accepted and respected by all outside powers.

There was much discussion on the lineage of Cabral's methods of analysis and guides to action. Some saw him in the direct ideological descendance of Marx and Lenin; others, rather more in number, found this too restrictive, and enlarged on the originality of his approaches to reality, as well as of the systemic ideas developed under his leadership.

What everyone seemed to agree upon was the centrality of Cabral's influence over a wide range of movements and peoples. Guests from Mozambique and Angola spoke of the trend of democratic transformation associated with 'public participation' in their own countries.

A delegate from the African National Congress of South Africa dwelt on the value of Cabral's thinking for the development of democratic processes in an eventually apartheid-free South Africa. A spokesman for the anti-Mobutu opposition of Zaire argued that the defeated Zaire rebellions of 1964 would have had a very different outcome if their leaders had possessed Cabral's understanding and ideas.

In 1960, I met Cabral during his initial visit to Britain, when he was living under a pseudonym and found almost no listeners anywhere. Eleven years later, he drew ardent audiences of many thousands at meetings held in London, Manchester, and elsewhere. His name had become a banner of hope and sanity wherever the issues of constructive social change were matters of serious discussion. Last month's gathering in Praia showed the same banner still bravely at its masthead.

A very model of bourgeois decorum

Richard Gott visits the Patrice Lumumba University   *Published 15 April 1983*

'Do we look like guerrillas?' said the pin-striped Ugandan student across the table. He was certainly a man who seemed, after six years studying international law at the Patrice Lumumba People's Friendship University in the suburbs of Moscow, to be in no great hurry to return to Kampala. Indeed he looked like someone who was hoping to get a highly paid job with some international organisation that would keep him out of Africa for a very long time.

We were sitting in the council chamber of the Soviet Union's Third World university discussing, with a group of students, their problems and prospects. And one of the things that really seems to irritate both students and staff is the apparently widespread Western belief that the university is a centre of armed subversion. It is a rumour about as accurate as the one that you sometimes still hear in distant parts of the world that the London School of Economics is a hotbed of Harold Laski socialism.

For the Patrice Lumumba is in fact the very model of bourgeois decorum and achievement. A hive of revolutionary activity it is not. Indeed one can imagine some Third World firebrand, having heard erroneously that the university offers course in rifle training, bomb fabrication, and urban guerrilla tactics, being somewhat surprised to find himself following academic lectures on economics and law, history and philology, all conducted in Russian.

Doubtless there are places in the Soviet Union where you can be taught to be a guerrilla, but this is not one of them. Indeed, if you enrolled today, the chances are that your country's insurrectionary movement would have been victorious or crushed by the time you emerged clutching your degree, six or seven years later, from the university's august portals.

The rector for the past dozen years has been Professor Vladimir Stanis. He is also a professor of political economy, and before he became rector he was a deputy minister of higher education. He is a senior member of the Soviet power elite. He has receding grey hair, blue-grey eyes, wears a three-piece blue suit with an embroidered shirt and, like many academics, he likes to use his spectacles for dramatic effect.

He would be an unremarked participant in any gathering of the international development jet set, and indeed that is where he is often to be found. He is also extremely proud of his university and, as far as one can gather, he has every reason to be. Its new buildings, all concrete and glass, give it a flavour of Sussex in the snow.

The People's Friendship University was founded in the Khrushchev heyday of expansionism in the early 1960s, when the Americans and the Russians were busy preparing themselves to leap into the vacuum left by the retreating West European empires in Africa and Asia, and when the Cuban revolution had opened up the possibility of imminent and radical change in Latin America.

The new university, founded to supply higher education to Third World students, was started in 1960 and given the name of Patrice Lumumba, the murdered Congolese leader. His portrait still stares down from the entrance hall, joined now by half a dozen other Third World martyrs from three continents – Guevara and Allende, Mondlane and Cabral, Jumblatt, Taraki and Ngouabi.

At the time its inauguration caused an immense shock in the West. What could Third World students hope to learn from the Russians? Surely London, Paris and Rome were the right places to go? Surely the new colleges devoted to Afro-Asian studies that were burgeoning within the many universities of the United States would be more appropriate? And for years, when it wasn't being attacked for being a guerrilla training camp, the Patrice Lumumba was being denigrated – as a third rate institution only suitable for second rate people.

Professor Stanis takes much comfort from the fact that these slanders have now been mostly laid to rest, and the university has had a clean bill of health from such major Western institutions as the BBC and the Washington Post. But I suggested to him that a more serious slander was now current, namely that Third World students went to American universities and turned into socialists, while those that went to the People's Friendship University often turned into capitalists.

He was not amused, though he permitted himself a wry smile to indicate that he had heard the suggestion before. We teach patriotism, he said without blinking, and embarked on an impassioned speech.

'This university,' he said, 'not only teaches but elevates its students. It teaches them to be patriotic about their own countries. Western universities fail to promote patriotism because capitalism is cosmopolitan. It has no motherland. It breaks down all frontiers. Those Western universities foster the brain drain. The metropolitan states exploit the developing countries, and Third World students, when they study abroad, often do not go home.'

For Professor Stanis this is the worst crime in the book. 'We consider it the greatest evil of our work if a graduate of the People's Friendship University does not go back home. They must learn to appreciate that money is not the most important thing. They must work in their own country. That is the only way to make progress. Patriotism is a very important feature of our work.'

Professor Stanis believes that 70 or 80 per cent of the graduates of his university do in fact maintain links with the countries from which they have come. 'We are proud of the fact,' he emphasises, 'that our graduates return to work successfully in developing countries.'

Certainly the three students we talked to planned to go back, though the Ugandan, who had a Russian wife, was hoping for a job as a diplomat. An Ecuadorean lawyer from Guayaquil was expecting to return to a university or a government ministry, while a cheerful Indian with a Polish girlfriend (who had been studying Russian) was planning to go back to India as a translator.

The expansion of Russia's capacity to provide training for Third World students has been considerable. In 1957 there were only 134 Third World students studying at institutions of higher education in the Soviet Union. Twenty years later there were 30,000.

Nowadays, at the Patrice Lumumba itself, there are about 8,000, and about 2,000 staff. The students come from 107 different countries, and for every two foreigners there is one Russian student. All students are taught in Russian, and the foreigners spend their first year doing an intensive Russian course.

The university itself has six faculties: physics and mathematics; economics and law; history and language; engineering; agriculture; and medicine. The students, says Professor Stanis, do have some difficulty in adapting when they first arrive. The language is foreign, the climate cold. And there are even problems of discipline.

'The Latin American students, for example, used to fight the university administration in their own countries. Here they have to learn to cooperate.' An elaborate system of students' councils, as elsewhere in the world, seems to have improved things.

I tried to discover whether Professor Stanis felt that there was anything in the Soviet Union's own special development experience that was of peculiar relevance to the needs of developing countries. He was horrified that anyone might dare to

suggest that the Soviet Union itself exhibited certain characteristics of Third World countries.

'It is not suitable to talk of there being under-developed
regions in the USSR,' he said, 'but it is important for developing
countries to keep in mind the example of our Asian republics
– Kazakhstan for example – where socialism has been built
without passing through a capitalist phase.' When the students
go there on visits, 'they are really surprised by what they see
there. The level of these republics is very high.'

Professor Stanis pointed out that although he personally
wanted everyone to become a communist, and that education
at the Patrice Lumumba (as in the rest of the USSR) was based
on Marxism–Leninism, there were nevertheless students with
different ideological attitudes.

'There are mullahs and Buddhists studying here,' he explained. 'They are believers, religious students. We don't make
fun of them. We treat them with patience and respect. We
recognise that a Buddhist monk cannot be a communist.'

As in so many institutions in the Soviet Union, even those
of a relatively recent creation, it is difficult to get those in
authority to discuss their reason for existence.

Clearly it is useful for the Russians to have people in the
Third World who know their country and speak Russian. And
no one would begrudge Third World countries the right to have
some Russian speakers and to have technical experts trained
wherever they can. But whether the People's Friendship University is any longer the right vehicle for these aspirations –
any more than its counterparts in Europe and America – is a
question the Russians are, perhaps understandably, reluctant
to examine.

Rawlings under pressure within and without

Victoria Brittain   *Published 17 June 1983*

The revolutionary process in Ghana, set in motion by Flight-
Lieutenant Jerry Rawlings after a coup at the end of 1981, is
coming under acute economic and diplomatic pressure from the
United States. After months of deteriorating relations, the
small amount of US aid to the Ghana government has now
been cut off – at a time of acute famine. Valco, the most powerful

American company in Ghana, has abruptly hardened its position during the long-running negotiations with the government about the price it pays for the use of two kinds of Ghana's hydro-electric power to smelt aluminium. Talks have now been broken off.

Next month's meeting of the IMF board is scheduled to approve a loan of $300 millions initialled in Washington in January. Many Western diplomats believe that the much-needed loan is unlikely to go through if the United States opposes it. Ghana might then be placed on the unofficial IMF 'black-list' recently revealed in a Congressional report – and join countries like Cuba, Vietnam, Nicaragua and Grenada.

The Rawlings government came to power with an avowedly anti-imperialist rhetoric, and an economic recovery programme that seeks a fairer deal from foreign companies. The current attempt to bring economic pressure to bear is clearly designed to persuade the government to stem the strong anti-American feeling among Ghana's urban workers. In recent weeks such workers, particularly in Tema, have grown increasingly militant, accusing the government of being too soft on the internal right-wing and their external patrons. There has been a flurry of anti-American statements, and such incidents as the recent seizing of a US embassy car by workers on the campus of the university of Legon give a flavour of the present mood.

At governmental level, relations between Ghana and the United States have become seriously strained. US officials openly maintain contact with sections of Ghanaian society known to be trying to bring down the government. The US influence has become clear around parts of the trade union leadership, the student leadership, the judiciary and the church which have been pitted against the government in battles over policy – chiefly the economic programme. The violent struggle for power now going on between Ghana's old middle class and the urban workers particularly from the docks and industry of Tema too is almost unique in Africa. If the urban working-class wins, American economic interests – which have thrived on agreements such as those made with Valco by successive governments – would be directly threatened.

A diplomatic crisis erupted two months ago when the government accused US ambassador Thomas Smith of being personally involved in a well-funded political destablisation campaign. The various coup plots which have threatened the revolutionary government throughout its 18 months in power have also, it is alleged, involved the Americans. The United States has denied the charges. But Ambassador Smith is shortly to leave Accra, to be replaced by another old Africa hand, Robert Fritts, late of Rwanda and Khartoum.

Three major plots have been uncovered so far – in October and November last year, and, most recently, last February. A treason trial, at which those allegedly involved in the November plot have been arraigned, has now produced evidence which shows a clear connection between the right-wing civilian opposition and a core group of soldiers who have participated in the various plots.

In the February coup an American connection was clear. A car normally used by the US military attache was used to take the American wife of one of the alleged plotters, Dr Antwi, away from the house where arms and plot documents were found.

This was not the first occasion that the Ghana government has produced evidence of foreign plotting. During the past year four foreigners resident in the country have been asked to leave after intelligence reports linked them to the opposition.

Early last year two Americans and a West German, employees of Valco, were expelled. Radio equipment was seized and it was claimed the three foreigners had been in radio contact with members of the previous regime's security forces, planning counter-moves. The CIA's use of Valco as a payment conduit during the Nkrumah period in the early 1960s has long been well-documented.

In another case a Dutch diplomat, Mr Johannes Landmann, was expelled just a few weeks ago. He had apparently been an associate of the former chief of the defence staff, Brigadier Nunoo Mensah, as well as of Kwame Pianim, now on trial in connection with the November coup attempt. Mr Landmann was also allegedly involved with two other men now in custody for their alleged part in the November events. Both also participated in the inquiry by the Special Investigation Board set up to look into the circumstances of the political murder last June of three High Court judges. The SIB team, led by former Chief Justice Azu Crabbe was drawn from the most conservative elements in Ghanaian society – a naive choice by the government in such a polarised society. It became a weapon in the arsenal of the Ghanaian right.

Information now available from published reports of the SIB has brought into the open the connections between the old guard political establishment now believed to be sponsoring coup plots, and the SIB itself. From the treason trial, too, a murky tale emerges of internal conspiracy, with international links, aimed at bringing down the Rawlings government and replacing it with a moderate pro-Western military regime. This strategy has been openly discussed by Western diplomats in Africa who cite the case of Sergeant Doe of Liberia as a success story for this kind of scheme. More recently the coup within the Upper Volta government succeeded in removing radical leaders who, like Rawlings, have connections with Libya.

Many Western diplomats and intelligence services, partly for historical reasons, have close associations with today's right-wing opposition. Yesterday, of course, it was Ghana's establishment. The Bar Association and the Christian Council are two of the most significant and vocal members of this opposition. Both are represented on the SIB, and have close links with the London-based opposition group, the Campaign for Democracy in Ghana.

Political crises triggered by these groups (on three occasions exploiting elements of the report being prepared by the SIB) coincided with three of the several coup plots. The pattern has been the same every time. Rumours sweep Accra of shoot-outs within the small group of top left-wing officials close to Rawlings. On the most serious occasion, last November, the coup attempt was preceded by the resignation of the chief of defence staff. His resignation letter said the alleged involvement of top officials in the murder of the judges was one of his reasons for resigning.

Rawlings subsequently emphasised his concern over the implications to be drawn from the timing of this resignation. News of the resignation had been given to newspapers and agencies in Europe by Mr Landmann, at that time in Lome, before Rawlings had even seen the letters.

At a press conference in March, Captain Kojo Tsikata, one of Rawlings' closest associates, said the government's accusations against the Americans were supported by a secret West German embassy report. He produced a copy of a report sent to the German government in Bonn and signed by the German ambassador in Accra, Dr Gottfried Fischer. American tactics to weaken the Ghanaian government, wrote the ambassador, were to exacerbate tribal differences, especially within the army, and to involve influential tribal chiefs in the internal anti-regime campaign. (The use of northern soldiers in the various coup plots, as well as the recent anti-government campaign in the conservative Ashanti region, lend weight to the ambassador's revelations.) Although the Germans made a routine denial that they were reponsible for this report, Dr Fischer has not returned to Ghana since it was made public.

Captain Tsikata also said mercenaries paid by the CIA and Israeli intelligence were preparing an imminent invasion. And it is now known that soldiers who fled from Ghana after the coup plot in February went to northern Togo where they still are. In 1980 and 1981 there was serious inter-tribal fighting across the Ghana/Togo border in the remote north. A recurrence would be a major blow to a regime struggling for survival on so many fronts.

A year and a half of coup plots and destabilisation has not managed to sap the government's ability to govern, but it has postponed the reforms of the civil service and parastatals necessary to curb the power of the old Ghana establishment – now fighting hard to retain its past privileges.

Nevertheless the German ambassador, who had derived his information largely from conversations with Ambassador Smith, concluded in his report that 'it would be a mistake to predict that Rawlings and his regime will soon come to an end as some of my American informants seem to believe.'

US and Ghana relations

Letter to the editor   *Published 8 August 1983*

Sir, The article by Victoria Brittain entitled 'Rawlings under pressure within and without' (17 June) contains some serious errors and omissions regarding relations between the United States and Ghana.

Miss Brittain states that 'The small amount of US aid to the Ghana Government has now been cut off.' This is not true. Aid continues to be given to Ghana. In particular, a gift of American food distributed by Catholic relief services to nursing mothers and children all over Ghana continues. The programme is currently valued at $4.7 millions annually.

The negotiations between the Government of Ghana and the Volta Aluminimum Company (VALCO) were broken off by the Ghanaian Government, not by the company.

Miss Brittain states that US officials openly maintain contact with sections of Ghanaian society known to be trying to bring down the Government. She implies that the sections of society she has in mind range from leaders of the trade unions and the students of the judiciary and the churches. Such individuals and organisations are normal contacts for any diplomatic mission.

Miss Brittain recalls the 'diplomatic crisis' which resulted from unwarranted and groundless allegations by the special adviser to the Provisional National Defence Council on 31 March that the United States is recruiting mercenaries for an invasion of Ghana and otherwise seeking to destabilise the Ghanaian Government. Miss Brittain correctly reports that the

United States denied the charges but fails to mention the fact that these allegations were publicly withdrawn by the Ghanaian Government on 26 May in a statement acknowledging that the so-called report from the West German Embassy on which they were based is a forgery and concluding that 'the Government . . . has no further reason to believe that the US has recruited or is recruiting mercenaries to attack Ghana or that she is engaged in any way in activities aimed at the overthrow of the Ghana Government.'

This statement by the Ghanaian Government makes nonsense of most of Miss Brittain's article. *The Guardian*'s readers deserve full and factual reporting and informed dispassionate judgments. Apparently, Miss Brittain's article contained little of either.

Philip W. Arnold,
Counsellor for Public Affairs,
United States Information Service,
US Embassy, London W1.

Victoria Brittain writes:
First, the article says that US aid to the Government has been cut off. This is true. The continuation of US aid to church organisations underlines the article's description of the continuing influence of the US in Ghana.

Secondly, as the article says, the Valco talks were broken off because of the hardening of the US company's position, as the Ghana government statement makes clear.

Thirdly, Mr Arnold refers to a 26 May retraction of the West German document with its description of US attempts to overthrow the Ghana Government and the accusations of the US funding of mercenaries in a neighbouring country. The statement carried briefly on Accra Radio was withdrawn from the news bulletin by the Secretary for Information and not authorised for use in the Ghanaian press because, according to the secretary, Ms Joyce Aryee, it did not reflect accurately the discussions held between Ghana government officials and the US ambassador in which he sought to discuss the future of US aid to Ghana.

Two days after the *Guardian* article appeared an elaborate coup attempt was mounted from Togo, linked to the previous ones described in the article. One of the coup leaders sought help from the West German embassy after the coup failed.

Third World through Second World eyes

Richard Gott *Published 14 October 1983*

Ryszard Kapuscinski is one of the world's best foreign correspondents. (He was the prototype for Wajda's film *Rough Treatment*.) Yet his name is hardly a household word. West European newspapers will often clog their pages with dispatches from American reporters, but no one reprints syndicated columns from the Polish Press Agency. Which is perhaps a pity. For Kapuscinski, over many years of far-flung travel, has made a point of trying to explain what goes on in the Third World to a Polish readership, and his insights deserve a wider audience.

Fortunately, his extraordinary book on the court of Haile Selassie is now available in English—to reveal a writer who is not only a master of journalistic enterprise and skill, but also a creative artist of great power and originality.

Haile Selassie: desperate reaction to the erosion of power

Sent to cover the slow unfolding revolution in Ethiopia in 1974, Kapuscinski devoted his time not to trying vainly to understand the confused dynamic of the conflicting revolutionary forces that eventually coalesced around Mengistu Haile Mariam, but to use his privileged position in Addis Ababa – and his friendship with former members of the Emperor's court – to discover what really went on under the ancient regime.

The result – in a series of brilliant snapshots – is a unique portrait of a declining despotism. For it is the sycophants that speak – the courtiers, the yes-men, the officer in the Ministry of Ceremonies (Department of Processions), the cloakroom attendant at the Imperial court, the man in charge of the Imperial lapdog, and His Most Virtuous Highness's pillow bearer for 26 years.

Still unable quite to believe that their world has gone beyond recall, they give a glowing account of their years in Imperial service. And so telling is their picture that it seems to illustrate earlier experiences of despotism – France before the Revolution, Russia under the Tsars. The nearest equivalent is the demolition job done on dictators by a host of Latin American novelists. But this book is not fiction, but fact.

From beneath the fawning adulation – hero of the League of Nations, and paladin of African unity – Haile Selassie emerges as a weak and evil man, propped up by sentiment and invented tradition, and surrounded by rippling circles of spy networks.

Nor is this a static portrait. It jumps jerkily over the last 15 years of the reign of the Lion of Judah like a magic lantern show, illuminating the Emperor's increasingly desperate reactions to the erosion of his power.

Finally, like the Shah, he throws all his eggs into the basket marked 'development', vainly hoping that foreign money and foreign ideas will somehow give his archaic system a new lease of life. He holds an 'Hour of Development' every afternoon. 'He received processions of planners, economists, and financial specialists . . . and His Indefatigible Majesty would ride out to open a bridge here, a building there, an airport somewhere else, giving these structures his name.'

The result of course, was merely to speed up the process of disintegration. 'Grumbling students' began 'to speak unreasonably and insultingly against the Palace.' They demanded reform. But how, one veteran in the service of His Imperial Majesty asked rhetorically into Kapuscinski's tape recorder 'do you reform without everything falling apart?'

And collapse it did. And as the revolutionary forces grew stronger and the temple walls came tumbling down, and the final Gotterdammerung loomed closer, the Emperor had a new fad. A team of Swedish doctors arrived to teach the court calisthenics, as though deep breathing would keep the revolution at bay.

In the last month or so there existed the old revolutionary scenario of dual power. By now, throughout the country, the revolution had swept away the old order, and in Addis Ababa the military committee – the Dergue – was in place. Yet the Emperor still remained installed in his Palace. And the Palace came increasingly to resemble a refugee camp.

It was a scene from Dante, with the scions of the nobility sleeping 'side by side on the carpets, sofas, and armchairs, covering themselves with curtains and drapes'. The Emperor would comfort them, but then, 'if he met a patrol of officers in the corridor, he encouraged them as well.' Finally the refugees were swept away, leaving the Emperor alone with valet – stuffing dollar bills into old bibles and under the carpet.

This is a wonderfully written, humorous and humanitarian book, which suggests that Eastern Europe is capable of being at least as well informed about the Third World as we are – and perhaps more so.

The Emperor: Downfall of an Autocrat, by Ryszard Kapuscinski, is published by Quartet Books.

Aid grows a crop of problems

Derek Warren   *Published 2 December 1983*

Over 50 per cent of all official aid goes to the 66 lowest income countries. However, much of this aid is tied to the donor country's goods and services and these projects run the risk of increasing future dependency on imported technology, draining scarce foreign currency reserves, disrupting traditional patterns of production and subsistence and failing to involve, or improve the living standards of, the poorest sections of the population.

A recent case study of a Canadian project illustrates some of the pitfalls of an aid programme placing heavy emphasis on commercial and political benefits to the donor country.

In 1970 the Canadian government committed Canadian $7 million (£3.8 million) to a programme designed to help Tanzania become self-sufficient in wheat production, with the intention of beginning a phased withdrawal of support some five years later.

The Canadian way may not answer Africa's needs

Thirteen years on, Canada has now committed a total of $33 million to the programme with no prospect of Tanzania being able to run it independently in the foreseeable future. The Tanzanian government's contribution has at least matched that of the Canadians, yet the project is still producing less than a quarter of the country's demand for wheat. In fact, due to a variety of other factors, Tanzania is estimated to be producing less wheat than when the project began.

Annexation of the land for wheat production has displaced pastoralists who previously used the area for grazing. Intensive farming techniques are depriving the soil of nutrients and may soon require an expensive input of fertilisers. Meanwhile severe erosion threatens to turn the whole wheat-growing area into a dust bowl within a decade.

The Tanzania Canada Wheat Project started in November, 1970. Canada's contribution is administered by the Canadian International Development Agency (CIDA) and Tanzania's involvement is through the National Agricultural and Food Corporation (NAFCO).

CIDA is providing the agricultural machinery, transport, technical experts and technical training for Tanzanians. The Tanzanian government, through NAFCO, is committed to providing (Canadian) spare parts for the equipment, the development and operating costs of the farms (including fuel), labour charges, buildings and water supplies.

The research centre, on 850 acres near Arusha, involves about a dozen Canadians and twice that number of Tanzanians. They have been testing soil conditions and plant breeds and analysing soil and crop management techniques to determine the best methods of wheat production. Results, in this respect, have been very good, with average yields increasing dramatically from seven bushels an acre in the early 1970s to 25 bushels an acre by 1980 on farms established with CIDA assistance.

There are currently six of these farms, covering a total of 60,000 acres in the Hanang district of north-central Tanzania, south west of Arusha. These are the production components of the project. The intention is to bring another 10,000 acres under wheat production during the 1980s. Each of these six farms costs Tanzania $600,000 per annum in foreign currency for running costs with 100,000 litres of fuel per farm accounting for much of that bill – and this at a time when rising oil prices have crippled the Tanzanian economy.

The project had fairly modest beginnings, with the acreage under wheat still only 7,300 by 1976, but it took on much greater importance following severe food shortages in Tanzania in the mid-70s and a coincidental shift in the emphasis of Canada's overseas aid programme. Canada's earliest involvement in Tanzania was in large-scale infrastructure projects such as railways, port facilities and water supplies. In common with many of the major aid donors, Canada introduced into its aid strategy in 1975 a commitment in principle to aiding the poorest people in the poorest countries, with the accent on rural development.

However, the aid programme is firmly tied to the purchase of Canadian goods and services. Canada has no specialised experience in the problems of tropical agriculture or peasant production. Its domestic agriculture, characterised by a growth of agribusiness – large farms using capital, skill and energy-intensive techniques of production – could not be further removed from the experience of rural, socialist Tanzania. When Canada offered to respond to Tanzania's plea for extra assistance in food production, wheat growing in the state farm sector was really the only option open to them.

In terms of benefit to the poorest people, the wheat scheme has been criticised on several counts. First, while more than 80 per cent of Tanzanians still live in rural areas, bread is a staple only for more affluent urban dwellers, expatriates and tourists. Even for poorer people in the towns, bread is something of a luxury, with the price of wheat soaring from 31p a kilo in 1972 to £1.03 in 1981, far outstripping the cost of the major staple, maize.

The farms have also done little to provide employment for

people in Hanang District. The high technology emphasis of the project has meant that all the Tanzanian research staff and many of those recruited for the farms are drawn from the educated middle classes. Seventy NAFCO staff have been sent to Canada for technical training over the past five years, though 50 per cent have failed to continue working on the wheat scheme after their return.

CIDA's commitment of $44 million, matched by a similar contribution by Tanzania, has created a total of only about 250 skilled jobs. About 100 local men are recruited as casual labour on the farms at harvest time and paid 17.50 Tanzanian shillings (97p) a day – their wives are able to make almost twice that (30 shillings) scavenging for grain behind the combines.

All the land annexed for the farms, on the Basuto Plain near Mount Hanang, was previously occupied and utilised by a pastoral people, the Barbaig. Unfortunately, what was considered to be the best wheat land was also their prime grazing land. They presented a petition as early as 1968, protesting at the initial takeover of their land, but without success. Deprived of pasture, they are now overgrazing the land around their villages to the detriment of the quality of their herds. In moves to expand the project, more pastoral areas in Masai land are now being considered for annexation.

The initial intention of accepting Canadian aid in order to work towards self-sufficiency in wheat production was easily squared with the doctrine of 'socialism for a self-reliance', but in reality the $1.5 million spent on equipment per farm (including several combine harvesters) has only increased dependency. According to Roy Button, Canadian project manager for the scheme, based in Arusha, 'It is not now possible for the project to make Tanzania self-sufficient in wheat production'.

Button also expressed 'reservations' over NAFCO's ability to take on the running of the farms, independent of Canadian involvement, in the foreseeable future. A Canadian mechanic involved in the scheme was less diplomatic; he considered there was not 'a hope in hell' of Tanzania ever running such a high technology project without back up.

While demand for wheat in Tanzania is rising by 5 per cent per annum, the project's ability to provide it is under serious threat. Initial increases in yields encouraged project staff to speculate that they would be producing 35–40,000 tonnes per annum by 1984, but they had failed to account for the problems of erosion and soil degradation.

The six farms have been laid out prairie-style, with huge 160 acre fields (1 mile x ¼) and no natural wind breaks. Tropical downpours during the rainy season have washed huge gullies through some of the fields and severe erosion now threatens the whole future of the project. After spending over £22,000 on one farm trying, unsuccessfully, to fill one gaping gully, the project now faces the prospect of enormous expenditure to switch to the type of contoured strip farming of wheat traditionally employed by small wheat farmers in Tanzania before the Canadians' arrival.

In a report, *Agricultural and Livestock Production in Arusha Region*, produced in 1980, Merritt Sargent was scathing about the prospects for the project: 'The technology being applied to these large-scale, fully mechanised operations is alarmingly similar to the technology used in Western Canada which contributed to the catastrophic soil erosions (dust bowls) of the 1930s. Even if, in the short run, these farms do produce some wheat, there is a very strong probability that this will be at lower and lower yields (and also less and less efficiently) and that there will be no soil left when the operation terminates.'

While the project gained some stature as a showpiece in the 1970s, with visits from two Canadian Prime Ministers (Trudeau and Clark) and from President Nyerere, present Canadian disenchantment bodes ill for the future. CIDA's present commitment expires at the end of 1984 and an independent review team has just completed an assessment of the project prior to negotiations on future Canadian involvement. Tanzania is likely to request greater rather than reduced Canadian funding, just to preserve present levels of production.

If the Canadians do withdraw their support and the project fails – as it surely will – they will face much criticism and adverse publicity. For Tanzania, the implications are infinitely more serious.

Two-way bet on progress

Basil Davidson *Published 16 December 1983*

Thirty-one years ago, in a book which I called *Report on Southern Africa*, I allowed myself a prophecy. I said that the white minorities of the sub-continent faced an urgent choice. This choice – and forgive me for quoting myself – was between 'waging bitter and perhaps bloody struggles as the Africans step by step assert their rights: or of conforming intelligently to the needs of those social and economic forces which white civilisation has itself forced into motion.'

Without exception, the white minorities chose the first

course, and, in the last two decades, have brought more violence and destruction to this whole wide region than ever before seen in history.

Things being as they now are, it is easy to forecast still more misery and destruction, and tempting to forecast nothing else. One is therefore bound to feel uneasy, not to say vulnerable to accusations of irresponsibility, in proposing that progress in Southern Africa remains, even now, even at this late hour, a real alternative to the disaster which seems imminent on every hand.

All the same, my own belief is that progress – by which I mean a process of far-reaching and therefore constructive change – is not only possible today; but has, in fact, become possible for the first time since the shaping of modern South Africa more than 100 years ago.

The reality of 'separate development' is, as was said as long ago as 1944, by the African scholar Z. K. Matthews, 'the separation of black and white, not with the idea of protecting each group in regard to its basic interests, but the separation of the groups in order to facilitate the subordination of one group to the other – the exploitation of one group by the other.'

The so-called 'independent homelands' are an organic part of that exploitation. Their acute and often helpless poverty is another guarantee of ample supplies of black labour for the 'white economy': another contribution to the profits of overseas investors. To suggest that these 'black areas' are zones of development is to propound a grim absurdity.

Official propaganda claims that apartheid provides for the development of Africans inside their own homelands: inside, that is, the old Native Reserves – some 13 per cent of the land surface – now often known as 'Bantustans'. The facts speak a different language.

Census estimates of 1980 showed that 54 per cent of Africans – perhaps 12 or 13 million people – were living in the Bantustans. But these so-called 'homelands' scattered about the country within an otherwise meaningless jigsaw of boundaries are no more viable today than they used to be when they were Native Reserves.

They have long been little better than rural slums: in the words of a Government White Paper of 1936, when their condition was better than today, they are – and I quote – 'congested, denuded, overstocked, eroded, and for the most part in a deplorable condition.'

Such is the system. Can it change: or, rather, can it change itself?

I was once among those who thought that it could and indeed would. I thought that the sheer expansion of the white economy must call for ever larger supplies of skilled labour, substantially black skilled labour, and that this would break through industrial colour bars, bans on black enterprise, and all the various barriers of apartheid. Many other observers thought and have continued to think like this, but they ceased to include me a long time ago.

The record shows that with every expansion of the South African economy – since 1910, but more especially since the long boom began in the 1930s, and above all since the 1950s – there has come a further tightening of the screws of an instrumental racism.

The numbers of black skilled workers has certainly increased, but *pari passu*, along with that, the colour bars and other weapons of discrimination have sharpened and grown heavier. Something like the embryo of a black 'middle class' has come into existence, but only as the helpless puppet of an immensely more powerful white 'middle class'; as may be seen, today, in the rag-tag-and-bobtail of sinister stooges who run the Bantustans on the rules laid down by apartheid.

In 1970 an industrialist as authoritative as Mr Harry Oppenheimer of the Anglo-American Corporation and De Beers could sadly conclude – quote – 'There is no evidence so far that economic integration has led to any improvement in political or social integration.' Everything that has happened since 1970 – not least this latest constitutional referendum of 1983 – has confirmed that Mr Oppenheimer's judgment remains accurate.

So far, in short, the system has revealed, within itself, no self-correcting mechanism capable of beginning the dismantlement of apartheid. Much has been lately said about reforms. Concessions have been made to the existence of black trade unions, though not yet in law. Steps have been taken to reduce some of the most minor aspects of discrimination in matters such as the segrgation of telephone kiosks or benches in parks. More white people than before accept that the system spells disaster for themselves as well as for non-whites; they remain, at best, an exiguous minority.

Nothing has been done, or promised, or even discussed at governmental or National-Party level, which in any way dismantles the overall system.

A white parliamentary assembly is to be 'partnered' by an Indian assembly and a Coloured assembly; but all effective power will remain with the white assembly. The 10 or 11 million Africans in the 'white areas' remain utterly disfranchised, and, by the laws relating to the Bantustans, are now denied any rights of citizenship in 87 per cent of the country. Nothing, in any essentials, has changed.

There may still be those who think that the apartheid system will fall apart from its own internal contradictions, even from its own inherent absurdity. Even today, when the black majority numbers only some 25 million, a white domination of fewer than 5 million people can pursue apartheid only by brute force, and sustain it only by ever more painful laws and practices of oppression.

Within a generation, there will be upwards of 45 million black people in South Africa; and one may well wonder what conceivable system of organised servitude will be able to contain them.

Yet to imagine that the system will fall apart of itself – or even, of its own volition, change against itself – is to fall into the illusion which held, years ago, that expansion of the economy would be enough to reduce and eventually to end apartheid.

The system will not fall apart of itself. It must be made to fall apart. That being so, the course of wisdom must be to make it fall apart in such a way that the violence of the system is displaced, as rapidly as possible, by movement towards a democracy of genuinely equal rights and duties.

To that end, only two pressures can be real factors on the scene.

The first and decisive pressure is that of the black community. To the extent that black people struggle for a genuine freedom to participate fully in representative institutions with genuine powers – political parties, national parliament and government, trade unions, integrated types of education, and the rest – they will be able to open the way for a democratic and therefore peaceful country.

This, of course, is what the representative organs of black opinion, and most comprehensively the African National Congress, have asked for and urged since the very foundations of modern South Africa. For decade after decade they have relied on peaceful argument and passive protest or resistance: always, invariably, in vain.

Now they are reduced to illegality or legal/subjection, and they have turned as a last resort, as did the black people of the Portuguese colonies and of Rhodesia, to an armed struggle of counter-violence to the violence of the system.

We should deplore that counter-violence if it were a black racist response to the provocations of white racism. But all the evidence shows that it is nothing of the kind, and that it is aimed not at replacing one apartheid by another, but, precisely, at winning a society of equal rights and duties.

This being the case, I do not see how governments or peoples who condemn apartheid can fail to give their active support to the African National Congress and its companions. To tolerate a system of violence while rejecting the planned and restrained use of counter-violence – of course, as only one means of securing change – is morally untenable.

Last 23 May, Mr Francis Pym, certainly a Conservative and certainly a statesman, warned in relation to Southern Africa that 'There is a desperate need to break the vicious circle where violence begets violence, and to seek peaceful solutions to the region's problems.'

Even the present American Administration, whose pro-apartheid stance remains a major source of strength for the apartheid regime, now adds to the chorus of alarm. Thus Mr Lawrence Eagleburger, American Undersecretary of State, told a San Francisco audience last 23 June that – quote – 'a cycle of violence has begun: unless it is reversed, the interests of the region and the West will be severely damaged.' Even the International Monetary Fund says that it is worried.

If such attitudes are more than pale hypocrisy, they demand action.

Anti-apartheid action by the outside world is the second and supporting force that can make for removal of the system which is the origin, maker and motivator of this 'cycle of violence' so rightly deplored by Mr Pym and Mr Eagleburger.

This means whatever positive action may be possible to support and encourage the opponents and critics of apartheid inside South Africa, whether these be Africans, Coloureds, Indians, or Whites.

It also means positive action to reinforce the independence of the nine Southern African Development Coordination Committee countries, and, very urgently, to help protect them, and protect themselves, from the aggressions of Pretoria: so that they can pursue a national and regional development to which, eventually, a democratised South Africa could bring its skills and wealth.

Further, it means a combined programme – far more effective than any so far envisaged – of what may be called negative action: action aimed most deliberately at isolating the apartheid regime. This means a comprehensive and resolute programme of sanctions against apartheid – political, cultural, military, and, above all, economic.

These extracts are from Basil Davidson's Canon Collins Memorial Lecture organised by the British Defence and Aid Fund for Southern Africa.

Why Shagari couldn't last

Wole Soyinka   *Published 3 January 1984*

The detailed, incredible story of the Nigerian exercise in democratic elections, 1983, will be published soon. This is only
an interim statement. The actual figures compiled from the
Returning Officers' forms at the polling booths and counting
centres will be published side by side with the figures announced by the Federal Electoral Commission (FEDECO),
which awarded the Presidency to the incumbent Alhaji Shehu
Shagari, and a number of state governorships to candidates of
his party. The discrepancy on these figures, running in millions,
will startle the democratic world, they will startle even nations
which are effectively one-party states. Yet even these figures
will not have told the entire story.

**Wole Soyinka, Nigeria's leading playwright, novelist, poet,
1986 Nobel Prizewinner for Literature and Professor of
Literature at the University of Ife**

For instance, will the figures reveal that in Sokoto, the home state of the President, there was hardly any voting except by his own party, the National Party of Nigeria (NPN). Shagari's credibility as leader had to be saved at all costs in his home state where the little support he ever enjoyed had been eroded by four years of neglect and manifest corruption, not to mention traumatic events like the police massacre of peasants at Bakolori, right on Shagari's doorstep.

It was saved by the simple process of flooding his home state with the fearsome special units of the anti-riot police who savaged would-be supporters of the opposition parties, arrested their party agents on sight, and even baton-charged lines of voters in obvious strongholds of his main opponent, Dr Audu Bayero.

Hundreds of booths were starved of ballot papers, so that queues of would-be voters waited in vain from seven o'clock in the morning to six o'clock at night when polling officially ended. Photographs taken of such scenes in the Nigerian newspapers, plus television coverage, more than testify to the reality, not merely in Sokoto State, but in at least 15 of the 19 states where the NPN knew that it faced certain defeat.

The ignorance of the outside world regarding this Nigerian 'democratic' reality is only to be expected; correspondents from other nations continue to present their audience with a primitive image of democratic understanding in Nigeria.

Discredited, rejected, even loathed by the majority of Nigerians, the National Party of Nigeria, buoyed by the image-building of its leader Shagari by the Western press – meek unassuming, de-tribalised, the guarantor of peace and stability – went confidently ahead to commit the most breathtaking electoral fraud of any nation in the whole of Africa. At every level – from acts of brutal ejection of the opposition at the polling booth by 'law-enforcement' agencies to the simplest but most daring motion of all, swapping the figures at the very point of announcement—the scale of the robbery was unprecedented.

Where all other measures failed, the Secretaries to the States Electoral Commissions simply announced the wrong figures; alternatively, the Federal Commission in Lagos announced the forgeries, claiming that these were the figures passed on by the state offices.

I have two sets of results (incomplete) for Oyo and Ondo states in the governorship elections. They were compiled from the form known as EC 8, that is, the forms for each polling booth, signed by the party agents and the Returning Officer. By the time of my departure from Lagos on 18 August no such compilations were available from the Federal Electoral Commission, yet both governorships in these states had been awarded to the NPN. The final figures for the NPN had simply been inflated by over a million votes.

In FEDECO's attempt to build up a credible accumulation of votes towards the final, pre-programmed figure, that method was uniformly applied all over the country, and particularly to the Presidential elections. Throughout the electoral areas, five copies of the form EC 8 held by the opposition parties will be found to contain identical scores while the sixth and seventh, held by the NPN and the FEDECO will be found to have the figure one – or two or three – in front of its correct figure.

A death-toll of 83 during the elections has been estimated by the Western press. That figure does not account for the total casualties in Oyo state alone.

There has been violence in Borno state, where a policeman fired on a crowd of protesters and was promptly lynched, and in Bauchi, Anambra, Gongola. In several states the election results have been rejected outright by all five non-NPN parties. In Sokoto, Cross River and Bendel, where no answer could be found immediately to the unexpected and brutal partisanship of the police and some of the army units, three, four or all five parties jointly resolved to boycott all future elections. Yet normally responsible newspapers such as *The Observer* continued to delude the world that a normal, peaceful, even democratic event was going on in this populous nation of the African continent. The irrepressible Shagari even went so far as to hope that ours would serve as an example for other African nations to follow!

While FEDECO delayed the results, meeting frantically with NPN leaders and law-enforcement officers, it was the state-owned radio and television stations which kept up a poll-by-poll announcement of results, leaving the arithmetic to its listeners; day and night broadcasts alerted the electorate and urged constant vigilance. For example, during the second week of elections – that is, during the preparatory week for the governorship elections – Ogun State Broadcasting Service repeatedly broadcast a secretly taped conspiratorial meeting between the NPN hierarchy and top officials of FEDECO. There was no anonymity—names were named, with official positions, assigned roles, methodology of rigging and contingency plans.

It was a dramatic catalogue of human greed, lust for power, abuse of position and felonious conspiracy to subvert the law and the constitution. Denial was impossible and was never attempted either by the NPN or by FEDECO, that impartial national arbiter of the political competition.

Certain programmes of anti-NPN sentiments constantly irked Shagari's clique—two of my songs virtually became political anthems for some of these stations. Not surprisingly, the government moved unconstitutionally to silence these stations. Bendel and Ondo Stations were seized and closed down by troops on the order of Shagari, and a further threat was made to close down further stations because of their 'inciting' attitudes.

The move towards the closure of those state-owned media was foreseen. The rehearsals took place at various periods during the past four years in pursuit of the assignment given to Inspector-General Sunday Adewusi, head of the Nigerian police force and well-known storm-trooper against the free press. The contempt with which Adewusi's command treated the Judiciary during Shagari's tenure of office removed the last doubt about Shagari's plans for civil liberty or the constitution.

While hundreds were being killed over these elections – the majority of them caused by the indiscriminate, cowardly firing of automatic weapons by Adewusi's uniformed thugs – *The Observer* correspondent, filing from Lagos, continued to image-build Shagari fooled – genuinely I hope – by the Hyde face of Shagari's Jekyll-and-Hyde political personality. Much of his (Shagari's) success can be attributed to his ability to project himself above his party – indeed almost above politics – which are far less popular than he is. His tolerance, modesty and personal integrity have also helped and he has managed, as no other Nigerian leader has, to reach across the still formidable barriers of tribe, language and religion.

That is the image which the Western press wants its reader-ship to accept. Every act, and nearly every pronouncement, of Shagari since he took office belies these claims. Shagari's anti-tribalism was no doubt proven when he campaigned in his home state of Sokoto, and appealed crudely to both religious and tribal sentiments that most papers castigated him, including the non-partisan and widely respected (Nigerian) *Guardian*. His tolerance has been underscored by his constant threats to use a 'big stick' on those who opposed him and by his habit during campaigns in hostile states of warning that they would continue to lose benefits because of their 'confrontational' attitudes.

Perhaps his silence over hideous police massacres such as took place in Bakolori and the numerous political assassinations carried out by his party during the countdown before elections is his way of being above party and politics. Shagari regained his voice only after the elections began and the opposition began to strike back with its own violence; and then of course his answer was to close down the state-owned media and order the police to 'shoot at sight'.

As for 'personal integrity', if it is true that we know-a-man-by-the-company-he keeps, it must be doubly true that a leader is judged by the company he gathers around him, as the Chief

Executive of a nation. There is no Nigerian child living today who does not know that Shehu Shagari has presided for four years over the most unscrupulous and insatiable consortium that the nation has ever known. His post-election bravado of calling for the resignation of all his Ministers and other political appointees is the typical gesture of a convicted leader who wants to pass the buck to his followership for past notorious misconduct. No Nigerian is fooled.

Nor are Nigerians under any illusion about the existence of Shagari's blueprint for fascism. Nigerians are a politically sophisticated people; they are not content to accept travesties of democratic processes which no sane party in power in the UK, or the US would dare to foist on even its own under-privileged sections of the population. Talk to those gnarled peasants and workers, ancient patriarchs and matriarchs, patiently waiting on the voting queues for hours in Nigeria and they will astonish you with their grasp of the political issues under contention.

It is insulting and patronising to ask the average Nigerian to accept what the factory worker in the Midlands would not tolerate all in the name of the 'nascent' condition of democracy in the Third World, a media fantasy of the Western world, a residue of the Western justification for colonisation and post-colonial interventions.

Time and time again, African peoples have been thwarted in their resolve to create a new social order. Every time the Western press with its love of the status quo, has found arguments of double standards for legitimising the intolerable, even if 'democracy' has had to be redefined in the process. When the extreme consequence – violence – can no longer be ignored, it is either underplayed or libelled as the eruption of tribal antagonisms.

Straw figures are decked out in appropriate virtuous terminologies and the masses, in effect, invited to admire, adjust, and count their blessings. Not this time! Our reading is that this time round, with a background of a costly civil war and 13 years of military rule, for the masses of Nigerians, half a loaf is no longer better than anything ...

It was not the Western press alone that was guilty of the programme for Shagari's international acceptance. Radio Cameroon, in what could only be understood as preparatory softening up of international opinion for an act of sordid collusion, can claim discredit for being the first African radio station to broadcast the false results, barely 24 hours after the end of polling.

Judging by the vanity of political leaders everywhere and their need for some kind of international acceptability, however spurious, we cannot totally ignore the possibility of the effectiveness of the international media on specific actions of some leaders, the extremes of which they may help to avoid, and their early recognition of the danger zone of brinkmanship.

If, for example, even Shagari's most ardent admirers among election-watchers had had the courage to point out to him that no one anywhere in the world would believe that the population of an obscure ward (Modakeke) within a constituency (Oranmi-yan North I), a ward with no industry, no labour-intensive project of any nature whatever, a ward with under 700 dwell-ings at the last count, many of them abandoned because of the perpetual feud between the Ife people and the Modakeke—if Shagari's international praise-singers had cautioned him that his fellow-Nigerians are not such cretins as to accept that such a ward, in effect a disaster area, would leap from a population of 50,000 in 1979 to 220,000 in 1983; from 4,500 recorded voters in 1979 to a purported 188,000 in 1983.

If this common-sense caution had been administered to Shehu Shagari at the appropriate time, seven prominent politicians would not have been burnt alive in a Kombi bus just before the elections; some 30 Ife/Modakeke citizens and policemen would not be lying in the mortuaries at this very moment and scores of buildings in that area would not have been turned to rubble.

I teach in Ife. I know Modakeke like the palm of my hand and it cannot boast even 10,000 citizens of voting age. A thou-sand and more Modakeke were created in the voting register of Nigeria, spanning the entire land, in order to provide Shehu Shagari his 'landslide' victory. A ghost population of millions to defy the political will of several millions, flesh-and-blood, who braved unbelievable brutalities to cast their votes for a change. It is obvious that Shagari is living in a world peopled by ghosts; the sad prospect is that he is equally bent on trans-forming the nation into a land of ghosts, a ghost of itself, a ghost of its potential and logical expectations.

A civil war has been set in motion by Shehu Shagari and the hierarchy of the NPN. The preliminary skirmishes should be recognised for what they are – mere skirmishes. The responsi-bility for bloodshed is unambiguously that of a rejected misfit who bungled his chance to make a positive contribution to Nigeria's history, and who abused the state machinery to re-entrench himself and his unpatriotic party in office.

This is an edited extract from an article which first appeared in Index on Censorship, No. 6, 1983.

Chronicle of a Kenyan massacre

Abdi Khalif   *Published 23 June 1984*

*In February this year 5,000 men of the Degodia Somali people
of north-east Kenya were seized by Government forces and many
of their homes burned. Within a week, it is alleged, at least 800
of the men were dead; 80 children have since died of starvation,
and approaching half a million livestock have been lost. In this
first full-scale report, A. S. Khalif describes the sequence of
events:*

On 16 January twelve Degodia Somali leaders in Wajir were
arrested and held without charge under the so-called 'North-
eastern Province and Contiguous Districts Act', passed in 1966.
This allows the Kenya Government to hold persons without
charge for up to 56 days. These leaders were held until well
after the events detailed below.

On 5 February Kenyan Government officials denied access
to all sources of water to all livestock, including cattle, camels,
sheep and goats belonging to members of the Degodia clan in
the vicinity of Wajir, the administrative centre of Wajir district
in North-eastern Province of Kenya. This lasted for 10 days.

Beginning at midnight on 10 February about 5,000 male
Degodia Somali living in the area of Wajir were rounded up by
Kenyan Government security forces – including the Special
Branch, the Kenya police, the Kenya army, and the Administration Police – and taken to the tarmaced and barbed-wire
fenced Wagala airstrip, about nine miles west of Wajir. Initially
security force personnel numbered about a hundred, but these
men were later reinforced by others from Moyale, on the Ethiopian border, and Mandera, on the border with Somalia. The final
total was about a thousand men, all armed with automatic
weapons.

On the same day Degodia women and children were told to
vacate their homes which were then burnt to the ground.

The Degodia taken to the airstrip were forced to remove their
clothing and remain without shade in this desert area where
the air temperature at this time of year reaches about 105°F
at the height of the day and approaches freezing at night.
For four days they were denied food and water and were not
permitted to say their Muslim daily prayers.

On 10 February Major Mudogo, of the 7th Battalion of the
Kenya army, addresses the group, telling them to produce
illegal weapons, which the Kenyan Government asserted was
the cause for the problems in the area.

A number of those present stated that there were no illegal

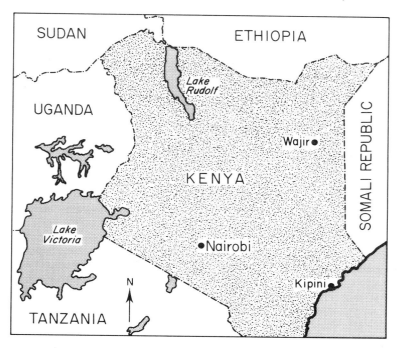

weapons to be confiscated. According to Kenyan government accounts, the other three clans which had been involved in the unrest preceding the Wajir incident – the Murulle, the Ajuran, and the Garre – had all turned in their arms, a number of which had supposedly reached the area during and following the Ogaden conflict between Ethiopia and Somalia. According to Degodia accounts, most of these arms had been turned in prior to the Wajir events.

By the evening of Saturday, 11 February, eight of the people detained at the airstrip had been killed by security forces. On 14 February, action was stepped up. People were shot, bludgeoned with axes and blunt objects; petrol from jerry cans was poured over some who were then incinerated. The Degodia stampeded and attempted to escape. Many did, in spite of the barbed-wire enclosure. Of those who remained, 307 had been killed, and about 600 were too weak to escape.

On the evening of the 14th, Benson Kaaria, the provincial commissioner of North-eastern Province, who gave the original order to detain these people, found out about the massacre and ordered the killing to stop. This order also commanded the security forces to remove those remaining at the airstrip, both the living and the dead, to places as remote as possible from

Wajir, some as far distant as 200 miles. One tally by observers in the area states that 855 people died, including the living who were dumped in the desert. The toll may be as high as 1,300 according to members of parliament from the area.

One reason why it is difficult to arrive at a definitive count is the magnitude of the massacre. Another is the removal of bodies to remote points in the desert. When members of voluntary agencies and missionary groups attempted to recover, first the wounded and, second, the dead, they were prevented from doing so. Nevertheless, about 70 of the weak or wounded were brought back to Wajir town.

One of the people who took lorries out to recover some of the dying was arrested and the vehicles confiscated. After three or four hours she was released, but placed in a camp where she was prevented from resuming her efforts.

The Sahel is once again suffering from a drought which in the area of Wajir is said to be the worst since 1970. The Somali are a pastoral people who keep cattle, camels, sheep, and goats as their sole means of livelihood. During the period when security forces prevented waterhole access, approximately 150,000 cattle, 75,000 camels, and 250,000 goats and sheep perished, thus depriving the Degodia of both food and financial support from livestock sales.

Because of the drought, international relief agencies have attempted to send food to the area. All of this has been stopped from reaching the area by the Kenyan Government. Somali trucking firms and independent truckers are volunteering their vehicles and services to expedite the movement of food to the area. Some 3,500 bags of maize provided by the Kenyan Government has reached the area but government administrators charged with its distribution have prevented members of the Degodia Somali from receiving any of it. Some of this food is rotting in government stores.

Representatives of Oxfam, the International Red Cross, Food for the Hungry International, AMREF, and the World Food Program have stated privately that their organisational policies prevent them from intervening in the politics of the distribution of relief supplies.

The International Red Cross has succeeded in sending food relief once to Wajir. When it arrived, government personnel insisted on distributing it. The Red Cross refused to allow this and insisted that the food be sent back to Nairobi. At this point government representatives relented and allowed the food to be distributed by a voluntary agency.

In addition to food, there is a great need for shelter, since the widows and children of many of the deceased have had their homes burnt by government forces.

**A Somali girl waters her herd: in February access to
waterholes in the Wajir district was denied for 10 days**

According to reports reaching Nairobi from Wajir late in
April, 587 Degodia children who were previously attending
school in Wajir District have been expelled. Their situation is
desperate since many of them are the children of the Degodia
clan members killed by government forces and have no bread-
winner in the family. For others there is no home, and for yet
others, there is no food, both because of the death of livestock
and because of the Kenyan Government's preventing Degodia
from receiving food aid.

On 5 May, a list from Wajir reached Nairobi which contained
the names of the 80 children who have died of starvation since
the Wagala massacre, in part as a result of the withholding of
relief supplies. This list was signed by elders of the Degodia
clan. Another report received at the same time claimed that
468 families had reported to Wagala from the bush in the
hope of finding food and shelter. Many of these families were
composed of the widows and children of men killed at Wagala
airstrip.

Foreign correspondents have been refused police clearance
to fly into the affected area. There have been non-Kenyan
whites in the Wajir area who have provided information to the

press. Journalists in Nairobi are wary of criticising Kenya too heavily, since Nairobi serves as either East African or African regional headquarters for about 80 foreign press corps members.

In the Tipis report (*Daily Nation*, Friday, 13 April), there is mention of 'diplomatic representations' by the United States and 12 other countries requesting the Kenyan Government to expedite the distribution of food donations to the North-eastern Province. Unofficial sources present at the 'representation' stated that the Kenyan Government was urged, first, to be forthcoming about the events of 10 to 15 February and, second, to allow food relief to reach the area.

It has now been reported that Kenyan Government officials directly concerned with this matter, have been removed as of 6 May, although the Kenyan Government has denied this. Military units involved are said to have been broken up and personnel reassigned to other areas of Kenya. This information has not been confirmed by official Kenyan Government sources.

If the Kenyan Government continues to prevent relief aid from reaching the survivors of Wagala it is not unlikely that thousands more, particularly women and children, will perish.

Abdi Sirat Khalif was one of 12 men detained without charge in January and released without explanation a few weeks later, after the events described here. He is the brother of Ahmed Khalif, MP for Wajir West, who was one of the few prominent Kenyans to have protested to the Government in February 1984 about events in Wajir.

Sankara's promise of a real revolution

Victoria Brittain   *Published 24 August 1984*

Two decades after independence half of Africa is ruled by military regimes and most of the rest of the continent by one-party states. Both forms of government are responses to the desperate search for authority capable of confronting the unprecedented economic and social crises these countries face today.

But wherever these military or civilian governments have taken a radical nationalist line and promised revolution – in

Mozambique, Ethiopia, Angola, Zimbabwe, and Ghana, for instance – external pressures and the resistance of remnants of the overthrown regimes have eroded the central authority and forced compromise with the new leaders' anti-imperialist and democratic ideals.

The young army officers now in power in Burkina Faso (formerly Upper Volta) believe the history of their revolution, in one of Africa's very poorest and most remote countries, will be different. This week's dissolving of the government, apparently in an attempt to end an internal power struggle with some of the civilians, shows, however, that a tough fight for unity still lies ahead.

Captain Thomas Sankara: sobering lessons in the months out of power

Some key differences between Burkina's starting point and those of their African friends appear to give Captain Thomas Sankara's government a rare opportunity to carry through the deep social change promised. First, in contrast with Mozambique, Angola, and Ethiopia, the army is highly educated, disciplined, and it is not at war with well-armed dissidents. Second, unlike Zimbabwe and Ghana, the country never had a bourgeoisie with Western links and tastes that now feels threatened by the new ascetic order.

The contrast in style between the National Revolutionary Council headed by Captain Thomas Sankara and the previous regime of colonels is stunning.

Scene: summer 1982, the Officers' Mess, Ouagadougou. A grand dinner washed down with wine and water imported from France is enjoyed by most of Colonel Saye Zerbo's cabinet, a handful of aid donors, and a few journalists. It has been a hard day touring dusty desperate villages where emaciated peasants heaped goats and other presents into the visitors' cars at every stop.

After dinner the Minister of Planning prompted by a whispering civilian official at his elbow, responds with an unconvincing air of confidence to questions on the seemingly hopeless economic prospects. That year 360 aid missions had visited Ouagadougou. Life expectancy was 32 years, the per capita income $110 a year, less than 10 per cent of the people were literate.

Today that official with two decades of experience of projects which died in Ministers' air-conditioned offices, is himself the top man in the Ministry of Planning – Eugene Dondasse. Except for Wednesday's Council of Ministers meetings Dondasse spends his time in the countryside where 95 per cent of the people live. His brainchild is a 15-month rural development programme due to start in October. It is based on small-scale projects and is completely decentralised.

To the new leaders it is the key to the future success of the revolution. 'For years in the Ministry of Planning I gave advice which wasn't listened to and drew up plans which were never implemented. Today we have a regime which should be the aid donor's ideal: we know exactly what we want, we have rigorous discipline with the finances, we, at any rate at the top, *really* work.'

Scene: summer 1984, the Officers' Mess, Ouagadougou. One hundred and two young soldiers and civilians from Revolutionary Defence Committees all over the country in unison solemnly dedicate themselves to a lifetime of 'selfless sacrifice in the service of the people'.

The modest ceremony ends a four-week series of seminars on politics, economics, and philosophy. 'We CDR militants, like our soldiers, would be just reactionaries or worse, criminals in power, without serious political education,' said the group's spokesman, addressing the Head of State, a number of Ministers and soldiers from the ruling Revolutionary Council.

Eugene Dondasse's rural development plan's success will largely depend on the dynamism young men like these (and a few rare women) can inspire and maintain in CDRs throughout the country. Each of the 25 provinces has a target of building 10 water reservoirs, one bakery, one light agricultural industry, one poultry farm, and one cinema-cum-cultural centre. In a successful first test of local mobilisation, 20 houses were built by each province before the first anniversary.

'For 23 years our people have been taught to wait passively for the government to bring them "development" but from our first day we called for Defence Committees to form themselves and simply start work. I use the radio ceaselessly to urge the people to start all these things on their local initiative and not wait for officials from Ouagadougou,' says Captain Pierre Ouedraogo, Secretary General of CDRs.

Burkina's CDRs are a similar system of reorganising power in society to Cuba's committees for the Defence of the Revolution, the *kebelles* of Ethiopia and the People's Defence Committees set up under the Rawlings Government in Ghana. So far in Africa such attempts to give 'power to the people' have been a very partial success. A new spirit of popular mobilisation and self-sufficiency has proved hard to maintain.

In Burkina Faso a strong moral line for the new leadership at national and local level was spelt out last year in the 'Political Orientation Address' which is the ideological touchstone of this regime. The tone matches the traditional peasant values of this conservative rural society. And though there have been some abuses of power by the CDRs for personal goals these have largely been a problem of urban areas.

The capital, Ouagadougou, has a long history of feverish political life by a tiny minority. Captain Sankara once described the 'democracy' of an earlier era as 'nine political parties, each run by three individuals – 27 people with the same interests, linked by the same political and financial deals to the foreign business world, getting their election funds from abroad, buying consciences, and getting millions of our people voting to order.'

And as the regime's number two man, Captain Blaise Compaore, has put it, 'immorality in our political life is a direct cause of continued under-development'. The corrupt political network of the past appears to have been crushed by the People's Revolutionary Tribunals which have fined or imprisoned 100 former officials. However, the foreign business community remains sceptical that the change is more than temporary.

Another traditional politicised minority is in the fragmented labour movement and some tiny Marxist groups which have surfaced noisily in recent power struggles. 'Our little Left groups in fact represent no-one but themselves,' says Dondasse, himself a long-standing member of one of them. 'The people are responding to something quite different in this country's politics – Sankara.'

However, a cult of personality is strongly discouraged by Captain Sankara himself and the other young officers at the top. Asked who are the members of the ruling National Revolutionary Council the captain said, 'Do our people really want to know the actors? They are much more interested in the performance. We prefer to live in a country where the leadership spends its time working, not polishing its public image for opinion polls – ours is not a society for personality cults.'

In early 1983, in the first phase of his group's rise to power, Captain Sankara was elected Prime Minister by his fellow soldiers. But he served under a timid head of state, Major Jean Baptiste Ouedrago, who was afraid of him and had him arrested within months. The unusual and moving speech of dedication to the people which Sankara made on taking office in 1983 revealed the uncompromising principles of his group. They are the basis of today's home and foreign policy.

Captain Sankara's two-and-a-half months out of power in mid-1983 were, he says, a sobering lesson in what is at stake in a bid to make a nationalist revolution. The French hand behind the arrests in May, 1983, of Sankara and Major Jean-Baptiste Lingani, now Defence Minister, was barely concealed. 'Our relations with France could certainly be better, and we want them to be better,' said Sankara recently.

At the same press conference the first question to the Head of State from a local journalist revealed something of the unusual relations of this regime with its people. 'Comrade President, could you spell out in detail the errors made during this first year of the Revolution?'

Captain Sankara replied simply that errors had been made every day.

But the most important lessons this group of single-minded soldiers believes it has learned are those of other honest and charismatic African leaders. From Nkrumah to Nyerere, early hopes of economic independence, health, and education for their people have dissolved under myriad compromises made in response to external economic pressures.

Love in a paranoid climate

Sylvia Vollenhoven talks to David Beresford about her life *Published 21 August 1984*

I was born and brought up in Cape Town. My father is a driver at a furniture store. He is half Indian and half Dutch, I think – that's why my surname is Dutch. My mother was mostly of Hottentot extraction, although her father was also Indian.

I met Bob in 1979. He is an electronics technician, working for a private company. I didn't really have white friends and didn't socialise in white society. I grew up in a housing area and a high school which was fairly politicised. Fraternising with whites was frowned upon.

We got married about a year after we met. We went to England to get married, in a tiny place called Harlington, near Luton, where Bob's family live. It turned out to be fairly complicated, because his parents were going through all these arrangements and they didn't know I was black. They phoned one day and said there was just one legal requirement – I had to get a document from the authorities in South Africa to say that there was no bar to my getting married.

Bob said: 'Well, you see, we can't do that, because Sylvia is black.' His father was so angry – not because I was black, but because nobody had told him – otherwise he wouldn't have been giving such stupid advice.

So we went over there. I remember trying to tell the bishop's secretary at St Albans that I could not get a letter from the South African embassy, because in South Africa I am black and I am not allowed to be married to him. She kept on saying: 'But you don't understand, dear, it is all right here.' Anyway, eventually we got an affidavit from a local advocate to say I wasn't already married because that was all they were really worried about.

A few weeks after the wedding we flew back to South Africa. It was a bit depressing – we had had a very happy and jolly wedding and a happy-go-lucky honeymoon and here we were back at Jan Smuts (Johannesburg's international airport) with those dour officials and men in green uniforms wandering around and saying in thick accents: 'Where have you been?' You suddenly realise the kind of paranoia you are going to live with every day. You think: 'My God, I don't know if anyone is going to stop us and question us.' Of course, they probably hardly ever would but there is that feeling that you have done something horribly illegal and that any minute you could get questioned and slapped into gaol. I just said I'd been overseas on holiday.

The day we got back from Britain we went to a café in Johannesburg with a friend. This Portuguese guy came roaring over and started shouting and screaming at Bob: 'Get out of this fucking place. How dare you bring these kaffirs in here, fuck off out of this place.' I was shattered. I'd been asked to leave places before – you know: 'We're terribly sorry, but we can't serve you,' and that jazz. I thought it might just be a patron who had lost his head. I asked a waiter and he said it was the owner who'd just recently come from Angola. Obviously these Portuguese had come to South Africa thinking it was the last bastion of racialism and they were going to fight for it every inch of the way. When a foreigner stands there telling you to fuck off out of the place in your own country, that to me . . .

We had to give up one of the two flats. Most of the flats in black areas are very expensive, roughly twice the amount of flats in white areas. So it made a lot of sense to move into Bob's flat, which was half of what I was paying and much nicer and much closer to town anyway.

It all went OK until I became pregnant – visibly pregnant. And then the neighbours started getting a bit twitchy, because I think they suddenly started having visions of hundreds of black kids running all over the show. One of the neighbours must have complained – that is all I can think – because one night when I was about seven months' pregnant the flat was suddenly surrounded by policemen at about three o'clock in the morning.

I saw them shining torches through all the windows and I went and woke Bob up. They were demanding that we open the door and saying we had drugs and things. Fortunately we didn't. They were searching all over the place and couldn't find anything. There was a very young policeman who was very agitated. He started trying to rough Bob up. He insisted he saw some paper floating in the toilet that looked ominous. Bob told him to get stuffed. He was very angry, being woken up at three o'clock in the morning. The cop didn't like the tone of voice Bob was using and tried to stuff his head down the toilet. I flipped and said if they touched him I was going to sue them and write a story about it. They said: 'Ah, you're a journalist. You can come with us.'

I thought they were just going to take me for a rough ride, down to the police station, but the young constable insisted that he had found drugs – the slip of paper he found in the toilet – and that I had to be locked up. Bob followed the police van in his car, but he lost them, because they were screeching through red robots. I was being flung around in the back of the van.

After we got down to the station they let Bob into the white side. I was on the black side, but we could shout across. Bob was asking me for the name of a lawyer he could phone. I was giving it to him when this policeman came up to him and said: 'I would prefer if you did not communicate with the prisoner.'

Bob said: 'The prisoner. God, that's my wife.' The whole station just burst out laughing – you know, 'Ho, ho, tell us another one.' They told him to go or they would lock him up as well. The magistrate eventually dismissed the case, he said he couldn't understand how it was brought, because there was no evidence.

We decided that we would have to get out of that white area. Whites regard me as too African-looking to be acceptable in their areas. There are lots of Coloured people who live in white neighbourhoods, but the fairer you are the better chance you have of assimilating. They would know you were coloured, but accept it. The darker you are the more of a threat you are to everything, from property prices to their own little security.

It took us six months to find a house in a black neighbourhood. Nobody there knew, or cared what anybody else was. Everybody got to know Bob was a Brit., but not once did even the kids mention that he was white. It was totally relaxed. Then we bought a house, in what would be considered a 'grey' area. Technically the street we live in is supposed to be white, but I don't think there is a white family in it.

There was a bit of a fuss, because for a lot of reasons we wanted to buy the house jointly. First of all we couldn't get a bond – they are meant to take a wife's salary into account, but they wouldn't take my salary into account. The building societies get generous money from the Government and it would go against the Group Areas Act if they took my salary into account. It would be acknowledging we were living together. But the banks are much more professional when it comes to lending money.

We applied to a bank and got turned down three times. Eventually, I thought, well, it is an international corporation, if I vaguely threaten to embarrass them, I wonder what their reaction will be. So I went in and saw the manager and said: 'I don't care what you say, I don't think you will lend me money because my husband is white and I am black.' He hummed and hawed and said he would have another look at it. And about a day later he phoned up and said it was OK, we could have the loan.

The battle with the baby was getting him a birth certificate. Bob wanted him registered at the British Embassy, to get him a British passport. When I was in hospital the staff were most perplexed. The procedure is that the hospital administration registers all the babies born in that hospital. I said: 'These are my husband's particulars and these are mine.' A woman came to me with these forms every day and told me what her problems were and every day I'd send her away and say: 'Just send them in, it's not your problem.'

A month after I left the hospital I got a letter from the Government saying the child was inadequately registered and I had to present myself with my husband at the Department of the Interior. We felt it would complicate things if we both went. So I went in and spoke to a clerk. She said my husband had to come in. I said he was overseas and if she would give me the papers I would send them to him for signature.

She said: 'No. Pretoria does not work like that.' She was very embarrassed, she couldn't say that they wanted to see what he looked like because in South African law the child assumes the race of the father. But in this case the child clearly, after looking at the mother, could not be white. She said she would have to send the forms to Pretoria. As I was leaving she called out after me: 'You know the child will probably have to be registed Coloured?'

It sounded like a threat. I said: 'Look, you can register him as navy blue if you like, but just give him a birth certificate.'

Eventually, about a year later, I got a full birth certificate, but in the place where all the father's particulars were meant to be given there was just a line through it and at the bottom it said the baby was illegitimate. So I sat down and wrote a long letter to the Minister of Internal Affairs, saying: OK, I'd coped with the fact that even a marriage in a Christian church was not recognised and if they wanted to decide my son was a bastard that was also fine, but that surely they could acknowledge the fact he had a father and give him a proper birth certificate. The British authorities said they could do nothing with that birth certificate. They were meant to be issuing the baby with a passport on the basis that the father was British, and here South Africa was saying he did not have a father.

Eventually, the embassy leaned on them and we got a letter from the Ministry asking us to go in. We thought, what the hell, and went in. We saw this very senior and serious official who was so charming. He was almost apologising for the Mixed Marriages Act. In fact, he called it 'just a little quirk in our law'. So now the baby has a British passport in his father's name, but he is registered as a Cape Coloured.

Apart from that time I was arrested we have not had any problems with the police. One of the best things we did was move out of a white area, because the people who have problems are almost always in a white area, where the neighbours complain. But I think people place too much emphasis on hassles with the police. The real hassles are with day to day things you can't do, like financial dealings, trying to secure a loan, or buy a house jointly. And people's attitudes are so important.

Conservative South Africans are always ready to point out to you that racialism exists in all parts of the world. That's true, but not to this degree. In other cities you would not feel constrained in hugging your husband, or holding his hand in the road. I consider myself fairly confident and fairly brave, but it would be asking for trouble, especially when it is holiday season in Cape Town. We never have so many whispers and stares as at the end of the year when all the northerners come down to the Cape.

One Christmas, I remember, I was working and Bob came to fetch me. We were driving home along the highway. A Mercedes with a Transvaal registration with four big, heavy Boer-type guys in it were just passing when I leant over to kiss Bob. They hooted and waved and made all kinds of rude signs. Bob ignored them, and they dropped back and tried to force us off the road. We were terrified – they were big guys. Bob accelerated. They chased us, trying to cut us off. Eventually we lost them. But that is always something we fear.

Social attitudes are really the worst. Like shopping in a supermarket: you consult each other in a supermarket and suddenly you bring a whole aisle to a standstill, people dropping their toasties. Or buying clothes – they won't let him into a cubicle with you. In the beginning it used to send me into a rage, but then I started to get very philosophical about it and sorry for those people, thinking: Christ, what sort of mentality it must take to live in that kind of world.

I think we've been very lucky, because we met at a time when the Government had already started turning a blind eye. I was worried, but not that worried. I knew that, especially in Cape Town, if you did not interfere too much with your neighbours and lived in the right kind of area, where you were accepted, they did not want the kind of publicity that came from putting constables in a tree outside your bedroom. They had stopped going that far.

I used not to know many mixed couples. But it's like owning a VW; suddenly you realise how many others there are. Since we got married – I think because we are so open and upfront about it – a lot of people have introduced us to mixed couples. But we tend to shy away from them. I hate the sort of attitude that says we have to form some sort of club. In any case, the kind of people who traditionally went into mixed marriages, or mixed liaisons, I don't really like. They tend to be ex-beauty queen types who have run off with German lovers. I find them fairly mindless and hate to think people link me with them.

Bob is a typical Pommy. He has got a healthy disrespect for authority. The fact that he came to this country when he was fairly mature means that he did not feel the sort of intimidation that I used to feel. And that has rubbed off on me. He would say: 'Well what can they do? This is a civilised world, in the twentieth century.' He couldn't understand how paranoid I was and as a result I've become a little less paranoid than I used to be. He lacks any fear of authority. Authority is there to serve you, as far as he is concerned, not to scare the hell out of you.

I think the Immorality Act and the Mixed Marriages Act may go, because it will be a handy sop to the new Coloured and Indian chambers in Parliament – to show people that they are effective. But it won't make any difference to my life. All it will mean is that we will have to pay joint taxes.

I don't think the new constitution is an advance. I think it is a step backwards. I mean they are looking for ways of improving the Group Areas Act, of making it tighter and stricter. I've looked very carefully at how the new system will work, but I can't see any evidence that this massive structure they have been building up is really breaking down. The Mixed Marriages Act and Immorality Act affect so few people. The majority of South Africans – 99 per cent – do not care either way about those two bits of legislation, because it does not affect their lives. What is more important is the Group Areas Act and housing.

Property prices in black areas are so artificially inflated. The rates in a place like Rylands Estate – an average kind of area, but the only Indian estate in the Cape Peninsula – are the same as Bishop's Court, the richest area in Cape Town. There is such a demand that it pushes up prices and pushes up the rates. And so black people who should be able to rent decent accommodation can't because it is so scarce and expensive. Black landlords run amazingly corrupt schemes, you virtually have to bribe a landlord to rent a property. The middle class is growing and getting better salaries, but they can't afford accommodation. We are paying half our combined salary for the house we're living in.

In the last five years in Cape Town, because of the fast-growing middle-class – not out of goodness of their hearts or anything, but because businesses have suddenly realised there is a market there which can be tapped – most restaurants in the metropolitan area and most hotels are open. But that is only so in a place like Cape Town. Move 10 kilometres out to Bellville and the Wimpy won't allow you to sit down.

I think I stay in South Africa because I don't feel like giving up. There is a constant black drain and I would hate to contribute to it. I would feel like a coward.

It is very much more comfortable overseas. But I don't relate to the social issues. I read the British papers and I think to myself: 'My God, is this really what they are worried about? Can Arthur Scargill really have the nation in uproar because he fell against a police shield or whatever?'

I think one needs to have a commitment to the issues in a society to feel part of that society. And while I can have a holiday fascination with the United States or Britain, I know that if I lived there I would be very depressed. I would feel homesick.

A hundred years of struggle

Victoria Brittain interviews Swapo's leader Toivo Ja Toivo   *Published 14 September 1984*

'No country can give passports to its enemies,' Andimba Toivo Ja Toivo was told last week by Mr Sean Cleary, South Africa's key official in Namibia. So the delegation of the South West Africa People's Organisation (Swapo) left Windhoek for London without him. Ja Toivo, Swapo's newly-elected secretary-general, is a survivor of 16 years on Robben Island, imprisoned for leading the struggle for independence in Namibia, and Mr Cleary was only prepared to hand over a passport in return for a statement that he now rejects violence.

'Cleary was the man who came to gaol to persuade me to leave,' says Ja Toivo. 'I told him then they would have to force me out if they wanted to. I haven't deviated from the path which led me into a Pretoria court – I have people to lead – I'm not shifting.' Ja Toivo speaks softly, but his gentle manner does not hide an unyielding determination, unbroken by the years of torture and prison.

After a Kafka-like series of exchanges between Pretoria's ministries, Windhoek's bureaucracy, and Swapo's lawyers, South Africa lost the latest round of their 20-year war of nerves with Ja Toivo. The old trade union organiser, sentenced to 20 years' imprisonment for 'conspiracy to overthrow South African rule' in Namibia, did not sign Mr Cleary's non-violence statement, but he eventually got his passport anyway.

Last spring, South Africa unexpectedly released Ja Toivo
from prison as part of the web of US-backed diplomatic initiatives in the area. The plan included persuading Mozambique to
sign the Nkomati peace pact – an agreement which opened
Mozambique up to South African capital and deprived the
African National Congress of an important haven. For a moment it looked as if the end of the 18-year colonial war in
Namibia between South Africa and Swapo would be in sight.

Ja Toivo's strand of the web was, in the South African strategy, to lead a 'moderate' Namibia – inching towards independence on South Africa's terms. Mr Sean Cleary spelt out South
Africa's strategy for Namibia in a long article. The key, he
wrote, was to destroy Swapo's legitimacy by persuading its
leaders to link with the territory's internal political groupings
– gathered together in the South African-backed Multi-Party
Conference. Perhaps, the South Africans hoped, Ja Toivo need
no longer be an enemy.

But for all Cleary's hours of talking to Ja Toivo in prison, he
seems to have seriously misunderstood his man. Once free, Ja
Toivo refused to deal with the internal parties. He refused to
be frightened into exile, and he publicly backed the Swapo
leadership in its decision to escalate the guerrilla war against
South African occupation. His four months of freedom have
been devoted to uncompromising attacks on South African
policy and on the Reagan Administration. The 'pro-Western'
label sometimes pinned on him in the Western press merely
makes him smile.

'Since taking power in 1981 the Reagan Administration has
consistently sought to hamper progress towards Namibian independence. The so-called constructive engagement policy has
served to camouflage Washington's open embrace of the oppressive apartheid regime. Washington's preoccupation is to
keep Southern Africa safe for continued plunder of the natural
resources, and unmitigated exploitation of labour. This selfish
interest has led the Reagan Administration actively to support Pretoria in continuing its illegal and brutal occupation of
Namibia.'

The shuttle diplomacy in Southern Africa of Dr Chester
Crocker, the US Assistant Secretary for Africa, created a peak
of optimism about peace in the region in the wake of the
Nkomati accord in March. But Swapo, whose United Nations
representative coined the description of 'the master of contrived
ambiguity' for Dr Crocker, never joined in the optimism. Ja
Toivo explains why. 'We went to the talks in Lusaka in May,
and then later to Cap Verde prepared for a serious negotiation
on a ceasefire. The so-called Administrator-General (for Namibia) came to both lots of talks with no mandate to negotiate. He

simply reiterated the South African Prime Minister's assertion
that there would be no settlement (in Namibia) until the Cuban
troops withdrew from Angola.

Toivo Ja Toivo

The Americans have encouraged South Africa with this link-
age policy. United States foreign policy is in chaos – they have
failed in Lebanon, they have failed in Central America, they
need a success in Southern Africa. But the South Africans are
studiedly vague and tricky. If ever the Cubans left, they (the
South Africans) have already prepared the next excuse for not
implementing the UN Resolution on our independence. Why

have they not withdrawn from Southern Angola six months
past their own agreed deadline?' Ja Toivo believes that the
South Africans are still hoping to force the Unita rebels into
the MPLA government in Luanda.

The months since the Nkomati accord have been traumatic
ones for the Southern African liberation movements. But South
Africa's miscalculation in the freeing of Ja Toivo has, in part,
produced a psychological boost to off-set it. None of the Front
Line states has criticised Nkomati openly. The desperation of
Mozambique's situation is too well understood. But an independent Namibia under Swapo will not be born on the same terms,
Ja Toivo says. 'It is our duty and our responsibility to support
the ANC in every way – I have repeated this time and time
again to the South Africans. And as for the idea that we might
go to them cap in hand for economic aid, it is out of the question.
We are tied to them economically now, but in the future we
will work with them only on an equal basis. There are many
other friends who want to assist us, some are already assisting
us. And these multinationals in Namibia will find they have
to enter into new agreements with us. Our fight is for a better
life for Namibians; exploitative economic agreements will be
revised.'

Such uncompromising fighting talk might be dismissed as
unrealistic if it came from an isolated exile group. But recent
months have seen another psychological change in Swapo's
position inside Namibia. At the first meeting with the South
African Administrator-General in Lusaka in May, the Swapo
delegation was not only boosted by the presence of Ja Toivo,
but also by the Central Committee's decision to produce the
white Namibian lawyer, Anton Lubowski, as a voting member
of the delegation. Lubowski had long been an underground
member of Swapo. As he explained last week, 'it was the
moment to bring in the whites. Suddenly the middle-class
whites were worrying about the economic situation, declining
investment and so on under the present set-up, and people
began openly talking about Swapo. A psychological barrier had
been breached.'

Swapo is still now allowed to hold meetings and rallies inside
Namibia, unlike the various internal parties in the Multi-Party
Conference. But the diminishing coherence and credibility of
those parties appears even to be recognised by South Africa
now. At the Cap Verde meeting last month, for the first time,
the South Africans met Swapo alone without insisting on the
presence of the internal parties.

Six months ago South Africa was still at the stage of trying
to initiate talks between Swapo and the internal parties. But
as Ja Toivo explains, 'There was no point – we have no power,

they have no power, what were we to discuss? The conflict is between Swapo and South Africa, and negotiations will be on that basis.'

Swapo's status as 'the sole and authentic representative of the Namibian people' was recognised by the UN General Assembly as long ago as 1973. It has taken 11 years to force South Africa to the conference table with them. Colonial wars have usually unravelled fast once that bridge is crossed. Ambassador Noel Sinclair, the Guyanan vice-president of the UN Council for Namibia pointed out in London this week that 'Swapo is not simply a liberation movement now. In international minds the Organisation is being associated with statehood.' Ambassador Sinclair recalls that South Africa's occupation of Namibia has been declared illegal by the General Assembly, the Security Council and the International Court of Justice. 'What has prevented the Security Council from taking action against South Africa?' he asks. 'Wasn't it the vetoes of France, the United Kingdom, and the United States?'

It is exactly six years since the UN Security Council passed Resolution 435 in support of UN-supervised elections in Africa's last colony. Pressure on the United States and Britain to drop their support for South Africa's demand for a withdrawal of Cuban troops from Angola – as a precondition for Namibia's independence – will be considerable at this autumn's session of the UN General Assembly. The passport that Mr Cleary finally gave to Toivo Ja Toivo was not valid for travel to the United States, presumably to try to stop him leading the Swapo delegation to the UN, a meeting which promises to dent the image of the United States as a peace-maker in Southern Africa.

Songs from the desert

Simon Zhu Mbako   *Published 14 September 1984*

Like most of the African countries, Namibia is a land of more than one ethnic or linguistic community. The society's cultural heritage is many-sided and its way of life has many roots.

The most popular form of artistic expression is poetry and songs. There have been and are still poems and songs symbolising nearly every social activity.

The Khoisan, one of the ancient peoples of Namibia, have perhaps more poetry, tales, and proverbs than any other community. A rich legacy has been handed down from generation to generation.

The poetry depicts the old history of the Khoisan, including the legends of Heitsi Eibeb, their greatest hero. It explains their beliefs and their relation to the natural order: the moon, the sun, the stars, the wind, rain, drought, the trees, animals, sickness, happiness, love – and man.

It unfolds the Khoisan theory of the division of the social world into hunters, cattle herders and cultivators, and it shows how the Khoisan have survived in their environment – the harsh plains of the Namib and Kalahari desert, where life seems impossible. The poems also bring to light their 'understanding' of creation and death.

The original traditional poems were frequently acts of resistance to colonial domination, one example being *The Battle Song of the Herero* which is sung and recited in times of trial. This expresses the call for peace when 80,000 Hereros were exterminated by Germans in 1904.

Following the rise of the national liberation movement in Namibia of a quarter of a century ago, there has now emerged a new revolutionary type of poetry. This has found clear expression in the publications of two anthologies: *From Exile*, by Mvula Ya Nangolo, and *It Is No More Cry*, by Henning Melber.

Heitsi Eibeb

Oh Heitsi Eibeb
Thou our grandfather
Let me be lucky
Give me game.
Let me find honey and roots
That I may bless thee again.
Art thou not our grandfather
Thou Heitsi Eibeb?

The battle song of the Herero

Listen when the song of the frogs
Resounds from the marshes.
Listen to what they have to say:
It is good to come together,
It is good to reach agreement,
It is good to make the voices of many
The single voice of all.

Praise poem to the !Nara Melon

You round food
With many thorns,
You many-breasted
Foster mother of the Topnaar children,
Even if I am far away
I will think of you.
You food of my ancestors
I will never forget you.

I blame Kara — tuma

I refuse this thing
that we should have come
to be the last of all.
It gives me pain.
And I despise
that old man
of long ago
who caused it to happen.
I think if I saw him today
I would beat him
But he's dead now
And there's nothing to be done.

Animal World

When man became separate
from the animal world
all went wrong.
Before this
we were all people
together
But after this
we were divided
each to his own.

Portuguese in airstrip threat

Alves Gomes   *Published 16 November 1984*

Eight months after the signing of the Nkomati accord between Mozambique and South Africa, the question whether South Africa is prepared to fulfil its side of the deal remains wide open. The signs are contradictory. On one hand, this is the first year since 1980 which has not seen direct South African aggression against Mozambique. On the other talks have come to a stop, and the violence perpetrated within Mozambique by the Mozambique National Resistance (MNR)—also known as Renamo, still continues.

New evidence has appeared of the collusion of influential Portuguese politicians and businessmen with the MNR, and also of a recent attempt to create a new rear base for the MNR in Tanzania.

In June, when President Machel first made reference to a 'conspiracy against Mozambique's independence and sovereignty' involving 'personalities of governments which maintain diplomatic relations with our country' and 'circles nostalgic for colonialism', few outsiders were able to decode his diplomatically veiled allusions. But now the outline of the Portuguese connection with the MNR is becoming clear.

With it appears the concern of those who lost wealth and influence in Mozambique that the MNR, long seen as their means to achieving some return or at least of forcing Mozambique to make huge repayments for nationalised enterprises and properties, might actually disappear.

If South Africa were to fulfil its obligations under the Nkomati accord, the MNR would disappear. But this is the big unresolved question. Bilateral talks between Mozambique and South Africa have continued without the participation of the MNR since 11 October and on 12 October Foreign Minister Roelof Botha decided to go to Lisbon to sort out the Portuguese end of the MNR and draw the organisation back into the negotiations. At the last minute, however, the Portuguese Government made it known that such a visit would be unwelcome, and it did not take place.

Four Portuguese citizens were arrested on 20 August in central Tanzania. Under cover of hunting under licence in the area of the Selous Gorge near the border of northern Mozambique, they had allegedly been preparing to create rear bases, including air strips, to facilitate continued supplies of arms to MNR units operating in the north of Mozambique.

Three of the four have long connections with the MNR. Adelino Serra Peres, Senior, lived in Beira, Mozambique's second city, in colonial times. He was a close associate of the notorious pro-Fascist businessman and newspaper proprietor, Jorge Jardin, who employed as deputy administrator of his newspaper *Noticias de Beira* a pide/dgs (secret police) agent called Evo Fernandes. Fernandes is now the ostensible leader of the MNR.

Adelino Peres, Junior, another of those detained, then a member of the Rhodesian army, had been accused of taking part in the Nyazonia massacre of Zimbabwean refugees in Mozambique carried out by the Selous Scouts in August, 1976.

Another detainee is Carlos Cardeano, nephew of Peres, Senior, who is claimed to have been deeply involved with the Rhodesian authorities in the creation and early activities of the MNR in the late 1970s.

The Peres family in Lisbon, one member of which used to broadcast in Rhodesia for Africa Livre, the MNR radio station, and also worked as Orlando Cristina's private secretary, apparently has friends in high places. Deputy Prime Minister Mota Pinto bypassed the Portuguese Foreign Ministry in giving direct instructions to Portugal's ambassador to Mozambique, who also covers Tanzania, to secure the release of the detainees from the authorities in Dar es Salaam.

President Nyerere's position is known to be that an attack on Mozambique is tantamount to an attack on Tanzania. He has deplored the fact that anti-Mozambican propaganda and activities were allowed to be launched from Portugal. The four remain in detention.

Deputy Prime Minister Mota Pinto, who is leader of the Social Democratic Party (PSD), junior partner to Soares's Socialist Party in the Portuguese Government, interfered again in Mozambique's affairs on 11 October. His telephone call from Lisbon to Evo Fernandes in Pretoria, urging him to return to Lisbon before agreeing to anything, caused the MNR to withdraw from the trilateral commission set up in terms of the declaration announced in Pretoria on 3 October.

The commission, made up of representatives of the Mozambican and South African governments, and of the MNR, was aimed at bringing violence quickly to an end in Mozambique.

Evo Fernandes, who travels on a Portuguese passport, returned to Lisbon where he has been operating for several years as the public face of the MNR.

On the South Africa side Roelof Botha seems personally committed to making the Nkomati process work, or at least preventing it from being seen to fail. And he is one of the South African ministers who, having been denounced by Jorge

Correia, Fernandes's deputy, as being allied with Communism in Mozambique, has declared that obstruction of the Nkomati accord damages South Africa's own interest.

It remains to be seen whether those in the South African military who have been most closely connected with the MNR both before and after the signing of the Nkomati accord will feel themselves bound by the Pretoria declaration of 3 October.

The fact that on 3 November, two civilian planes from South Africa dropped supplies in Zimbabwe in an area close to a part of the Mozambique border where the MNR has operated in the past is a poor omen.

Alves Gomes was international editor of the Mozambican weekly, Tempo, at the time of writing.

Free to die
Victoria Brittain   *Published 8 February 1985*

Half a million people are being marched from the drought-stricken fields of Tigre, in northern Ethiopia, to the rocky wastelands of Eastern Sudan in the most determined effort yet by the Tigrean People's Liberation Front and its influential Western backers to break the authority of the Ethiopian regime.

The Ethiopian refugees' future in Sudan is desperate beyond imagining. Big irrigated agricultural schemes were painstakingly carved out of the inhospitable terrain by the Eritrean and Ethiopian refugees who have trickled into this area since 1967. The settlement schemes never fulfilled the hopes of self-sufficiency and are now themselves victims of the drought. The new refugees could never be absorbed into these fragile settlements. In leaving Ethiopia the Tigreans face a living death of subsistence on handfuls of cowpeas in conditions of utter degradation.

All liberation wars take a high toll of civilians. But few liberation movements have so compounded their people's suffering as the Tigrean leadership.

Since the international community belatedly responded to the starvation in Ethiopia last October, food for starving peasants has been brought into the towns and relief camps of Tigre, but the TPLF disrupted the government's food distribution as they have disrupted agricultural and water development projects in the province for nearly a decade.

Numerous Western aid agencies have helped the TPLF covertly through Sudan for the last few years. More recently the Front's Western lobbyists have come into the open. They range across the ideological spectrum from the ultra-conservative Horn of Africa Committee to the radical charity War On Want. All have encouraged the TPLF to enter a war they cannot win. The drought has made it a war they cannot sustain.

The strange alliances of the TPLF's backers have their roots in the geo-political power struggle over Ethiopia, once the West's key ally in this strategic position on the Red Sea. A tangled web of opposition factions confronted the military in the early years after the Emperor's overthrow in 1975. Most have been eagerly wooed by the West or the conservative Arab states of the Gulf who would like a pliable client in power across the Red Sea in Eritrea.

The only authentic anti-Derg movement then and now is the one with no external support – the Eritrean nationalist group demanding the independence of the former Italian colony annexed by the Emperor. The dominant group, the Eritrean People's Liberation Front (EPLF) has a fighting force of 20 years' standing, trained in the old anti-Emperor days by Algeria, Cuba and Libya, and an administration of health, education and agricultural services which is the envy of many independent African countries.

The drought has hit Eritrea's rocky desert as dramatically as anywhere else in Africa. But the Eritreans are receiving far less aid than anywhere else on the continent and meanwhile this war, which neither side can win, rages on with incalculable cost. The Eritreans have shown over 23 years that, unlike the Tigreans, they can organise their country and their army to meet any conditions. But Ethiopia's People's Army cannot in the current crisis.

Early on the military government in Addis Ababa made its fatal decision to fight not negotiate with the Eritreans. The EPLF, presumably on the basis that my enemy's enemy is my friend, aided the nascent TPLF.

But the TPLF's political demands are as different from their former mentors' as their spectrum of political alliances. The Tigreans are not an independence movement, but say merely that they want the Derg ousted and 'democracy'.

The TPLF justify their people's trek to disaster in Sudan by claims that the Ethiopian Government refuses food to their supporters and is forcing them into a resettlement programme. Such claims, so widely and uncritically broadcast, are one side of a much more complex battle for power in which food is a key weapon for all sides, and skilful propaganda a monopoly of one – the TPLF.

The Ethiopian and Eritrean people are paying a terrible price for the outside world's interest in their countries.

In recognition that dramatic moves are called for, the Derg is now resettling 1½ million people. Only peace can give them a chance of self-reliance. The Sudan can never give that to Ethiopians.

No end to the hunger

John Markakis   *Published 22 February 1985*

Are the causes of famine in Ethiopia as simple and natural as commonly presented? Is drought a sufficient cause of starvation, and will its passing resolve the problem of food scarcity? The answer to these questions is No.

The harsh fact is that the northern plateau, its land exhausted by an age-old process of erosion and continued cultivation without fertilisers, is no longer able to sustain an expanding population.

Living on the margin of subsistence, without reserves of their own, or access to the resources of the market, the peasants are prey to any interruption in production – drought, flood, locust, animal disease, or war.

Northern Ethiopia has had more than a fair share of such visitations and famine is not a stranger. A pattern of recurrent drought has been recorded, showing that major droughts are likely to occur every 10 years, and raising fears of enduring climatic changes.

The lethal potential of drought derives from the fragility of subsistence cultivation, which in northern Ethiopia has not changed since biblical times. As everywhere in Africa, the sector that produces food for the bulk of the population has been completely neglected in favour of export crops.

For this purpose, land and labour were withdrawn from food and nothing was invested in it. As a result food production failed to keep up with population growth, and while the urban sector made up for it through expensive imports, the rural population was pushed to the edge of starvation.

The present military regime won early acclaim with the enactment of a sweeping land reform that wiped out landlordism and divided land more or less equally among the tillers. This benefited mainly the mass of former tenants in the south, but had little impact in the north where land was already parcelled out in small-holdings.

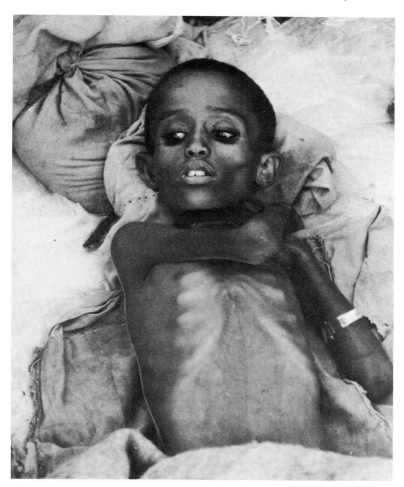

A starving past, a hungry future

Reform did not improve production since neither capital nor technological improvements were introduced.

The FAO estimates only 8 per cent of planned investment in agriculture went to peasant production, and the rest was allocated to state farms to produce grains for the townspeople and the soldiery.

Moreover, endemic warfare during its reign, the conscription of young peasants in the army, the flight of waves of refugees from the countryside, and the deliberate destruction of livestock in dissident regions, have dislocated agricultural production and have as much to do with famine as the drought. It is no coincidence that the worst affected regions – Eritrea, Tigre,

Ogaden – have been battlefields for years, and so has Wollo more recently.

The Imperial regime regarded famine as a natural and inevitable phenomenon and refused to acknowledge its existence in 1972–1974. The soldiers who toppled Haile Selassie from his throne in 1974 proclaimed that drought is natural, but famine is a man-made disaster.

Now, 10 years later, they are blaming drought for a famine 10 times worse, even though the Ethiopian Relief Commission sounded the alarm in time for the disaster to have been averted through concerted national and international action.

Foreign governments are justly blamed for not responding with alacrity. The same at least can be said of the Ethiopian Government, whose actions have yet to show that famine prevention is its highest priority. The war against half a dozen opposition movements has continued without let up, with an army amply equipped by the Soviet Union. Neither supplies nor badly needed transport was provided by the military for famine relief.

Nor did the regime requisition private transport for this purpose, as it did in 1976 to transport the militia to Eritrea. There was no requisitioning or rationing of food and the townspeople experienced no discomfort. In fact, 1984 was a banner year marking the tenth anniversary of the revolution and the founding of the Workers' Party of Ethiopia, followed by Ethiopia's hosting of the OAU Heads of State meeting. Following months of intensive preparations and great expense, these events were celebrated with an extravagance unimagined in the days of Haile Selassie.

How is this possible? The answer lies in the structure of African states where the peasantry is politically irrelevant. Peasants elsewhere, because they produce for urban consumption and export, have some economic leverage and a measure of political influence. Peasants in Africa can barely feed themselves, and the subsistence economy figures only notionally in national calculations. Far from being able to influence his rulers, the African peasant cannot even communicate with them, since they seldom speak the same language.

Ethopia's army has expanded tenfold since 1974 to become the largest in Africa, and consumes the lion's share of state expenditure. Its function is to defend the state and the incumbent regime. Its preservation is the Ethiopian Government's highest priority. Legitimate though it may be, it is directly responsible for allowing drought to turn into famine.

The traitors' plea to be recolonised

Wole Soyinka *Published 30 March 1985*

I am two years late for this engagement, but it hardly matters: the news is still the same—nought for our comfort. We live in the era of Nkomati, and no matter what minor variations we receive from time to time in the medical bulletin, Nkomati remains alive and well. Perhaps in future years the black children of Southern Africa will justify any psychosocial disorders by claiming that they were born under the Nkomati star.

The Nkomati syndrome will take its place in the medical dictionary to explain certain forms of aberrant conduct in African leadership. After all, a veteran member of the medical profession, Professor Lambo, who is also the deputy director of the World Health Organisation, did propose, a year or two ago, that African leaders should be subjected to psychiatric examination once every five years—something like that anyway. An experienced doctor in such a position, who interacts regularly with the power-wielders of the world, must have observed something, something we, as laymen, do not know.

What we do know however, and experience in our socio-political milieu, is the failure of political will throughout the continent. No one can disagree with President Nyerere's insistence that the failure which Nkomati represents is a failure, not of the signatory states but of the entire continent.

Salient events in Nigeria since 1975.

- **July, 1975:** Gen. Yakubu Gowon deposed in bloodless coup. Brig. Murtala Muhammed becomes head of state.
- **February, 1976:** Muhammed assassinated in attempted coup.
- **February, 1976:** Gen. Obasanjo becomes head of state.
- **August, 1979:** Alhaji Shehu Shagari declared winner in presidential elections and (**October**) Obananjo hands over.
- **August, 1983:** Shagari declared re-elected president.
- **December 1983:** Gen. Buhari takes power in military coup.

I go even further and insist that this failure will continue as long as African and black leadership continues to exhaust its limited fund of political will on creating internal structures of oppression against their own peoples, thereby isolating them from that communal endeavour which should reinforce them, at moments of crisis, in their undertakings against our common external enemies. To remain blind to this basic fact is to reveal total alienation from the organic forces which give a coherent identity to a people as a people.

Such leaders exist only as members of a select, secretive club, gathering from time to time to make deals above the heads of the people whom they claim to represent.

We know whose gun-ship helicopters, whose ubiquitous marines snuffed out the lamp of self-determination in Grenada, but what do we say of the consortium of black leaders who spread out the mat of invitation to Ronald Reagan? Who were these shameless so-called leaders who sent out the SOS which read: 'Recolonise us, *please!*' We know whose agency manufactured the dastardly instrument which terminated the career of Walter Rodney, but whose was the face beneath the reactionary mask which nodded in the Brigades, signed Rodney's death warrant, and emasculated his workers' movement?

As for the mother continent, it is pockmarked with vicious replications of apartheid structures, with the full machinery of arbitrary arrests and imprisonments, torture, 'disappearances', displacement and dispossession, and ingenious forms of dehumanisation which appear at times to strive to outdo one another across national boundaries. Is it any wonder that, gleefully observing these anomalies of black existence, the Ronald Reagans of the Western world continue to tip the wink at Pik Botha, who thereupon is emboldened to carry on business as usual?

Our literature must not fail to reflect the treachery of such alienators even as our people struggle on the actual terrain to reject them, enduring hideous mutilations, dying heroic but unnecessary deaths, experiencing the despair of seeing their victory over one fascistic imposition hijacked by yet another fascist opportunist, only ten times worse. The crumbs of solace which come our way need also to be elevated to legendary status to counter these agents of our pessimism—thus, even as we mourn Nkomati, we must celebrate Mandela. If we don't, the opportunist leeches, those discredited leaders, will claim him for their own. They will rhetoricise with his name, they will mouth his courage, name the odd street or two after him, then promptly forget the meaning, the challenge of his superhuman gesture.

And it is a frightening ... no, not gesture but act. It is a replete combative act on its own, the summation of that same revolutionary will that began over two decades ago when a group of committed nationalists decided that the word no longer sufficed, and took to other weapons. In these dark days of Nkomati, let us at least be thankful and humbled by Nelson Mandela's giant fist thrust out beyond Robben Island to smash a loud resounding 'NO' in the teeth of apartheid.

Together with other heroes like Steve Biko, Walter Rodney, Maurice Bishop and Malcolm X, around whom the festival has been organised, they remind us, confined or at liberty, living or dead, that the imperatives of struggle reach out beyond prison fortresses and beyond the grave.

This is part of Wole Soyinka's speech when he opened the fourth International Black Book Fair.

The playwright turns film-maker

Michael Simmons talks to Wole Soyinka
Published 30 March 1985

Wole Soyinka's acute concern for his country, Nigeria, and his flair for drama remain undiminished. Twenty years ago the trouble was that he had allegedly forced Radio Nigeria at gunpoint to broadcast an anti-government statement in place of one by an establishment chief. But it wasn't quite as the prosecution said, and he was acquitted on all counts.

Today, it is a film he has just made, severely critical of the Shagari years. As hundreds turned up at the National Theatre in Lagos for the premiere the other day, security officers stepped in and took the reel. *Blues For A Prodigal*, as it is called, depicts real events, and specifically the violent attempts to indoctrinate a naive young student. It amounts to an unambiguous indictment of what Soyinka now calls 'the crude hammer-blow fascists and the looters' who made up the Shagari administration. 'Make no mistake,' he says now, 'under Shagari, it was civil war.'

Clearly, he disapproves heartily, but of necessity guardedly, of the military regime of General Buhari which seized power in the coup of New Year's Eve, 1983. But he fails to understand the seizing of his film. 'Taking it,' he said in an interview in London this week, 'is a kind of admission of culpability. It is a way of identifying with the Shagari regime. The government has condemned itself.'

Still no reason is given, and officials remain silent. It is left to Lagos journalists – already treading their own tightrope under Buhari – to speculate. Soyinka has seen such things before, many times, and sighs heavily – but he and his backers are nearly £200,000 out of pocket.

Soyinka, the writer and thinker and some-time film-maker, is unavoidably the political activist as well. There is a universality about his work – he has adapted Euripides – but he is principally a chronicler of events he has lived through. His moods fluctuate between aggression and black despair, but are always permeated by the 'life-affirmative' force that sustains him.

No one knows for sure, but probably 100 million people – one African in every four – live in Nigeria. The country has been billed, just occasionally, as the continent's flagship for democracy, but is seen more often as a battleground for warring factions, tribes, federalists and secessionists always ready to tear at each other's throats. Soyinka talks, however, of the possibility, one day, of political coherence, of the truly sophisticated nature of the Nigerian electorate.

But he also talks of the dismal prospect presented by the 20 or so years since Independence. For every one step forward, he says, Nigeria takes 12 steps backward. There has been no real 'hey-day' since Independence, he adds, though there were tolerably better times under Olusegun Obasanjo and Murtalah Mohammed in the mid-1970s.

'We are guilty of our own crimes,' Soyinka argues, speaking of Africa generally as well as Nigeria. 'The first and the principal enemy is internal. The humiliation of Nkomati (the 1984 treaty between South Africa and Mozambique) was the price for failing to unite. We are fighting the reactionaries within . . .'

President Alhaji Shehu Shagari, he dismisses now as 'a traitor', at least in the latter stages of his rule. Did the West, seeing Shagari as a gentle moderate, let Nigeria down? Not exactly, Soyinka replies, but it was unpardonable that Western observers were so 'fooled' by the man, and that they therefore complicated the country's problems by demoralising the opposition forces.

To what extent does Soyinka rate himself a patriot? He paused. 'There is no shortage,' he says, 'of anti-life rogues. But I love life, and the human community is mine. It is for the Government to prove its patriotism, according to my definition.'

Soyinka is now 50, and when not writing has spent his professional life either teaching or as visiting lecturer at half a dozen of the world's universities. Three were in Nigeria (Ibadan and Ife twice over), one in Ghana, one in the US (Yale) and another in Britain (Cambridge). Now he talks of retiring from this part of his life at the end of the current academic year.

What next? More autobiography? He stopped the instalment so far published, called simply *Ake: The Year of Childhood*, at the age of 12 quite deliberately. 'Autobiography,' he says, 'is lies. You *have* to be selective . . .' He said when Ake was published he wouldn't add to it. Now he says perhaps he'll have to do so.

His most famous work outside Nigeria and a classic of prison literature is *The Man Died*, and will be reissued by a London publisher soon as a paperback. He has written a new introduction. It remains to be seen whether this will echo what he wrote ten years after the first edition – that, where a regime may be deemed culpable, each family should have a handy pin-up photograph of the nation's leader, so that, every day as a reminder, they could hurl the family slops at it.

More seriously still, he sees himself primarily as a playwright, and would like to write – given the time – and direct more of his own work. Whatever comes out, there will certainly be no complacency. 'Acquiescence in political crime,' Soyinka reflects, 'is a hideous form of surrender, very tempting but very contemptible.'

What he writes next will not be as stark as lines produced just a few years ago, saying 'Sodom and Gomorrah/Will seem quite paradisial/When this whorehouse comes to trial . . .' But it will almost certainly startle.

How to stop the fat of the land feeding off the poor

Mahmood Mamdani   *Published 10 May 1985*

I am sorry I have a rather bad cough today. You can say I am prone to disaster, unlike some of you in the audience who look rather resistant to it.

I remember hearing a story, during the Sahelian famine of the seventies, of a fat man and a thin man. Said the fat man to the thin man, 'You should be ashamed of yourself. If someone visiting the country saw you before anyone else, he would think there was a famine here.' Replied the thin man, 'And if he saw you next, he would know the reason for the famine!'

The simple point I am trying to make is that if you divide

our society into two, into the majority prone to disaster and that minority resistant to it, you are likely to find some sort of a relation between the two.

Last year, I was doing research in Lira District. I met a capitalist farmer in one village. She had over 500 acres which she had bought (technically leased). I wondered how she could buy land in an area where people observed clan right to land quite strictly.

She replied, 'The 1980 famine helped. People were in need. For the first time, they were willing to sell land, cows – things they wouldn't dream of selling in normal times.' Famine, it would seem, is a disaster for the poor but an opportunity for the rich. The former are disaster-prone, the latter disaster resistant.

Disasters are not natural but social catastrophes. They are the result of social conditions: deforestation, soil erosion, desertification. Lack of rain does not cause a famine, it is simply the occasion for it. It triggers off the famine.

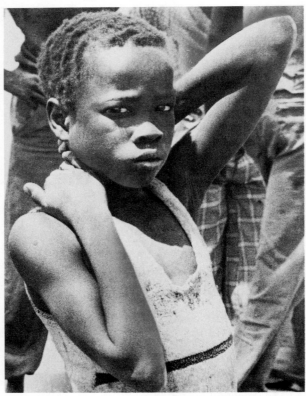

Among the disaster-prone

But why do people cut down forests? Why do they over-graze? Why do they work the same old tired land without resting it? Is it out of malice? Or sheer ignorance? Not really.

I am going to talk about Uganda because this is where we are. All Africa has become much more prone to disaster in this century, and particularly in the past two decades, than it ever was before. So, I want to begin with the impact of the colonial period on the major producers of wealth, the peasants, in this country.

An analysis of how this country was integrated into the colonial imperialist economy would show that there were two major forms of integration, depending on the region we may consider.

The first was where an area was turned into a cheap labour reserve. This was the migrant labour system whereby the wife remained a peasant producing food in the village, but the husband migrated as a worker to a plantation. He was employed only part-time, the rest of the year, he returned to the village and lived off the food cultivated by the wife.

The second was where an area was turned into a reserve of cheap raw materials. You take the above system, with the wife producing food and the husband cheap labour and collapse the distance between the husband and the wife.

● African countries with food shortages:

Angola, Burkina Faso, Chad, Mali, Mauritania, Niger, Sudan, Ethiopia, Botswana, Burundi, Cape Verde, Kenya, Lesotho, Rwanda, Senegal, Somalia, Tanzania, Zambia.

● UN estimate of emergency needs $1.5 billion including $1,078 million for food aid and transport and $81 million for water projects.

● 150 million Africans threatened by famine.

● Food production has declined by 15 per cent since 1981.

● Food imports feed 1 in 5 Africans

● Grain yields per hectare have fallen by a third in a decade.

● Industrial capacity is working at a third of its potential.

● Africa's interest payments are $15 billion a year.

With the wife still producing food and the husband producing an export crop, you now have a cheap raw material reserve. Cheap because the family produced its own food. The cash it got from selling cotton or coffee was just to pay tax and to buy a few manufactured necessaries.

Now, in Uganda, there were quite a few cheap labour reserves at the outset of colonial rule: Lango, Acholi, West Nile, Kigezi. But in the 1920s, as the Belgians increased exploitation in Rwanda, the Banyarwanda peasants began to emigrate to Uganda. In the late 50s again there was out-migration from Rwanda due to a political crisis. As a result, the British introduced cash crop production in Lango and Acholi in the 1920s and then in West Nile in the 1950s.

Today the only remaining cheap labour reserve is Kigezi. The rest of the country continues to be a cheap raw material reserve.

Now the whole system of cheap raw material production required two conditions. One, that labour meets a substantial part of its own cost of production (food cost). And two, that labour remains the major input in production; or, to put it differently, that the technological base remains low.

The above remains the general condition of the Uganda peasantry today. The Uganda peasant is essentially trapped in two main types of exploitation.

The *first* is exploitation through unequal market relations where you sell cheap and buy expensive. This is monopoly exploitation, whether by state or private agencies.

In July, 1984, I investigated the millet trade in Lira District and discovered that peasants received just 25 per cent of the final price of millet.

In December, 1983, I researched the coffee trade in Buganda. My data showed that the peasant received exactly 18.96 per cent of what the government got in the world market for the same coffee.

You would be surprised by how constant this proportion has been since the colonial period, whether in the first independent government or in the Amin period or now.

The details vary from region to region. But together, they amount to three types of forcible exactions. These may be *forced labour* amounting to as much as a quarter of the peasants' total labour in certain villages, forced crops, usually those for export, or forced cash contributions for the party or the church.

The result of this dual exploitation – that through unequal market relations and that through direct force – is that the peasant operates with a permanent handicap; his surplus product is regularly siphoned off. His cash income is barely enough to meet immediate needs; for tax, to replenish a hoe or buy some salt or medicine. Peasants don't eat sugar any more; in many villages in the north, they can't even buy soap any more.

The point is, that the peasant is forced to begin the production cycle each time with roughly the same or even a worse technical base than the previous time around. Walter Rodney wrote that the African peasant entered colonialism with a hoe and came out of it with a hoe. He should have added that the hoe the peasant entered with was locally produced, the one he came out with was imported.

To grasp the point better, let us look at the peasant's labour process. It consists of three elements: land, labour, and implements of labour. We have seen that the peasant has little choice so far as the implements are concerned; his technology is relatively stagnant. To get out of a crisis or to endeavour for prosperity, what does a peasant do? He uses whatever control he has, over land and over labour.

He works the tired land over and over. Why is it that periods of fallow are getting shorter and shorter in Kigezi? Or that cassava is replacing motoke and beans on Entebbe Road?

At the same time, the peasant has as many children as possible to maximise the labour at his disposal. For a middle class family, a child may be just a mouth to feed for 20 years, but for a peasant family after only four years the child is also two hands to work! People are not poor because they have large families; they have large families because they are poor!!

What is to be done? To begin with, it is necessary to safeguard against utopian thinking, against looking for a solution outside the parameters of the problem by introducing it from without. We must be realistic and find the solution internally.

From this perspective, we can correctly define the role of relief or foreign 'aid'. It can only be complementary to a local solution, not a substitute for it. Failure to understand this can even compound the problem. During the Sahel famine of the 70s, for example, 20 per cent of the population of Mauritania was entirely dependent on relief food by 1974.

Such assistance is not an antidote to disaster. It becomes a hand-maiden.

Only that relief is worthwhile which undermines itself in the long run; which restores the initiative of the victim, and does not strangle it; which sees victims not simply as objects to be helped, but as subjects potentially capable of transforming their disaster-prone situation.

My main point is that any strategy that claims to be a solution must seek to revive the creativity and the initiative of the people. Central to this must be to educate people about these relations which make them disaster-prone. This education must be based on investigation, concrete and independent.

If land is taken to create national parks, we must organise for the return of the land. If labour is maimed and shackled by administrative coercion, we must organise to remove that

coercion. If products of labour are appropriated through mono-
polistic market practices, we must organise to change these.

Simply put, we must organise concretely, organise on the
basis of a common education and educate on the basis of independent and popular investigation.

*This is the edited text of a talk given to the Uganda Red Cross
conference on disaster prevention in Kampala on 19 March,
1985. Within a month Dr Mamdani was deprived of his Ugandan citizenship by the government of Dr Milton Obote.*

A letter to the President of Uganda

Published 10 May 1985

Mr President – Dr Mahmood Mamdani, a Ugandan, an associate professor of political science and the acting dean of the
faculty of social sciences, Makerere University, Kampala, has
lately run into problems with your government for his committed scholarship and progressive political standpoint.

Around 19 April, 1985, while away in Spain attending a
conference with the permission of his vice-chancellor, Mamdani
received a letter from the Immigration Department purporting
to declare him an alien in his own country. The immediate
circumstances, Your Excellency, which appear to have led to
this arbitrary and unlawful stripping of Mamdani's citizenship,
thus rendering him stateless, is a talk he gave recently to the
Uganda Red Cross Conference on Disaster Prevention. The
conference was held in Kampala.

The speech, Your Excellency, infuriated the Minister of State
for Security so much that he singled it out for a vicious attack
in his closing address. Subsequently, the same minister appeared on television and repeated the attack.

Soon after, officials affiliated to the Ministry of State for
Security (the Criminal Investigation Department, Immigration
officials) interrogated him on his immigration status. Subsequently he received a letter from the Immigration Department dated 1 April, pretending to solicit certain information
for the purposes of, as it put it, 'updating the files'.

On 10 April, Dr Mamdani supplied the requisite information. On 13 April he left for Spain. On 19 April a letter was received purporting to declare Dr Mamdani an alien and asking him to surrender his passport.

Dr Mamdani has written extensively on his country. He is the author of *Politics and Class formation in Uganda* and *Imperialism and Fascism in Uganda.* He is the Editor of a leading academic journal *Mawazo* published by the Faculty of Social Sciences, Makerere University.

During the Amin period Dr Mamdani was in exile in Tanzania and he taught in this university.

In view of your Excellency's position as Chancellor of the University of Makerere and your known progressive stand on academic excellence and on rights of a citizen in a democratic society, we appeal to you to intervene and stop this harassment and restore Dr Mamdani's citizenship.

Dr K. I. Tambila,
Chairman of Dar es Salaam Academic Staff Assembly.

Pioneers in the fight against the desert

Victoria Brittain   *Published 21 June 1985*

Ten years ago when the Sahel was reeling from the great famine of 1973 the Nigerian writer, Amadou Ousmane, wrote a novel called *15 Years – That's Enough.* It was a classic portrayal of those days – post-independence hopes betrayed by a super-educated, Frenchified elite living in high style while peasants starved to death. The book ends with the night coup which brought an unknown 'strong man' to power in Niger. 'Long live the Army. Down with the Party' is the cry.

In real life he was Colonel, now General, Seyni Kountche of Niger. Like the leader of every military coup in Africa, Kountche vowed to end corruption and transform the underdeveloped economy and political structure of his huge landlocked semi-desert country. The same cry of 'enough' rippled too through barracks, school rooms and trade union meetings in Niger's neighbour, then Upper Volta, today Burkina. Successive governments talked weakly of change and crumbled from the inside until the present head of state, Captain Thomas Sankara, seized power nearly two years ago.

Those two West African regimes, often identified as 'pro-Western' (Niger), and 'radical' (Burkina) have in fact both set a new pattern of development which confounded the pessimism of many experts. Today there is even a cautious new tone of optimism among many of the United Nations organisations involved in the huge inter-state anti-desertification projects which must succeed here if the Sahelian people are to live.

As one expert in the UN Sahelian Office puts it after 10 years working in the area, 'We do have the technical knowledge to hold back the desert – we all know that and it has been done successfully in China. But in the Sahel, incompetence has reinforced fatalism and produced failure after failure. But now in Burkina you can see how an ambitious government in less than two years has done more than others achieved in 20.'

In Niger by 1983 the years of declining food production had been reversed and the country was self-sufficient in grain before the drought hit with new ferocity.

At the root of every World Bank and other analysis of what has gone wrong in African development since independence is the theme that the balance of power must be shifted from the 5 per cent who live in the cities to the 95 per cent in the countryside. Education, health, infrastructure and even food are concentrated in the cities. Lip-service is always paid to changing these priorities. Niger and Burkina have created political structures to carry such radical change through.

The style of the two capitals is however very different. The 'Balles Populaires', compulsory sport and exuberant informality of Burkina's Ouagadougou are unthinkable in the rigid efficient corridors of power in Niamey. Crossing the border northwards the Burkina greeting 'camarade' gives way to 'monsieur' or 'Excellence'.

Niger has spent these years under President Kountche constructing its unique 'Development Society'. Officials explain it as the obverse of the usual party system with power and patronage flowing down. Instead it is a pryamidal structure of village, regional, provincial and countrywide committees. Members are selected by their own community on the basis of how hard they work. 'This is a society with no time for passengers,' said one official. Decisions flow up as well as down.

Burkina's Revolutionary Defence Committees (CDRs) sprang up spontaneously in response to Captain Sankara's first speech after taking over on 4 August, 1983. He struck the note which has characterised this regime ever since – development lies in your own hands, the government will try to help you in anything you organise. Nationwide the CDRs have organised huge collective work projects.

Both governments have institutionalised styles of popular consultation. Last week President Kountche met his cadres in the gleaming modern hall dating from Niger's brief period of capital inflow when uranium from its northern mines was highly priced on the world market. The President briskly exposed three serious cases of corruption in top government circles, one of which he called 'the embezzlement of the century', announced heavy penalties for such behaviour, and revealed a mysterious commando attack on a small police post in the north which he said had come from Libya and been led by the son of the former head of state, Hamani Diori.

- Population: Niger 7 million, Burkina 7 million.
- Capitals: Niger's Niamey, Burkina's Ouagadougou.
- Life expectancy: Niger 45, Burkina 44.
- Children in primary school: Niger 23 per cent, Burkina 20 per cent.
- Economies: subsistence agriculture, herding, cotton, peanuts. Niger has uranium mines.

In Ouagadougou's Maison du Peuple, open debates on formerly taboo subjects such as the budget, land distribution and female circumcision have sometimes gone on all night with the leadership. More than 90 per cent of the population here is illiterate, one of the worst records in Africa, and currently debates are raging on the priorities of literacy campaigns for adults, increased primary school enrolment, and French versus national languages.

The impact of such symbolic changes has been reinforced in the rural areas by last month's opening of state People's Shops. Bicycles, paraffin lamps, salt, soap, oil, rice, Biros, hoes and seeds – commodities almost never seen before – have arrived in new village shops built by the community. New football stadiums and cinemas have also been built by the CDRs as fast as the dams, airstrips, wind and water breaks which now dot the parched brown landscape.

Now is the hottest time of the year with the rains already overdue. Early morning in the provincial capital of Ouallam, a barren desert town 50 miles north of Niger's capital, Niamey, finds the new breed of local top official, a colonel, out in the town's market garden. The colonel has sown his own land. Now he is encouraging tired townspeople who have spent the last six hungry months scraping a living in Niamey to do the same. 'The rain *will* come this year – be strong, work now,' he urges.

Here in Ouallam, Niger's typical dry season production of vegetables by civil servants, farmers and nomads watering small patches of ground by hand from boreholes or wells has spotted the uniform brown sand with green. Small gardening projects were introduced all over the Sahel after the 1973 drought by numerous non-governmental organisations. They became government policy last year in Niger to meet the drought emergency President Kountche himself forecast as early as January 1984. At the same time a cattle slaughtering and meat drying programme has prevented even worse pasture destruction moving south.

In both Niger and Burkina today it is striking how the traditional conservatism of peasants and herders gives way to creative innovation under the pressure of the drought. 'Give us seeds and teach us cultivation,' says one nomad chief after another at the sight of a foreigner. And Niger's Minister of Rural Development, Dr Ari Toubo Ibrahim explains that, after the 1973 famine when the country had been producing 200,000 tons of groundnuts for export, it was the peasants who decided to replace more than half that crop with cereals or the nutritious niebe bean. 'It was in their interest and they did it spontaneously.' Many experts are sceptical about such spontaneous change in agricultural patterns.

But change is being sparked on many fronts with unpredictable results. Burkina last year abolished the 'head tax' – a colonial legacy which contributed to the seasonal migration of about 2 million Burkinabe to the Ivory Coast to work in the cocoa plantations. Some of that labour may now choose to stay at home where it is badly needed for the infrastructure projects.

The present famine crisis reveals just how few of the infrastructure and transport problems of these impoverished landlocked countries have been solved since the last famine put the spotlight on them. The consensus from government and aid workers alike is that this year's much worse emergency has so far been better handled. But the real challenge is to end the days of crisis management in the Sahel by breaking the cycle of dependence and under-development. Both Niger and Burkina have begun, despite the drought disaster.

A blueprint for an Africa for Africans

Yoweri Museveni *Published 23 August 1985*

Africa's economic and social crisis has at last excited the interest of the world beyond the continent, but the starvation of millions is still too neatly explained by the experts. Population growth and spending on defence are not, as so many would have it, the fundamental causes of Africa's terrible backwardness. The causes of the problems are the distortion in economies which has been brought about by foreign domination, both past and present, and the incapable men who have been in positions of leadership since independence.

The economies of Africa do not produce for Africans. Instead of growing food for home consumption resources are devoted to the cultivation of export crops (tea, coffee, cocoa and tobacco). Africa is paid low prices for these products and much of the money goes to the advanced countries to pay for trivialities ranging from razor blades and sewing needles to perfumes, lipsticks, wigs, cars, and cornflakes for tourists. Africa is producing what is not vital for its survival, while neglecting what is vital. Expensive imports are used habitually even when there are cheap alternatives.

Uganda's presidents since independence:

● Milton Apollo Obote, 1962–71;

● Idi Amin, 1971–79;

● Yusuf Lule, April/May 1979;

● Godfrey Binaisa, 1979–80;

● Military Commission (three months) headed by Paulo Muwanga;

● Milton Apollo Obote, December 1980–85.

Population 14 million. Export crops: coffee, cotton, tobacco, tea, sugar. Between 1970–80 production of coffee dropped by half. UN High Commission for Refugees estimate of displaced people by 1984: 800,000.

For example, the countries of East Africa depend on imported oil. But there is an extremely cheap source of energy in the form of hydro-electric power from the Nile. Why don't we electrify the railways, build more of them, and start tram-services in the cities of East Africa?

This would save so much foreign exchange. At present, East Africa uses oil exclusively for its transport, and it is used most uneconomically. Monster trucks plough up the roads from the coast to Kigali in Rwanda and consume huge amounts of oil, when the use of rail from Mombasa through Kenya and Uganda to Rwanda and Burundi would save so much and would enable us to attend to other fields.

Who is responsible for making such poor decisions? Clearly it is the foreign interests that have dominated Africa for so many years, and in many cases the incapable and corrupt leadership that has been in power since independence.

Uganda is a classic case. Idi Amin was encouraged to take power from the dictatorial Obote, because Obote, out of opportunism, had started making confused noises about 'moving to the left' and trying to play 'Eastern interests' against 'Western interests' as if there were no *African* interests to cater for. We opposed Amin resolutely and he sought Libyan and Soviet assistance against us. This link with the Libyans and the Soviets caused his original Western sponsors to 'discover' that Amin was a 'monster'.

We hoped that after Amin outside interests would back the struggle for genuine democracy, having seen how much damage the lack of it had caused to Uganda. We were soon disabused. As long as Obote was clever enough to say that he was for these or those outside interests, much as Amin had done, those foreign interests would back him to the hilt. And back Obote they did, with economic and military aid, virtual news-blackouts on the regime's crimes etc.

The IMF involvement in Uganda provides an example. Obote accepted all the 'advice' of the IMF wholesale; devaluation, two-tier exchange rate, return of the Indians, and the unbridled free interplay of 'market forces'. The result was impoverishment of a rich country.

The story of Uganda is the story of so many other African countries that are now cap-in-hand. Many have had foreign economic 'experts' in their ministries of 'Economic Development and Planning' and in the central banks. For 15 years some of us have been warning that the haemorrhage of resources is bound to cause catastrophe. We have warned that the centuries old malformations in our economies must be re-shaped.

We have been labelled 'Marxists', 'radicals', but of course such labels do not matter. I would very much like to be a 'conservative' if I am shown something worth conserving. What should I conserve in the present situation? Jiggers, intestinal worms, malnutrition, a high infant mortality rate, a low average life-expectancy, a low calorie and protein intake, etc. in the population? Or the complete denial of basic human rights by the present regimes, including the security of human life?

What should we conserve of these things?

The new talk about 'the starving millions' overlooks that more people die as infants, from miscarriage, or disease than from outright starvation and war.

The way ahead lies only in refusing to allow disadvantageous terms in dealing with foreign interests and in rejecting incapable leaders who above all prevent the discussion of national issues, let alone their resolution.

In Uganda certain foreign interests are jittery about the emergence of the National Resistance Army and the National Resistance Movement. The movement challenges Uganda's old politics and old patterns of dependence. The self-reliance of the NRA means that it is not subject to foreign pressures. And the alliance of young educated people with peasants is a dangerous example to the rest of Africa, where it could be emulated by other down-trodden peasants.

If Africa is to break out of the present neo-colonial straitjacket its leaders must have independence in decision-making, bearing in mind the primacy of our interests. Secondly, Africa needs integrated, self-sustaining and independent economies that will be able to interact with the world economy on a mutually advantageous basis not on the present unequal one.

Thirdly, national economies must be integrated to ensure greater diversity of resources and wider domestic markets.

Without these factors being realised, nothing can be done to reverse the downhill drift of Africa's economic, political, social, and environmental situation.

Uganda, and much of Africa, is not poor, and does not need constant charity and relief.

Yoweri Museveni was interim Chairman of the Uganda National Resistance Movement at the time of writing this article. He is now President of Uganda.

A letter to Balarabe Musa

Rufai Ibrahim   *Published 30 August 1985*

I am sure you will understand, and excuse my choice of such a public forum as a way of reaching you. Your exact address at the moment is unknown to me and to all those from whom one could inquire about you. Not long ago, persistent though barely audible whispers in town seemed to point to the Kirikiri Maximum Security prisons as your place of confinement. But now that such whispers have fizzled out almost completely and, since, for what I hear, it is not uncommon to move or transfer detainees around the country's prisons, I haven't the slightest idea in which particular prison or guest house (some detainees are kept in guest houses?) you are now being held.

Anyway, wherever you are my hope is that your spirits are high. Those of us who have never been in detention for any considerable length of time can only imagine what your loss of freedom for such a long time must mean to you. I guess, though, that your freedom apart, there is not much else you are missing in detention, since you have always led a simple life – no alcohol, no cigarettes, no particularly high tastes. Only a couple of days ago former communications Minister Audu Ogbe was saying that he was well taken care of while in detention. It showed on his body too, and on the bodies of most of those released along with him early last month. You know, this government doesn't take prison affairs lightly. It's yearly food budget to the 50,000 or so of you in detention or serving various prison terms is a staggering ₦70 million. And contracts have long been awarded for the building of 47 new prisons, including four maximum security ones, in an effort to ease congestion in the prisons. No mean achievement, you must admit.

I have been itching to ask you this question: How do you kill the boredom of prison life? I know reading is your habit. But what kind of stuff do they allow in the prisons? The kind of fat novels that Ojukwu, the Ikemba of Nnewi, was reportedly holding as he walked into freedom after his release early October? Or just about anything, including radical stuff? I have in mind to send you a copy of Ngugi's *Detained*, and Onimode's most recent book (which incidentally was the only new publication from the Nigerian left featured at the UNIFE Book Fair a fortnight ago) *Imperialism and Under-development in Nigeria* in order to add to your collection. But I am not sure how the prison authorities will take it. As far as I know there is no decree yet against such books but this administration, you know, does not tolerate 'undue radicalism'.

Talking about books, I wonder if the authorities or anyone
sent you a copy of the book *Muhammadu Buhari, Nigeria's
seventh Head of State*, which was published by the Federal
Ministry of Information and released last month. I don't want
to say anything about it here for lack of space, but I assure you
the book received excellent reviews in the Nigerian press and
it is currently being serialised by many newspapers. You must
read this biography of our leader. And let your friends there
have it when you're finished with it.

I know that news about what's happening outside here filters
somehow in to the prisons. But if you can't make much sense
of all the little bits and pieces of information that come your
way, don't worry. Even for us, before whose eyes, and ears,
things are happening, it is not easy to keep track of recent
happenings, much less discern from the seeming contradictions
and confusion of onrushing events, their real essence. But we
are trying. Personally, what I do when I am beginning to get
confused about happenings in the country is to re-read George
Orwell's *Animal Farm*—between the lines of course. I find it
rewarding, and I recommend the same to you. Do you have a
copy with you there or do I try to send one to you?

I am not sure you are in the know, but we are now quite close
to getting the IMF loan, thanks to the negotiating abilities and
'no nonsense' posture of our present leaders. The Naira may
not, as the IMF demands, be devalued, but the government has
satisfied, or is busy satisfying, IMF's other conditions. Cut back
on public expenditure, mass retrenchments to trim the civil
services and even the private sector, introduction of all sorts
of levies and fees, the muzzling of all organised groups and
opposition, you just name it and the government has satisfied
it.

I know how painful it must be for you to see, in your own
lifetime, the re-introduction of the poll and community taxes
(which you abolished in Kaduna State on becoming governor
on 1 October, 1979), the introduction of all sorts of fees and
levies, and the elevation of traditional institutions—in short,
the complete reversal of the gains made by the tal akawa in
their struggle up to the end of the Second Republic. I can almost
hear you ask: Who then was the 31 December coup meant for?
Well, let's not forget that our present leaders had no idea of the
real extent of damage done to our economy during the Second
Republic and that, as the government often reminds us, these
are difficult times that call from each one of us, sacrifice—even
of one's right to differ.

But have you heard that the members of the Nigerian Army
are soon to get new wardrobes—with new uniforms, boots, caps
and all? It was former President Shagari's idea, of course, but

the present government has found it exciting and is implementing it. You must praise this administration for according defence its proper place in the scheme of things. Defence allocation in this year's budget, you know, is almost 1 billion (₦928,244,100) out of a total of ₦10.1 billion. And today we are proud producers of light personal arms and explosives —courtesy of the Defence Industries Corporation (DIC) in Kaduna. I know you must be wondering about morale in the armed forces. Well, I'll tell you it's very, very high, especially with the salary review of a few months back and the recent promotions. Only last week, fourteen fine officers, including SMC Chief of Staff, Brigadier Tunde Idiagbon, became generals—bringing the number of officers in the rank of a general to about 30 in our armed forces. Nigeria is doing very well in this direction, and as the Head of State said recently, we would win any war any time, anywhere.

Does Fela happen to be in the same prison as you? They got him at last, you know. He is now in for five years, for foreign exchange offences. And for this number of years, the 'suffering and smiling' masses of our people will lose a strong voice in their struggle for a better deal from their oppressors. I doubt, though, that this is 'Chickena, Finish' for Fela. He may, in fact, have been helped by the whole incident. But, let's wait and see how it turns out.

Do they supply you with the dailies? The papers may not always be worth your time and money, but they remain the best source of information on how this country was plundered during the Second Republic, through their coverage of the various probes and trials going in in the country, I am sure you have by now heard of the trial and conviction of the NYSC bosses—former Director Colonel Obasa and his deputy, Chief Kila. In between them, they 'chopped' almost ₦20 million in one year—(Colonel Obasa: over ₦7 million, jailed 21 years; Chief Kila: over ₦12 million, jailed for life).

About a fortnight ago, your friend Edwin Madunagu came out in defence of the Nigerian socialists in a two part article in *The Guardian* (issues of Monday, 5 November and Tuesday, 6 November, 1984). A very good defence, no doubt, I would have loved to summarise for you here Madunagu's main arguments, but this letter is already getting too long. Besides, I know you will consider it much more urgent at the moment to be briefed on how the left in Nigeria is faring under the present dispensation.

Well, as a long-standing and prominent member of the left yourself, you are already very familiar with the problems the Nigerian left was facing up to the demise of the Second Republic. Disorganised, lacking own medium through which it could make itself heard, crippled by the opportunism of some of its members, under-funded and too obsessed with bourgeoisie morality to take some necessary steps to improve its financial position, the left didn't make as much impact as it ought to have made even in the Second Republic.

Today the situation, I regret to tell you, is gloomy. The PRP which, its limitations notwithstanding, provided the left with a platform and a structure for mass mobilisation, is no more. The Kano-based *Triumph* newspapers which became the only media organs of national importance through which the left could talk to others, are not now what they used to be. And what is more, conditions today are simply impossible for any organised group. Students, labour, the left—the government has clipped their wings all.

You know, I think Shakespeare was right when he said there is no art to find the mind's construction in the face. But I also agree with those who say that if a man shows his friends you can tell who he is. And I think this can be applied to governments too. Let a government show its friends, or make its key appointments, and you can tell how its mind is working and where it is going. Were you opportuned to see the list of all the appointments so far made by this government? Did you notice how extra care seemed to have been taken to ensure that no name associated with any known radical featured in it? Incidentally your comrade and former secretary to the government, Yusufu Bala Usman, was the only known radical given an important appointment (membership of the governing council of Ife University), and I have it on authority that he didn't jump at it nor accept it.

This apart, I hear that the Federal Government has ordered that the universities too, embark on retrenchments of their staff. How badly bruised the left will emerge from any retrenchment exercise in the Ivory Towers, I leave you to guess. But I assure you those academic and non-academic staff believed by the authorities to be spreading 'undue radicalism' on the campuses aren't likely to go unpunished.

You see, the government has to show that it is the khaki men, and not the radicals nor any other forces or groups who are in control of the events in Nigeria. Otherwise the IMF loan, which the government believes is necessary, won't be forthcoming.

And where does all this leave the Nigerian left? Well, weakened and harassed members of the left are now, for the most part, reduced to talking to themselves in staff clubs or departmental or faculty seminars. For how long this will continue I cannot tell. But I know one thing: the left everywhere has a durable optimism on which it thrives. It is an optimism based on its faith, and, confidence that history is always on the side of truth, and it, no matter how long it takes, things will turn out fine in the end.

So please do not despair. Keep faith. I don't know why they are still keeping you behind bars. Is it because 'investigations are not yet concluded?' Don't you worry. After all, you have company. Former President Shagari, his Vice-President Alex Ekwueme, are still in detention—not released, not tried. And with so many decrees hovering over our heads, any of us outside here could join you any time.

Before I stop finally, I should remind you not to forget to read *Animal Farm* wherever you feel unable to sort out and make sense of the fragments of information that get to you. Bye for now.

On patrol with South Africa's peace-keepers

Published 6 September 1985

This article is by a national serviceman who has been with the South African Defence Force – the army – on township duty for the past four months.

When we first deployed for the unrest, it was to protect a white suburb for the duration of a large (black) funeral procession. But it was mostly a release from army camp and an opportunity to chat up the girls. Next time we were called out we began doing patrols with the police in the black townships.

As we entered one of the Port Elizabeth townships and began our run, the police express contempt at the rubbish and dirt around. But they keep their litter to dump in the township, throwing it out of the vehicle at pedestrians minding their own business.

The streets are busy: there is a funeral of someone shot by the police, and vehicles overloaded with blacks roar back and forth. The police respond to the chants and clenched fists with shouts of abuse and of 'white power'. They also keep watch for members of the media, especially cameras.

We come on a pick-up truck loaded with children and youths who show us the clenched fist salute. The cops go into action: the pick-up is overtaken and forced to stop. Black bodies spill off in all directions as the cops tumble out in pursuit. Soon, they return in triumph with their catch: a boy of about ten whom they hit and slap as they drag him into the vehicle, where they continue to slap and punch.

The pneumatic steel doors shut, and the vehicle moves off. They force him to slap himself with both hands, while telling us he won't show a black power sign again in a hurry. This, for me, is the central image of this time: a small black boy with wild frightened eyes (but no tears) slapping himself, and the sudden stream of bright, bright blood appearing from his nose and dropping from his chin on the carpeted floor of the vehicle. Drip, drip, drip. Slap, slap, slap.

A few blocks later we pause and he is dumped. For the first time, I look at the other guys. Only one shows any discomfort. On the faces of the rest I see only a leer. The young men are not afraid or confused. They are either bored or excited. They want action, they are callous, and they are enormously arrogant.

We trundle on. The cops talk about white politicians interfering on behalf of blacks. Helen Suzman and Molly Blackburn are mentioned. There is a loud 'dong' as a stone hits the armour and bounces in through the roof opening. The sergeant reacts immediately, sending off a 37mm gas canister. It lands on a house and the residents pour out coughing, eyes streaming. We go and watch briefly, the cops laugh loudly, pointedly. An old man wags his finger at us, and the cops bawl at him threateningly before we move on.

The funeral is over. The returning crowd starts to break up. Knots of people on street corners sing and shout defiance. The sergeant radios, asking permission to disperse a small crowd. A sudden hail of stones is what they've been waiting for. 'Yahoo, let's go!' and we launch into a hurtling, lurching circuit, past streams of panicking, running people, pumping out gas and rubber bullets.

It's over in a couple of minutes. The cops prepare for the second round but the crowd has dispersed. There is an atmosphere of sport: kaffir baiting, beating and hunting.

Eventually we return to the police station. The police brought in a man (ostensibly a stone-thrower) and derive much sport from beating and poking him with the sjamboks and truncheons, in front of the station and in the back of a van. After half an hour he was released.

The sjambok – traditionally a rhino hide whip – is perhaps the truest symbol of the police in South Africa: for herding humans, baiting and punishing them – the tool of a base and perverted shepherd. Bright orange government stock, mass produced, I have seen policemen wielding them on trapped and

cowering offenders with all their might. A wrist flick is enough
to produce a yelp of pain from my fellow soldiers.

Almost throughout these four months, the army has been
mixed with the police, with SADF members in police vehicles.
For the black population there has been no opportunity to
differentiate between the two forces, and the SADF almost
immediately inherited the lack of credibility and bad reputation
of the police.

It is not so much the acts of violence that shock as the level
of racism that allows them to flourish: so many people who are
normally fair and reasonable but who simply 'hate kaffirs'.
They have an attitude of hatred, loathing and contempt for
blacks and a complete lack of human feeling and compassion
towards them.

Action, especially for the young serviceman, is often a thrill,
an ego trip. There is a sense of power in beating up someone;
even if you're the most put-upon, dumb son-of-a-bitch, you are
still better than a kaffir and can beat him up to prove it.

My own guilt at my inaction in the face of this brutality, as
well as the sheer physical impact of it, created an enormous
tension and conflict of behaviour. My response was enough to
get me labelled a 'kaffir-lover' and a 'Communist'. The experience undid much of the nine months of training. Yet it is almost
impossible to isolate yourself completely – you've been living
'fart to fart' with the people for nine months, so you are forced
to compromise and, treacherously, you lose the sense of outrage.

One's superiors are not much help. Although they step in
when breaches of instructions become obvious, they seem not
to want to know what is going on and won't interfere with
another security force. Once we reported by radio that the cops
were beating up a drunk in full view of the community and the
HQ radioed a reply which amounted to: 'What must we do about
it?'

These generalisations are not just drawn from one day's
experience, but are based on incidents over a period of months.
Other surreal scenes come to mind. A stolen vehicle is spotted
– we give chase and, siren going, career through the alleys. We
catch up. Others already there, haul the man out and start
laying into him. As we leave, they smash his head into the
stolen car.

Another night, another fire. We hang around while the fire-
tanker does its work, when stones start dropping about us.
Suddenly one smashes a police windscreen and two cops with
shotguns bound off like dogs let off the leash. They stalk
the lone thrower and corner him. He continues his desperate
barrage. They shoot him dead. He is about 16.

As we arrive to take over from another group at one small

town, a policeman is whipping a black man. He is surrounded
by a small knot of army spectators. The officer in charge must
know what was going on, as the man's groans were clearly
audible. In another town a couple of army boys take to removing
the points from their ammunition and pinching the cartridge
closed to make blanks. There is also drinking on duty and,
more innocuously, 2 o'clock in the morning barbecues on the
township's outskirts. Many incidents stem from a lack of discipline.

This may all seem over-pessimistic. After all, great changes
are taking place in our society. But it has hardly touched the
reality of township life. The daily assault on the dignity and
self-respect of the black man goes on, if anything made worse
by the economic situation and the unrest.

The dream they could not destroy

Victoria Brittain *Published 18 October 1985*

An era ends in Africa next month as President Julius Nyerere
retires as Tanzania's Head of State. No Tanzanian cares to
estimate what the change is going to mean except Nyerere
himself who says briskly: 'The style is certainly going to change,
but not the policies.'

Hassan Ali Mwinyi, the Vice-President, who will take over
in November, is a quiet, little-known Zanzibari teacher. He is
a devout Moslem. He takes power as Tanzania sinks further
into economic crisis and its stability is threatened by the civil
war in neighbouring Uganda.

Tanzania's experience over the past 15 or so years is one of
the political landmarks of Third World governments' attempts
to confront the world's most powerful economic institutions.
Put simply, there has been a six-year battle between nationalist
ideals and the International Monetary Fund.

Tanzania's fight followed some famous defeats. In Chile Salvador Allende was killed and his socialist government replaced
by a military dictatorship; in Jamaica Michael Manley's
nationalist government was squeezed out like a wet rag. But
Nyerere is retiring undefeated to Dodoma, Tanzania's unbuilt
capital on the great Rift Valley plains.

Mwalimu (teacher), as he is universally known in Tanzania, will remain chairman of Tanzania's sole political party, Chama Cha Mapinduzi (CCM) which has the guiding role in the country's policies, though not their administration. His voice in world forums will still be the one the West least likes to hear. Unlike Fidel Castro, Mao or Ho Chi Minh, this mild-mannered liberal Christian cannot be dismissed as a Communist. His persistent call for sanctions to end apartheid and South Africa's occupation of Namibia, for a change in world economic structures, for an end to military spending, have earned him the hatred of the Western establishment. His commitment in the 1967 Arusha Declaration to building a Socialist state for impoverished peasants was greeted with a scepticism which has dominated international opinion.

Over 20 years Tanzania has poured the bulk of the generous aid funds it has received into social services and education. 'The health services are the best on the continent,' according to United Nationals officials. Seventy per cent of children live within five km of a health centre, there is universal primary school education, a countrywide vaccination programme will begin next year, adult literacy at 85 per cent is impressive compared with richer African countries such as Senegal with 10 per cent, Nigeria with 34 per cent or Kenya with 47 per cent.

But still 600 Tanzanian children under five die every day. Rare is the village with a milling machine or a biogas plant. Africa's rural poverty is as degrading in Tanzania as anywhere else. Ujaama villages, where peasants are grouped so that essential services can be shared, have not, in most cases, increased production. Though in Chamwino village, outside Dodoma, where Nyerere will live and till his patch of vines, bananas, maize and papaya, there is a communal vineyard and a herd of cows and goats, as sleek and well tended as in an English picture book farm.

The Dodoma region has had a bumper crop this year of sorgum, the staple food, but the foreign exchange crisis means that much of it will never be collected according to the Regional Commissioner Anna Abdallah. 'We have simply no fuel,' she explains. The economic crisis is reflected everywhere. In the University of Dar es Salaam there is no water, no new books, journals or magazines. Most industries are operating at about 30 per cent of capacity because of lack of spare parts or essential inputs. Agriculture is on a downward spiral and corruption feeds on this atmosphere.

'But we are not facing a *Tanzanian* problem, this is the problem of all sub-Saharan Africa. Unless there is a shift in policy so that massive international resources are poured into this continent the situation will simply get worse,' says Amir Jamal, formerly Finance Minister and now serving his last weeks in government as Minister of State in the President's office.

President Nyerere has said for years that if Tanzania were to implement a classic IMF programme it would mean putting the army on to the streets to control the anger of the population. The IMF riots of Sudan, Egypt, Tunisia and Morocco are seared deep into Africa's leaders today. 'The issue in this economic crisis is whether you can keep the democratic process or whether authoritarianism takes over and outside influences are drawn further into this continent,' says Jamal. For more than a decade his voice, like Nyerere's, has been warning that the collapse of producer prices spells catastrophe for a vast section of the poorest of the Third World. The latest World Bank proposals unveiled in Seoul go no way towards meeting this drama.

Tanzania's exports are 90 per cent agricultural. The world drop in producer prices means that the imports they could buy in 1975 were about twice what the same volume could buy today. And, as a result of downward spiral of inputs and efficiency, the volume available for export has dropped by more than one-third.

In addition, the six weeks' Ugandan occupation of northern Tanzania and the subsequent war against Idi Amin cost $400 million in 1979, according to Mr Jamal. That came on top of the collapse of the East African Community which cost about $200 million in new infrastructure. Tanzania's export earnings could not hope to cover costs like these and the second oil shock found the economy with no leeway. Government and people have been squeezed progressively every year. Two devaluations, cuts in the state sector (18,000 civil servants were sacked recently), a rise in producer prices and cuts in food subsidies have been carried out gradually since 1981. But none of this has been enough to persuade countless IMF missions to Dar es Salaam to release the $200 million stand-by credit agreed by the IMF in August 1980. Most other donors have held back waiting for the IMF stamp of approval from Washington. 'It is hard to come to any other conclusion than that the US under Reagan set out to force the collapse of Nyerere's regime,' said one official.

The battle with the IMF was just the open part of the pressures which destabilised the government. In Kenya a South African/Israeli/US influence on top decision-making has been on the increase for years and causes deep anxiety to Tanzania's leaders.

In 1983 a secret deal was made by the Kenyans with a senior

Tanzanian official which involved reopening the border closed since 1977 and returning some minor Tanzanian opposition figures in exchange for the two Air Force men who led the August 1982 coup against Moi. Without the knowledge of Nyerere the two men (executed in Kenya last July) were returned to Nairobi as were a number of Kenyan students with UN refugee status. The effect of the swap was devastating for the President's credibility with the Scandinavian aid donors who, with the Chinese, have been Tanzania's greatest support in its ambitious social services programmes. Scandinavian aid programmes have been under severe threat ever since. The World Bank/IMF prescriptions for Tanzania of devaluation, rise in producer prices, privatisation and import liberalisation have become the new donor orthodoxy where a commitment to aid the unseen areas of health, education and budgetary support ruled before.

Tanzania has, in fact, tried most of the World Bank prescriptions on agriculture and internal Party debate on these issues is sharp. As Prime Minister Salim Salim explains 'The CCM is not monolithic. There is a left and right on tactics and the interpretation of the Arusha Declaration, but what is never questioned is the commitment to socialism declared there.'

Salim Salim's infectious confidence is one of the few clear strengths of the uncertain era beginning. 'Agriculture will be the salvation of Tanzania given the change of emphasis we have put on it since last year. We *can* feed ourselves, *can* expand our cash crops, *can* improve the quality of education and productivity,' he says. Agricultural projects are about to begin, with North Korean labour-intensive schemes for cotton and maize with no foreign exchange input.

Nyerere describes the future more cautiously as, 'devising a strategy for survival'. Amir Jamal is more cautious still: 'there is much more belt-tightening to come. The world has turned out to be much harsher than we ever envisaged.'

Angola on the edge of the precipice

Victoria Brittain   *Published 20 December 1985*

In a deeply sombre mood the MPLA government in Angola is facing its most dangerous threat since it came to power in Luanda 10 years ago—economically, militarily and politically.

Then the South African army was 1,000 kilometres into the country advancing from the south, and within a few kilometres of the capital, to the north, were Zairean, Portuguese and rival Angolan forces of Unita and FNLA. The US had that year spent $32.9 million in covert support to those two groups in an attempt to keep the MPLA from taking power. Every administration in Washington has refused to acknowledge a final defeat for their protégés and withheld recognition from the MPLA government.

Today South African troops are again in action inside Southern Angola. The United States is virtually committed to 'covert' aid to Unita and four separate bills are pending in Congress which would give $54 million of military and other aid to Unita and variously prohibit loans, trade and new investment from the US to Angola. In its present precarious situation Angola's regime would find it almost impossible to survive such an economic onslaught. The US is Angola's biggest trading partner and has $500 million worth of investment in the country.

Officials say that in the last year three factors in Southern African politics have combined to make Angola once again, as in 1975, the major focus of US policy in the region. 'First, the escalation of the violent threat to Western interests in South Africa itself. Second, the success of our August offensive against Unita which demonstrated that without a new level of commitment to Savimbi from the US he could no longer make a plausible showing as a contender for power sharing. And third, what they believe has been the successful breaking of Frelimo in Mozambique.'

Angola's historic commitment to moral and material support for the ANC has always set it apart from the other frontline states as a particular threat to the white regime in South Africa. During the second Party Congress earlier this month, Joe Slovo, veteran South African Communist and a member of the ANC's fighting wing, Umkhonto wa Siswe, was treated to an extended standing ovation and a rare warm embrace from

President Jose Eduardo Dos Santos after a fiery speech thanking Angola for its 'shelter to liberation fighters given for ten years.'

The price, as Mr Slovo put it, has been that 'there has hardly been a day of peace here ... mercenaries are hired, bandit armies are created, the economy sabotaged.'

It has become a war impossible to quantify in figures though the latest United Nations fact-finding mission after the South African bombing attacks round Mavinga in late September and October calculated $36 million for that phase alone. Over a year ago President Dos Santos spoke of $10 billion worth of destruction since independence. One key target, the Beneguela railway, has been blown up again and again and suffered $60 million worth of damage. Every family knows the human cost.

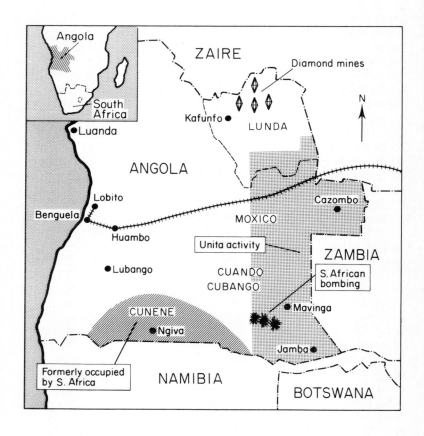

'The war has become routine to us—every day there is fighting, every day dying, every day prisoners, every day Unita boys giving up, every day peasants losing limbs,' said a young military officer, giving a briefing on the latest phase of the war. Increased South African involvement, particularly by Mirage fighter bomber strikes, stepped up sophisticated equipment supplies to Unita, and a new phase of undisguised US involvement against the MPLA government are expected to become the new everyday realities.

The handful of survivors of the helicopter crews shot down in the last days of the September fighting near Mavinga give a graphic picture of the war in the eastern area the Portuguese called 'the lands at the end of the earth'. One young sergeant, the son of a peasant, walked for two weeks following the sun until he got back to the operational base at Cuito Cuanavale. He described a vast empty plain where he met not a single person and survived only because he stumbled on an abandoned Unita base where he found a jerry can which he filled with water. Two lieutenants who had been piloting the M17 and M25 helicopters supporting the ground troops which confronted the South African 32nd Battalion at Mavinga said afterwards they walked 100 kilometres back to Cuito. In five days of blazing hot days and freezing nights they lost 25 pounds in that inhospitable no man's land.

Until this offensive, Unita convoys and South African air drops were unhindered in this eastern zone near the Sambian border. But Cazombo is now safely enough in MPLA hands to have been reoccupied by at least 20,000 of its former inhabitants returned from exile in Zambia. Unita has thus lost an important base area for actions against economic targets in the diamond area of Luanda near the Zaire border.

Unita's decision to try to hold Cazombo and Mavinga and fight a conventional-type war next to South African ground troops cost very high casualties which will be difficult to replace. The same tactic was tried once before (though with Unita then on the attack) in Cangamba in 1983. Then, too, Unita was rescued by a major South African air attack.

Unita's traditional pattern of war has avoided all contact with MPLA military targets. But the record of ambushes, economic sabotage and terrorising villages has dropped in the last two months since the eastern fighting, according to Angola military sources. However kidnappings and assassinations of local officials and journalists continue.

In his speeches in what should have been triumphal celebrations of 10 years of independence and the holding of the second Party Congress, President Dos Santos grimly emphasised that the war will continue. 'Because we are in Southern

Africa the policies of imperialism mean that we will continue to live in difficult circumstances for a few years. The hawks in the US encourage South Africa's policy of destabilisation and aggression. They will continue to force us to mobilise huge material and human resources. These are the sacrifices forced on us by imperialism . . .'

In 1960 the CIA station chief in the Congo cabled Washington, 'whether or not Lumumba actually Commie or just playing Commie game . . . anti-west forces rapidly increasing power Congo and there may be little time left to avoid another Cuba.' Now declassified US material shows how little Washington understood or could control the forces they unleashed against Lumumba's brand of African nationalism. John Stockwell, the CIA agent who broke with the Agency after running their Angolan operation against the MPLA, revealed later just how cavalier and cynical was the decision to support Unita and FNLA to bleed the MPLA nationalist movement more than 10 years ago. 'Nothing has changed in the US attitude to us,' said one official. 'But they have been battling for influence in the regime almost as openly as they have been battling to pull us down.'

The MPLA's early leadership posed a challenge to Washington not because they were 'Commies' who heralded 'another Cuba', but because they were highly-educated African nationalists with international authority. Only Algeria's post-colonial leadership in Africa has similarly dominated the intellectual philosophy of the continent. 'Our struggle is against imperialism and internal reaction,' said Dos Santos last week—many times.

For more than a decade they have been the words of Agostinho Neto and Lucio Lara in meetings of peasants and young soldiers in the frontline of the war all over Angola, and of former Foreign Minister Paulo Jorge in every world forum. Both Lara and Jorge were among the prestigious old guard leaders down-graded in last week's big changes in the Central Committee and Political Bureau.

President Dos Santos appears to have changed neither the language nor the MPLA's principles to meet the US pressures for negotiations with Unita and the departure of the Cuban troops defending Angola in its undeclared war with South Africa. But there have been numerous meetings between some of the President's closest associates and US officials such as Dr Chester Crocker—even since aid to Unita came onto the US public agenda.

And it appears that the President has chosen a new image for the leadership of a new era of Angola history though it is too soon to tell if changes of substance will follow the changes of personnel. The Western media, including the most conservative West European and American papers, are today surprisingly warmly welcomed in Luanda. Even Jeune Afrique, perhaps Savimbi's most loyal publicist over many years, had a 40-page supplement on the tenth anniversary. The President's new men in the Political Bureau have yet to show their hand.

Uganda tries again
Victoria Brittain   *Published 31 January 1986*

This week's takeover of power by the National Resistance Movement in Uganda is a new political phenomenon in Africa which has little in common with the familiar musical chairs of military coups. Instability is the most notorious product of Africa's two decades of coups, and from 1981, when Yoweri Museveni's response to Milton Obote's rigged election was to start guerrilla war, he declared himself against 'short-cuts like assassinations or coups'.

The 'protracted people's war from a liberated area' which he talked of then seemed like a romantic dream in the real world of East Africa's harsh power politics where under both Amin and Obote all popular participation in politics was cowed for years by detentions, killings, harassment, bribery or even the buying back of exiled opponents from the Kenyan authorities.

It is a measure of the degradation of Uganda's government under Amin and Obote that for the last decade some of the best minds in the university community chose an armed peasant's life in the bush under Museveni rather than the traditional African elite's life of perks, prestige and power in government or business under the patronage of the military.

For a decade and a half Museveni's group, first in Fronasa and then in the National Resistance Army, has attracted a broad spectrum of Ugandans who refused to accept that corruption and dictatorship were the political norms of their country. All over Africa intellectuals are in exile for similar reasons. Museveni, and his university contemporary, Colonel John Garang in Southern Sudan's guerrilla movement, have challenged the old authority from the inside with the gun rather than from the outside with the pen.

In Nairobi, during the 'peace talks' which preceded the collapse of the Okello regime, Museveni's rare public appearances were the occasion for enormous popular acclamation.

The NRA has gone out of its way to thank publicly President Moi of Kenya for his contribution towards peace. They need his goodwill.

The old order in Uganda still has powerful foreign friends and is not giving up without fighting diplomatic and economic rearguard actions even after the hopeless street battles have taken their huge toll.

Foreign interests have played a deeply destructive role in Uganda ever since independence. In particular, Britain's complicity with Amin's and Obote's death-dealing regimes will never be lived down. Six months ago Obote fled Uganda still able to keep a retinue of 150 people in exile in Lusaka.

Over the last five months a great deal of material and moral support was made available to try to turn the doomed junta into a government which could co-opt the NRA as a junior partner. Among the countries involved were close allies of the United States such as Israel, Egypt, Saudi Arabia and Zaire.

Last week, as the NRA commanders planned the move on Kampala and the junta was hoping for the arrival of Israeli crack units to hold the capital and Entebbe, the Reagan Administration had invited Yoweri Museveni to be in Washington for what US officials called a 'get acquainted' visit. If the NRA leader had made that visit the history of the last week might have been rather different with the junta still clinging to power and Israel having diplomatic recognition from one more African country.

The new broad-based government which Museveni has promised for Uganda will need massive support from Ugandans and goodwill from the outside world. Every carpet-bagger in East Africa turned up in Kampala to 'aid' Uganda in 1979 when Amin fell. International bureaucrats were in the finance and planning ministries within days telling the UNLF government how to get Western aid.

The NRA ran Western Uganda with its own local leaders. The powerful Western aid industry would do well to listen more humbly than usual before treating Uganda as a helpless victim again and creating another opportunity for the vultures to settle on Kampala.

Water Works

Mkwapatira Mhango
Published 14 February 1986

A Japanese television station is paying for 13 Japanese engin-
eers to teach Zambian villagers how to drill wells, using bamboo
instead of expensive machinery. The team of water experts
arrived in September to introduce a traditional method of
digging wells called 'kazusa-bori'. The technique enables wells
to be dug as deep as 500 metres without using electricity, fuel
oil, drilling rigs or pumps.

Nearly 60 per cent of Zambians lack access to safe drinking
water, with the figure much higher in rural areas. But even in
the cities, chronic water shortages are common, and economic
recession has ruled out large-scale investments to improve the
supply system.

The man behind the bamboo invasion is Seizi Kondo, highly
respected in Japan for reviving the traditional method of digging wells. He became concerned about African women who
walk long distances daily in search of water, and thought that
the 'kazusa-bori' system could save them this chore.

He launched an appeal through TV Asahi, a major Japanese
television company. Eventually TV Asahi itself was impressed,
donated $150,000 to enable his team to travel to Zambia. Kondo
chose Zambia for the first experiment because it is one of the
most politically stable countries in Africa, 'and the people here
have the eagerness to acquire new techniques for themselves.'

Drilling is done by one or two men equipped with conven-
tional hand tools. The only thing needed to dig a 'kazusa-bori'
well is a length of bamboo which is connected to an iron head,
and to a large flywheel made from bamboo and timber. The
bamboo drill piece is driven into the ground using only manpower, and acts as a conduit once water is struck.

Within five days of arriving, Kondo's team had sunk a well
in a remote Wenela village in Mongu District, 361 miles west
of Lusaka. The well now supplies water to the villagers, who
are ready to teach the techniques which they have mastered to
people in other villages.

The permanent secretary for the Western province, Reuben
Chinambu, said the government was interested in the 'kazusa-
bori' technique because it would not require scarce foreign
exchange to be spent.

Lack of money and expertise limits rural Zambia's efforts to
increase drinking water supplies. Mongu and other districts in

the western province have a chronic shortage of water during summer, but villagers there are now hoping that the Japanese technique will allow them to make the land green again.

Rapid urban growth has overwhelmed water supply and sanitation services. For some time, Zambia's principal aid donors – the World Bank and countries such as Canada, West Germany and the Scandinavian nations – have concentrated on improving rural water supplies. Urban areas like Lusaka, Ndola, Kitwe and Chingola have not had the money to improve their water and sewerage networks.

Lusaka, with a population of 800,000 is critically short of water. The director of the water and sewerage department, Dr Carl Haffke, says that nearly all the expansion projects that have been undertaken are ad hoc measures which have not kept pace with the city's growth.

At present, Lusaka receives 160,000 cubic metres (5.6 million cubic feet) of water per day, 25 per cent of which is lost through leakage. Maintenance of pipes is inadequate due to lack of foreign exchange for importing spare parts and the situation is steadily worsening.

The use of bamboo technology is becoming increasingly popular with Africans. In Tanzania's southern province of Iringa, for example, nearly 500 acres of land have been put under irrigation using bamboo and wood pipes.

Bamboo offers Africa the opportunity of 'growing' its own pipes, providing an alternative to expensive iron pipes and water tanks which most countries desperately need and few can afford.

Polisario's battle for the wall

Victoria Brittain on 10 years of war in the Sahara desert   *Published 21 February 1986*

'Piccadilly Circus . . . Camberley . . . Sandhurst . . . the English ways . . . these are the things I have dwelt on between games of chess and bouts of reading for six long years . . .' said Captain El Mazouari el Glaoui Abdelkrim.

This highly educated son of an aristocratic Marrakesh family is one of 2,000 prisoners held by Polisario guerrillas with whom Morocco refuses to negotiate after 10 years of war in the Sahara desert.

The captain is held in a huge military compound full of more tangible memorials to his officer training in Sandhurst.

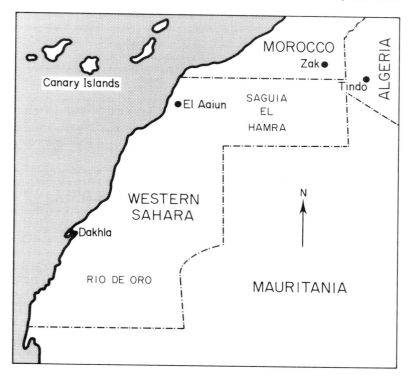

Captured Moroccan equipment ranged from British 105mm mortar cannon stamped with ERII Honi Soit Qui Mal Y Pense, US, French, and Belgian tanks, napalm shells, fragmentation bombs, parts of helicopters, French Mirages, US F5E fighter bombers, and even armoured personnel carriers with the origin scraped off everything except the shock-absorbers which were inscribed 'made in South Africa' in English and Afrikaans.

'Of course, most of what we capture we use at the front – Morocco's friends are our best suppliers,' said the Polisario officer in charge of the exhibition.

Ten years ago, as Franco lay dying and Spain's politics were in turmoil, its Saharan colony was abruptly handed to Morocco and Mauritania in a secret deal pre-empting a UN mission's report favouring independence for the Saharaouis. Polisario promptly launched a liberation war of reckless hit-and-run raids and ambushes. Now it is an expensive stalemate.

Morocco has a 120,000-man army in the Western Sahara strung out behind a 2,000 kilometre wall enclosing two-thirds of their territory. Support from the US, France, Israel, and Saudi Arabia is critical in maintaining the occupation.

Polisario's secretary-general, Mohamed Abdelaziz, in a carefully measured analysis of the 10-year war, blamed the Reagan Administration for increasing military aid to Morocco during 1981–3 'just when we believed a political solution was possible. Mauritania signed a peace treaty with us and then, in a meeting with the Moroccans in Bamako we felt they, too, were ready to make peace. The increased US aid put off that chance of peace.'

Several hours drive south of the Algerian town of Tindouf lies Polisario's own Sandhurst – the El Ouali Military Academy, named after the movement's first secretary-general who was killed in the early days of the war.

Polisario's army is only one tenth the size of Morocco's. It is supplied by Algeria with hardware, but its soldiers and officers are trained at home in schools like this – a complex of rose-pink traditionally made buildings hidden in the folds of rock and sand hills.

Freezing nights and sand-blasting winds make the area virtually uninhabitable. 'If it wasn't for our national pride and self-respect we would leave nature to drive the Moroccans out – even for Saharaouis this is a difficult place,' said Taleb Ahmed Mahmoud, the school's director of training, a veteran of many Polisario attacks on the wall.

The school's Political Commissar said: 'The wall holds no psychological terrors for our boys – they've studied the Challe and Morris lines the French built here during the Algerian liberation war. I've talked to many veterans who say they were much tougher than King Hassan's sand wall.' Through a long afternoon the school's leaders talked of their war.

'The five walls (and we expect them to build a sixth and maybe more) were a response to the crushing military defeats of 1978–9. In that phase there were engagements when we took 200 prisoners and as many vehicles,' said one.

'Today there are daily exchanges of fire anywhere along the wall. We also concentrate on one specific area so hard that the radar overworks and breaks down. It takes a week usually before French or US technicians arrive to mend it and in the meantime we overrun their forward positions which are 15 kilometres apart. They always signal they're about to give up by calling in the F5s for a bombing raid.'

Last week, hundreds of miles farther South along the wall's East/West axis, Polisario's Defence Minister, Ibrahim Ghali, led an offensive which successfully occupied a stretch of it, according to Mohamed Ould Salek, secretary-general of the Presidency.

Next week marks the tenth anniversary of the liberation movement's declaration of independence as the Saharan Arab Democratic Republic. Nothing illustrates the fiercely independent nationalism of the Saharaoui better than the fact that their declaration, made deep in the desert on 27 February, 1975, took their Algerian protectors completely by surprise.

That day, in Addis Ababa, Algerian diplomats were trying to get Polisario recognised as a liberation movement in the Organisation of African Unity.

Today the SADR is recognised as a state by 63 countries, including non-aligned heavyweights such as India and Yugoslavia. It is a full member of the OAU.

'Over this 10 years we've proved that our state is viable. Not only in terms of our fighting forces but with our international weight,' said Mohamed Abdelaziz, who is both Secretary-General of Polisario and, by the constitution, Head of State of the RASD. Last year, after Morrocco withdrew from OAU, the rest of the continent unanimously elected Abdelaziz one of the organisation's vice-presidents.

The SADR would, if not two-thirds occupied, be one of Africa's most economically viable states. The population of less than a million would control the world's second biggest phosphate industry (Morocco has the biggest), and a fishing potential of two million tons a year. Iron ore, tungsten, platinum, gold, managanese, garnets, tourmalines, and zircons have all been found. Off-shore oil exploration was started in the 1960s, but appears to have been halted by the war.

King Hassan has pushed ahead with a kind of development behind his wall: 100,000 Moroccan settlers have been brought into the Western Sahara and on a recent trip to Paris the King unveiled plans for a Club Mediterranee holiday resort at El Ayioun.

'For the Saharaoui that is roughly equivalent to installing a Turkish belly-dancer next to the Vatican,' said an Arab observer. The SADR Minister of Information, Ibrahim Hakim, condemned the project as 'pornography'.

- Beginning of Spanish rule
- Founding of Polisario
- 1975 14 November, Madrid Accord – Spain ceded its colony to Morocco and Mauritania
- 1976 27 February, Polisario declared independence of Saharan Arab Democratic Republic
- 1979 Mauritania pulled out of Sahara
- 1983 OAU summit peace plan
- 1985 Morocco withdrew from OAU and refused further UN discussion of Western Sahara

In Southern Algeria there are refugee encampments holding about 165,000 Saharaoui who fled from the disputed territory in Western Sahara when the Moroccans invaded in 1975–76. The careful preservation of the traditional and Islamic culture is a priority in the camps. A cultural evening at the 27 February vocational school for women saw groups acting out traditional wedding ceremonies no longer practised since their flight, and songs of praise to Allah, to love, to education, and to 'home'.

The war has transformed women's lives with extraordinary speed and, as some husbands admit, it can be difficult to accept their enormous social responsibilities running the refugees' five provinces and 24 towns of tents.

'The men run the combat, the women run the rear bases and production,' said Fatima Balla, one of the teachers at this girls' college of 1,800 pupils.

In the school's sewing and weaving workshops, in the town's experimental market gardens, in the impressive boarding schools of over 2,000 children, in Mohamed Abdelaziz's sparse office, everyone is dressed in anonymous fatigues and heavy army greatcoats. But inside the rows of tents in the towns, the Saharan women, in spite of their new responsibilities, wear the traditional long-flowing dresses, spend hours on the ceremonies of tea-making, and in their rug-filled tents burn incense on tiny braziers and lovingly decorate each others' hands with intricate patterns of red henna dye.

In a record unequalled in Africa everyone is now literate after four summer campaigns organised by the youth movement and specially targeted on women.

Education is the backbone of the Saharaoui strength. In the 9th June school (commemorating the day of El Ouali's death) mixed classes of 10-year-olds study the Punic Wars or the history of Africa in Spanish, and algebra and botany in Arabic.

'But we teach the Koran and Islam as the fundamental cultural values – otherwise the society would simply reject us and them,' said the headmaster, a typical polymath of this leadership, speaking four languages and much given to intellectual debate.

Colonel Gadafy, the Polisario's first backer with Algeria, is one of the Saharaouis' favourite subjects of discussion. In 1983 he made a surprise alliance with Morocco. Instantly the Saharaoui removed 4,000 children from schools in Libya and had to rely on the generosity of Algeria and Cuba to absorb them.

'That Oujda Accord was one of the most serious setbacks of this 10-year period,' said Abdelaziz. 'However, looking back on it, it has not been so very negative; King Hassan has not got the results he hoped for. Gadafy has not done the complete policy volte-face that Sekou Toure (of Guinea) did under Moroccan guidance, and thanks to other Third World friends, and some West European governments through non-government organisations, and our increased self-reliance, we've managed to make up for the Libyan aid.'

Earlier this month, when US threats against Libya appeared serious Gadafy visited Algeria and had a meeting with President Chadli. For Abdelaziz the meeting was a 'highly positive sign' that 'Gadafy and the Libyan revolution are discovering the opportunism and manoeuvres of King Hassan' and turning back towards their 'natural allies, the Algerian and Saharaoui people'.

El Ouali, Polisario's first secretary-general who was killed in the early days of the war

But the old Libyan alliance is one of the factors which has earned Polisario relentless animosity from the US and France. US military assistance grants to Morocco for the current year are estimated at $45 million, and France is studying a request from the king for the new Mirage 2000 fighter bombers. 'But those are not planes suitable for use against Polisario – they open the door to a regional conflict,' said Abdelaziz.

The Secretary-General underlined the potential for increased regional instability. 'By his own direct contacts, or those of his close military collaborators, the king has sought the experiences of Israel and South Africa in aggressions against neighbours.'

However, Morocco's internal instability as a result of the strain on resources caused by the war is likely to restrain the king from widening the conflict. 'King Hassan is now in virtually total diplomatic and political isolation, living on credits from Saudi Arabia and certain Western countries. How long can this go on?' said Abdelaziz.

Morocco's external debt is now $13 billion and the US has refused some recent requests for more credit. Meanwhile, in another ominous sign for the king, a trickle of Moroccan deserters has recently begun to brave the empty desert beyond the wall. The lucky ones have been picked up by Polisario Land Rover patrols. The unlucky have been found dead.

2 ASIA

Korean poet's protest
Letter to the editor
Published 21 May 1982

Sir, I am a Korean poet living now in America. At home, I was a member of the editorial staff of Seoul Shimmun, the leading newspaper in Seoul, and a special professor of literature at Dong-Kuk University. I have written five books. My collection of poems, *Night Bombing and the Birds*, was banned and I lost my jobs when the army took over the government in 1979.

As you know, Korea is a divided nation. You may not be able to imagine the pain of people who must lead their lives in the midst of a blind ideological struggle, the pain of people living under a communist dictatorship and under an oppressive government that calls itself a democracy. As a Korean poet, fighting for freedom and democracy, I ardently wish to make known to others the sorrowful voices of the Korean people, who long for freedom and unification.

According to its constitution, Korea is a democratic nation and, in fact, compared with communist North Korea, it over-flows with freedoms, but not the freedom to criticise every falsehood. But without freedom of criticism and thought, how can real democratic government exist?

I think that intellectuals have a right and duty to ponder not only the present and future of Korea, but also the threatening problems of the whole world, and to write about them freely and openly. In fact, however, many freedoms in South Korea are strictly limited. Its newspapers have become almost government newspapers. As a result, our country is going to fall into an age of collective blindness.

In the last 20 years, many professors and newspapermen have been expelled from their jobs, although they did nothing wrong. Therefore, why did a so-called democratic government purge them?

We are living in an age of fraud and oppression. Yet the United Nations Committee on Human Rights sleeps in a cosy

place that no one knows of and free nations keep their mouths shut because of political and economic interests.
Sincerely,

Chul Bum Lee,
West Los Angeles,
California.

Gen. Zia's last ditch

Eqbal Ahmad   *Published 26 August 1983*

In spite of General Mohammad Zia ul-Haq's last-ditch attempt to forestall it, in Pakistan the autumn of the dictatorship has begun. The opposition had appealed for public demonstrations to reclaim democracy on 14 August, Independence Day. General Zia ordered widespread 'preventive' arrests of suspected organisers, threatened harsh punishments, and renewed his oft-broken vow to restore constitutional government. The banned demonstration, unexpectedly large in major cities, was attacked by the government's armed right-wing supporters. A week later the Army continued its bare-knuckled crackdown on the civil disobedience campaign. These events point toward a decisive polarisation; the alternative to an early restoration of representative government is strife and disintegration.

Like many Third World countries, Pakistan suffers from a four-fold crisis of legitimacy, democracy, development, and integration. A government must be judged in terms of its contribution to reducing these fundamental crises. By this basic criterion, General Zia's regime must be deemed a dismal failure.

The crisis of legitimacy has been compounded by the ruling junta's record of betrayed promises, and violations of human rights. On 5 July, 1977, General Mohammed Zia ul-Haq overthrew the Prime Minister Z. A. Bhutto, whose constitutional government he had sworn to obey and who had promoted him Chief of Staff. General Zia's other putschist colleagues, too, were beneficiaries of Mr Bhutto's promotions. In April, 1979, they executed their benefactor, violating personal trust, a cherished norm of Pakistani culture. To legalise the murder, Zia rigged the higher courts and inaugurated the process of destroying Pakistan's relatively independent judiciary.

Pakistan has had a distinguished judiciary. Over the years of political turmoil, the higher courts had continued to legitimise governmental authority and arbitrate conflicts between individual rights and state power. Confrontations between the executive and judiciary had occurred; compromises were made. But all governments, including Mohammed Ayub Khan's military regime, had respected the judiciary's independence; when enjoined, they bowed to court orders. Judges were rarely dismissed on political grounds and without the Chief Justice's recommendation. Under Zia, this tradition was broken.

The tanks that brought General Zia to power patrol the streets of Karachi

On 25 March, 1981, 19 Supreme Court and provincial high court judges were dismissed for declining to endorse a 'constitutional order' which restricted the civil courts, outlawed political parties, declared as crime the advocacy of secular ideologies, and empowered General Zia to amend the Constitution at will. Among those who refused to swear allegiance to this 'constitutional order' were the Chief Justice of Pakistan, four of the six Supreme Court judges, and the Chief Justice of Baluchistan. Twelve provincial high court judges suspected of integrity were not 'invited' to take the oath; they 'automatically' lost their posts.

Pakistan's besieged Bar Association protested: 'A country can put up with laws that are harsh or unjust so long as they are administered by just judges who mitigate their harshness or alleviate their unfairness . . . Nations fall when judges are unjust because there is nothing people consider worth defending.' For their defence of the rule of law, lawyers have been treated more harshly than judges.

What distinguishes Pakistan from other contemporary tyrannies is not its actual excesses but General Zia's assault on the country's legal framework, and his militarisation of society. The Bill of Fundamental Rights has been suspended indefinitely. Unlike previous military governments, Zia's has deprived the judiciary of its power to review the decisions of martial law courts. Citizens have no recourse against violations of legal and human rights by these military courts, which exercise wide civilian jurisdiction. The bureaucracy, which in the past had lent a civilian note to military rule, is being systematically militarised. By junta orders, 10 per cent of all positions in the higher civil services must be filled by army officers; today soldiers occupy important civilian positions in government and in state-owned industries.

Military laws have replaced the laws of the land. These draconian decrees bear no resemblance to law. Consider Martial Law Regulation 53. This prescribes the death sentence for 'any offence liable to cause insecurity, fear, or despondency among the public.' Crimes punishable under this measure include: 'any act with an intent to impair the efficiency or impede the working or cause damage to public property or the smooth functioning of government', abetting 'in any matter whatsoever . . . the commission of such an offence'; and failure to inform the authorities of the 'whereabouts or any other information about such a person'.

Thus, one is guilty not only of what one does or says, but also of what one does not do. Furthermore, the decree provides that a 'military court on the basis of police reports or any other investigation alone may, unless the contrary is proved, presume that this accused has committed the offence charged with'.

Thus, in General Zia's Pakistan, one is guilty until proved innocent. Martial Law 53, promulgated on 27 September, 1982, applies retroactively: it 'shall be deemed to have taken effect on 5 July, 1977', that is, the day the ruling junta broke its oath of allegiance to Pakistan's constitution.

General Zia's crackdown on justice reflects his government's insecurity. Its primary cause is his betrayal of the oft-repeated promise 'to organise free and fair elections' by October, 1977. Following Mr Bhutto's execution, General Zia abandoned the pretences of being a caretaker and, seeking a legitimising platform, launched his campaign of 'Islamisation'. But his Islam does not elicit popular support because it is reduced to a medieval penal code and outdated social practices; above all, it is shorn of the spiritual, moral, and civic virtues that had assured Islamic civilisation its richness and humanity.

Historically, the questions of democracy and distributive justice, not of Islam, have been central to Pakistani politics.

The following pattern is discernible since independence in 1947: first, Islam has been most vigorously invoked by insecure governments; religion has not been exploited by the secure ones. In two instances, the shift from temporal to Islamic rhetoric occurred in a single regime, at the height of their power both Marshall Ayub Khan and Mr Bhutto spared Islam crude politicisation; but when confronted by popular opposition both turned to religion like medieval mullahs.

Second, while Islam has been the refuge of weak governments, it has not served them well as an instrument of legitimisation.

Third, politicians and parties with 'Islamic' platforms have been consistently and thoroughly beaten at the polls by their populist and reformist rivals. Typically, the Army has staged *coup d'états* to prevent the affirmation of popular demands.

Fourth, central to Pakistan's political crises – in 1954, 1958, 1969, 1971, 1977 – has been the unresolved tension between authoritarian institutions and their allies (the military and bureaucracy, the feudal and the clerical classes) and popular demand for democracy and equitable distribution. This historic tension, vastly augmented under General Zia, is sure to explode.

Pakistan faces a severe crisis of national integration. Even after the secession of Bangladesh in 1971, it remains ethnically and linguistically divided into four diverse and insurrectionary peoples. Decades of unequal development and the unwillingness of the Punjab-dominated ruling elite to share power have compounded the problem of integration. It is aggravated by contiguous Baluchi and Pakhtun population in Iran and Afghanistan, by the recent influx of Afghan refugees, and by the fact that Mr Bhutto came from Sind, the most oppressed and potentially the most explosive of Pakistan's four states.

The military is ill-equipped to promote integration. It consumes 50 per cent of Pakistan's budget; it is the largest employer in a country with 40 per cent male unemployment. Status and privileges accrue to members of the armed forces. Yet Baluchis and Sindhis have negligible representation in it; 80 per cent are Punjabis largely from a few rural districts. For the non-Punjabi, 42 per cent of Pakistan's population, the army symbolises inequality and Punjabi domination.

The junta's preference for a strong, centralised government increases anxiety in the minority provinces, which regard meaningful provincial autonomy in a federal, parliamentary system as the best guarantee for redressing their grievances. Similarly, the advocacy by General Zia's regime of a fundamentalist religious ideology alienates not only Christians but also Shi'ite Muslims who together constitute some 25 per cent of the population.

Economically, Pakistan gives the appearance of muddling through the world-wide slump. A succession of good crops and about $2.5 billions annually in receipts from Pakistani workers abroad, have even produced some optimism. But just beneath the surface are a stagnant economy, a skill-drained workforce, and a dangerously mortgaged nation.

Eqbal Ahmad is a Fellow of the Transnational Institute, Washington and Amsterdam.

The instability behind the new boom in agriculture

William Hinton   *Published 27 September 1984*

Over the last four years China's leaders have steered the countryside through a vast change of course. Having reversed the collective emphasis of the previous 30 years, they are pushing the privatisation of production, if not of ownership, by way of a 'responsibility system' that allocates resources on a long-term basis to individual peasants or peasant families to be exploited by them for personal gain.

Communities now contract out not only land, livestock, and big machinery (tractors and trucks), but ponds, pastures, forests, local industries, dispensaries, clinics, and in some cases even schools to individual operators or specialists as many of them are now called. Concurrently the Government is relaxing controls on almost everything in the countryside from production quotas to prices and markets, thus freeing people to enrich themselves in any way they can.

This combination of privatisation and relaxation has led to an impressive rise in agricultural production, particularly special products including livestock products, and also in services, handcrafts, and many small industries. Rural incomes are rising, peasants are building houses by the millions, and starting to buy big consumer items like television sets and washing machines.

The daily press regularly prints individual success stories like that of the chicken raiser who became the first peasant in China to buy a car, and the reed mat seller who made a profit of 30,000 yuan and presented his neighbours with a free clinic. The slogan is 'some must get rich first' and all media concentrate on the process of the vanguard.

Nevertheless, the current emphasis on personal enrichment in the countryside raises many serious questions. Starting with technical matters such as the environmental impact of free-for-all raids by individuals on natural resources, the fiscal impact of land fragmentation on all economies of scale in crop production, and the barriers to capital construction on the land thrown up by the need to pay cash wages for all labour, the list moves quickly to more disturbing fundamentals like the revival of Confucian culture with its appalling denigration of women and accelerating economic polarisation.

Proponents of the new system argue that polarisation cannot take place because the main productive resources – starting with land – remain in the hands of the local government and nobody can accumulate them as leverage against others. But since there is no limit to the amount of land or other resources that an individual may contract and since there is no binding limit to the number of people an ambitious contractor may employ, the question of ownership has become, for all practical purposes, irrelevant. What counts in the vast concession system that makes up China's rural reconomy today are use rights.

Long Bow Village in Shanxi province, organised as a collective, built six truck gardens of six acres each where teams of vegetable growing specialists, 12 to 15 strong, raised fresh produce on contract for a nearby State-owned market and shared earnings based on accumulated work points. In 1982 when Long Bow Brigade leaders, under orders from above, contracted out the resources of their cooperative, they auctioned off the six gardens to those individuals who agreed to pay the brigade the highest fee for the operating rights or users' rights —a euphemism for cash rent. Each contractor then hired ten or a dozen people to work the gardens and paid them wages roughly equivalent to the work point earnings of vegetable growers in the past. In the course of this transaction six people became managing employers and 60 or more became day labourers. For each individual who stepped up the ladder of opportunity, at least ten stepped down. None of the labourers to whom we talked to in 1983 would say how much they were earning, but all agreed that the boss paid them only when he felt like it.

The question here is not simply one of the equalisation of earnings—I will prosper first and you will catch up later. It involves the polarisation of a certain proportion of the village population into classes with diametrically opposed status *vis-à-vis* the means of production. There are those who have nailed down enough use rights to extract surplus value from the labour force needed to exploit them, and there are those who have missed out in contracting for use rights and have to work for others for wages. Knowledge that in the middle there are large numbers of petty contractors who exploit minor use rights with their own individual or family labour, and still others who pool resources for cooperative production, hardly makes the polarisation less disturbing.

So far, aside from fear of an eventual settling of accounts sparked by 'Conservative' peasant egalitarians, the only road-block to capital accumulation is taxation. But too extreme a levy on profits will undermine the direct material incentive that is the *raison d'être* of the privatisation policy. State leaders are not likely to opt for a tax system that snuffs out the ambitions of those with a talent for self-enrichment. In any case, regardless of what officials do on this front, the newly rich will find creative ways to evade whatever taxes are levied.

As long as production goes up, does all this make any differ-ence? From a socialist point of view it certainly does. If private initiative were the only way to develop productive forces, there would be nothing to say, but well led collectives showed extra-ordinary ability to transform nature and create wealth. If collectives as a form had been given the same autonomy in production and the same freedom to develop markets that private producers now enjoy, would they have lagged behind? It seems unlikely. In the meantime the new policy is unlocking a pandora's box of questionable side effects.

Once a class accumulates enough economic clout, it can begin to warp all terms of reference to its advantage. Official statements constantly reiterate that all is well. Each time there is a public outcry over some particularly crass new development in capitalist style production or market relations, higher bodies send investigators down. But their function seems to be to quiet the clamour by giving Central Committee approval to whatever controversial new mode of enrichment is under scrutiny. It is hard not to conclude that, all moral exhortations notwithstand-ing, the real policy is 'anything goes'.

Have Party leaders decided then to develop capitalism in the countryside or in China as a whole? That appears unlikely. What they have decided to do, it seems, is to revive the agenda of the 1950s and reconstitute 'New Democracy', a stage of development characterised by a mixed economy that combines state, cooperative, private and joint State-private ownership.

The problem with 'New Democracy' is that it is unstable. Mao urged socialist transformation of the countryside in the 1950s primarily to forestall class polarisation and ensure that the peasants all came up together instead of splitting into rich and poor, exploiters and exploited. He also foresaw that restriction of the bourgeoisie (and of capitalist development) and resistance to restriction would be the main content of political struggle in the whole nation in the ensuing period. That prediction was accurate and presumably holds to this day. Everyone could have more confidence in the new policy if the media discussed more realistically what is happening now limitations have been relaxed to the point where 'anything goes'.

William Hinton is the author of Fanshen, a classic account of revolution in a Chinese village where he lived in 1948. His second book, Shenfan, came after a return visit in 1971.

Capital failure

John Gittings *Published 21 December 1984*

Marx, so the Chinese have recently reminded us, only wrote a thousand words or so about what is actually supposed to happen after the revolution. Engels added that the State would wither away and would become as obsolete as the bronze axe. Lenin briefly thought that the transition to communism would take just a few years, but soon changed his mind.

It might have been better if Marx had said nothing at all rather than leave a deterministic skeleton of theory on which the post-revolutionary societies have tried in vain to put some flesh. There was a lower phase of communism, he said (which is usually called socialism), and which retains some of the 'birthmarks of the old society' such as unequal reward for labour.

There would be a higher phase of communism where society would inscribe on its banner the brave words 'From each according to his ability, to each according to his needs.' The problem of how to get from A to B, added Marx, would have to be answered scientifically, but he left that task for others.

The theory was developed by Lenin, Stalin, and later by Mao along lines which have entered the school textbooks of almost a third of the world's population. The requirements for achieving communism were material abundance based on public ownership and planning, plus a high level of communist awareness. Meanwhile the party would stay firmly in charge of the transition.

In saying now that Marx's 'tentative ideas are not necessarily very appropriate' for the present time, the Chinese are really throwing doubt on the whole shape of this scheme. One of China's leading Marxist scholars, Professor Su Shaozhi, recently told a British audience that he and his colleagues have no idea what the 'higher stage' may consist of.

'Marx and Engels did not establish a model of communism,' said Professor Su. 'They only thought about what might happen. I cannot imagine the real situation in a communist society. The main task in socialist society is to develop production, and we did not stress this sufficiently before.'

Post-revolutionary developing countries like China, Vietnam, and Cuba have followed the same pattern, painfully casting away illusions about the possibilities of transformation. The early years of the Soviet Union saw a similar progression from the Utopian enthusiasm of Preobrezhensky's and Bukharin's ABC of Communism to the NEP.

The real casualty has been the loss of confidence in the ability of human beings to transcend material limitations. It was natural at first to transpose the revolutionary ethic – where man was more important than weapons – to the new society, and to seek to infuse it with new socialist ideals.

The human element also seemed to provide the missing link between Marx's A and B. Briefly in the late '60s and early '70s it seemed as if an entirely new model of socialist development was being sketched out on a clean sheet of paper.

Responsibility for the death of Mao's new socialist person is a subject deserving much more attention that it has so far attracted. Was it just that Marxian theory was inadequate? Or was the fatal blow struck by imperialism whose enmity and blockades encouraged the new Socialist states to develop an alternative model but then crippled their ability to sustain it materially? Or was it caused by the dictatorship of the party masquerading as the dictatorship of the proletariat—for which we should blame Lenin?

The most common assumption among Western commentators is that capitalism is bound to prevail and that people in Peking and elsewhere are beginning to grasp the fact. This is not only the dubious proposition in the light of the West's economic crisis. It is also a glib assumption about the 'real' opinions of leaders and some of the rank and file. As Isaac Deutscher wrote about the Soviet Union, 'the heritage of the revolution survives in one form or another in the structure of society, and in the nation's mind'. Mr Deng Xiaoping says he is still a socialist— and believes it.

The final defeat of capitalism, wrote Lenin soon after the revolution, would require the patience of the scientist who has tried '605 preparations before he developed a 606th which met definite requirements'. Here lies Mr Deng's real problem. How much patience is there left when it is necessary to go back to square one and start again?

Wanted—money from home

Ahmed Rashid *Published 4 January 1985*

Strict censorship in Pakistan means no public debate about the
state of the country's economy. It is indisputable that it is one
of the few developing countries with as much as $4.2 billions
in its foreign aid pipeline over the next three years, but is
unable to complete a five-year plan. So when the Planning
Minister, Mehbubul Haq, announced recently that the
country's sixth plan (1983–88) had been dropped, the audience
was shocked. The move had been on the cards for nearly a year.

Pakistan went to the top of the list of countries favoured by
western aid donors after the Soviets invaded Afghanistan in
1979. Sudden front-line status in the cold war gave the unstable
military regime and fragile economy a much-needed boost. Over
$10 millions were spent in drawing up a vast plan conceived by
the World Bank, which was revised downwards three times
before an expenditure of 490 billion rupees (about $33 billions)
was announced.

'It was unrealistic and grandiose right from the start,' says
Akmal Hosein, Professor of Economics at Punjab University.
'Independent economists criticised it for being more suited to
IMF demands than to Pakistan's needs.'

The Government has now scrapped it and launched a three-
year rolling plan costing $12 billions, down 15 per cent from
the sixth plan's spending targets. The reason is a staggering
$2 billions short-fall in expected government revenues until
1988. 'Put simply, it means the Aid to Pakistan Consortium
and the World Bank is prepared to give us the dollars for
projects but we ourselves cannot raise the rupees,' Hosein says.

The internal economic crisis has been fuelled by a number of
factors—a low savings rate, a drop in exports by 20 per cent, a
high and unstable rate of inflation, and a reduction in remittances from Pakistanis working in the Middle East.

Remittances by an estimated two million Pakistanis working
legally in the Gulf and another half a million illegals, reached
nearly three billion dollars in 1982–83, at roughly 53 per cent
of the country's foreign exchange earnings and on a par with
export earnings. More important, they support a consumer
orientated economy in the rural areas in the politically sensitive provinces of Punjab and North-West Frontier.

Thousands of rural families have moved to cities where
women and children live off what the men send home. Haq's
plan expected an annual 10 per cent rise in remittances reach-

ing $4.5 billion by 1988. Just the opposite has happened. A recent ILO report for the Government reveals that remittances have fallen by 4 per cent this year.

Planning officials now talk of a 10 per cent drop with an even higher figure predicted for next year, as the Gulf War drags on and the Gulf countries cut their spending. The ILO report says that 600,000 workers will be forced to return home by 1988 and they will face unemployment and disorientation after the higher living standards they became used to. 'We have been unable to channel remittances into constructive investment,' says a vice-president of Habib Bank, the country's largest nationalised bank. 'We Muslims cannot save, we spend what we earn.'

The lack of savings is what the planners have learned to their embarrassment. Pakistan has a savings rate of only 7 per cent, one of the lowest in the world and on a level with countries like Nepal and Afghanistan. 'Planners had envisaged a rise in all kinds of savings to nearly 23 per cent,' said a professor at Islamabad University. 'But that was just wishful thinking.'

Numerous government schemes to promote savings have not proved successful while the black economy has boomed as luxury goods continue to be imported. The money is inside the country but is not being tapped effectively.

While the sixth plan envisaged a growth rate of gross domestic product at 6.5 per cent, GDP for 1983–84 stood at only 4.6 per cent. Bad harvests, mismanagement, and acute power and water shortages have led to a decline in agricultural production. Pakistan has little heavy industry and depends on the export of agricultural goods, but between July and September 1984, exports were down 20 per cent from last year. Even industrial investment has suffered because of the unfavourable investment climate. 'Although there is so much project aid lying around, industrialists are just not interested in putting up long gestation projects,' said a Pakistani vice-president of an American bank.

Censorship means that bankers, economists and politicians have been expressing frustration at not being able to have their views heard. The Majlis, an assembly nominated by President Zia, has become a rubber stamp body where even annual budgets are not debtaed, but many bankers are even more uncertain about government plans to Islamicise all banking in the country by next July. The process began on 1 January. No interest bearing account will be permitted; instead a profit and loss sharing system will give a return to depositors based on the banks' profits over the year.

Bankers are heavily divided on the issue, although once again, there has been no public debate on the pros and cons.

Senior officials with the country's nationalised banks insist that Pakistan is making the first truly Islamic banking system and it will become an example and inspiration to the rest of the Islamic world. Younger bankers, and certainly all the 17 foreign banks operating in the country, are extremely sceptical. 'Banking is much more than just the elimination of interest,' says a Pakistani president of a foreign bank.

The State Bank has issued a list of permissible methods of financing, of which the most important are mark ups on trade financing, hire purchase, and leasing for capital equipment, and participation term certificates or debentures but with a fixed rate of repayment. Other modes are Musharaka, a partnership for sharing profits and losses between the borrower and the bank, and Mudaraba, venture capital for a fixed time provided by the banks with a sharing of profits and losses. The last two have been in operation on a voluntary basis since 1981, but only a dozen such arrangements have been carried out since then and they have not proved successful.

However there are entire areas in the complex world of modern banking that the State Bank has not provided any answers to and this is already creating confusion in the minds of bankers and many big borrowers. 'Let's face it—nobody is in this business for sharing profits and losses. It is only profits we are interested in,' said one leading Pakistani banker. If banks avoid potential losers or small businessmen with few assets in their corporate lending, the investment climate and the economy will suffer even more. Another obvious, contradiction is that normal interest will continue to be paid on the country's enormous $11 billion foreign debt, but eliminated inside the country.

Both the economy and banking are going through a period of great uncertainty at the moment. However in the past Pakistan's economy has demonstrated a resiliance and ability to survive even worse crises, such as the trauma of Partition in 1947, the collapse of the Ayub regime in 1969, and the division of the country when Bangladesh was created. However, much now depends on the political direction that the military regime pursues and the defusing of tensions on Pakistan's borders with Afghanistan and India.

To create a saving psychology or to persuade illiterate workers in the Gulf to invest their earnings creatively; to develop heavy industry or to put a stop to the black economy which is fuelling inflation, needs a government that has the confidence of the people.

Ahmed Rashid is a Contributing Editor to Euromoney magazine.

The new Islam signals danger in paradise

Richard Gott   *Published 18 January 1985*

The strength and power of the Muslim revival, so much a feature of the rest of the Islamic world, is now much in evidence in Malaysia. Support for radical Islam has grown so quickly that it threatens to play havoc with the country's political system—and with its whole future as a multi-ethnic state.

I was first forcibly made aware of it as a significant phenomenon in the course of a meeting held in a provincial university. A veiled young woman in black came to the rostrum to denounce Western feminism. 'I like to wear the hejab,' she said. 'I use it in my defence. I feel safe behind it. I feel very independent.' It soon became clear that this was no isolated phenomenon. She was speaking for her generation of Muslim students.

The hejab as worn in Malaysia is a veil that goes over the head and shoulders but leaves the oval of the face uncovered. Not unlike the garb of a Christian nun, it gives the wearer – in the eyes at least of a Western male – a somewhat saintly, even seductive, look. It certainly appears less sinister than the defiant chadors of the Iranian revolution, with their vizored echo of Norman armour-plating. And it is practical, no obstacle to participating in modern urban life—as the veiled women on motorbikes testify, weaving their way through the heavy traffic of Penang or Kuala Lumpur.

More significantly, the veil is becoming fashionable. In a revolt of extraordinary complexity and importance – anti-Western, anti-consumerist – the Malay women of Malaysia, particularly the educated ones, are turning to Islam. And they are subscribing not just to the tolerant observances of the Sunni sect that have long characterised life and worship in the Malay archipelago, but to the new fundamentalism springing up all over the Islamic world that has its origins in Khomeini's Iran. In multi-ethnic Malaysia, it is a phenomenon of potentially cataclysmic dimensions.

For a country of 14 million people where different races mix but do not mingle, Malaysia is astonishingly peaceful and good-humoured. Yet this gentle paradise is poised permanently above a precipice. Unlike so many Third World countries, overt violence is at a minimum. People expect to get home safely in the evenings. There is no great display of soldiers and police in the streets.

But this calm atmosphere, this intensely agreeable feeling

of amity that it engenders, is only surface thin. It is based on a strange consensus that has been long established and enforced —and is not now discussed. Indeed it is not allowed to be discussed.

Under the Constitutional Amendment and Sedition Act of February, 1971, all sensitive political issues are removed from the realm of public discussion. Even in parliament there are certain matters to do with the country's racial balance that MPs are not allowed to raise. Under the consensus, the Chinese (36 per cent of the population) retain as much economic power as their inherited skills and abilities allow them to—which is a lot. But the Malays (45 per cent) have entrenched themselves as the political rulers.

For 14 years the system has survived without challenge, but the balance of the aspirations of the two groups is never far from breakdown. If you are a Malay, you tend to shrug your shoulders at the thought of this structural imbalance. If you are Chinese, you nurse a certain lasting dissatisfaction.

The present consensus is accepted, not just because the government carries an iron fist within its velvet glove, but because there is a folk memory of the price of breakdown. Knowledge of the precipice is always present. In May, 1969, after elections in which the Malay-dominated ruling coalition received a reduced majority, communal rioting broke out in Kuala Lumpur on a scale that gave the lie to those who believed that Malaysia was a model of inter-ethnic harmony and cooperation.

'Malaysia's most significant achievement,' an American academic (James W. Gould) had written that year, 'is in racial cooperation.' The country, he went on, 'seems to have discovered a way of permitting three ancient cultures to continue their great traditions but to work together in harmony.'

In May, 1969, this seemed a somewhat roseate and romantic view. Riot, arson, and sudden death were followed by curfew, the setting up of refugee centres for the Chinese, and the establishment of a state of emergency. The actual death toll was not large, a few hundred, but the event left a lasting image of what could happen if the consensus were again to collapse.

And herein lies the importance and significance of Islam. For the Muslim revival and resurgence is eroding the power of the increasingly secular Malay elite—for whom Islam has never been more than a social and cultural veneer.

Politically, the challenge to the government comes from PAS, the Parti Islam SeMalaysia, the party that seeks to establish an Islamic state. If PAS, with its fundamentalist message, were seriously to split the Malay vote (which at present goes mostly to UMNO, the ruling United Malay National Organisation), the Chinese could theoretically once again become arbiters of the future of the nation.

Even a sniff of such a possibility would be enough to rekindle the flames ignited in 1969. But the appeal of Islam is extraordinarily powerful.

In one celebrated case recently, given much publicity in the government press, a religious teacher in Selangor told children to destroy the family television set, purveyor of infidel propaganda. It would be right, he said, for the children to execute their parents should they be prevented from carrying out his order. In such circumstances, beheading one's parents would not be regarded as a sin.

In any society this would be the voice of extremism, but in Malaysia it is a voice that increasingly has followers, and a voice that the Government cannot altogether ignore, as the challenge becomes more open and more politicised. Fundamentalist zealots can be laughed at, or locked up, but what of the preachers who denounce the Malay government itself as infidel? What if the people are taught to believe that it is a sin to vote for UMNO?

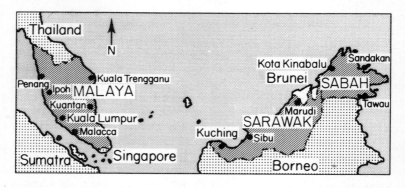

The government's reaction has been to emphasise more strongly its own enthusiasm for Islam, and to try to co-opt the more moderate leaders of the Muslim revival. One of these is Anwar Ibrahim, formerly the fiery head of the Islamic youth movement and now the Minister of Agriculture. Ibrahim knows what a difficult course he has to follow: proclaiming Islamic values on the one hand, imprisoning Islamic extremists without trial on the other. But what else can we do, he asks? 'If they appear in court, 20,000 people would turn up, shouting, "God is Great".'

So Ibrahim is now a moderate. 'Muslims should see Islam as a source,' he argues, implying that there might be other valid sources of indigenous values. Malaysia needs 'to objectively evaluate and select'. And he takes issue with those fundamentalists who wholly turn their backs on the West. 'It is absurd to imagine that after hundreds of years Western civilisation needs to be rejected in toto.'

- At the 1980 census Malaysia's 13,745,241 inhabitants were spread through the 13 states of the federation.
- 83 per cent lived in the peninsula: 54 per cent of those were indigenous Malays (bumiputras), 35 per cent Chinese, and 10 per cent Indian (from India, Pakistan, or Bangladesh). In 1983 the population was estimated at 14,744,000.
- Most bumiputras are Muslim, rural and work in traditional agriculture. The Chinese are mainly Taoist or Buddhist, urban, and have the major roles in the more modern industrial and commercial sectors.

The difficulty for the Government – and indeed for any kind of secular opposition – is that the Islamic revival has subsumed a number of other traditions. Often seen in the West as a resurgence of the Right, Islam is also embraced by those who might at other times have been of the Left. 'No one's interested in socialism any more,' said one old socialist professor. 'They're obsessed with Islam.'

So if you're a radical Malay student with the usual Third World concerns about cultural colonialism, American imperialism, and government corruption, the chances are that you'll see Islam as a vehicle for change—and if you're a woman you'll be wearing the veil.

All this leaves out a significant aspect of Malaysian life. As Anwar Ibrahim points out when discussing the zealots, 'these so-called religious leaders are oblivious to the fact that this is a multi-racial, multi-ethnic society. There are people here of all races and all religions.'

In particular, there are the Chinese, too large a group to be dismissed as 'a minority'. The Chinese, too, are not immune from the sense of cultural nationalism that is affecting the Malays. For although there is Chinese representation in the government (through the MCA, the Malaysian Chinese Association), the Chinese as a whole have little political power.

A small segment of the older generation has been satisfied with retaining considerable economic power, but most of the younger generation have to struggle with their Malay contemporaries who were awarded structural advantages under the post-1969 carve-up. As the young Malays turn to Islam, so the young Chinese have begun to rediscover their own roots.

Symptomatic of this development has been the row over Bukit China, a controversy that could do immense damage to the government. Bukit China – Chinese Hill – is an old Chinese graveyard in Malacca.

But Bukit China is not any old graveyard. It is the largest Chinese graveyard in the world outside China. According to legend it was once the residence of a beautiful princess from the Ming court, Hang Li Po. She arrived in Malacca in the fifteenth century.

Ambivalent though the Chinese may be about death, they do not like anyone monkeying around with the graves of their ancestors. Which is exactly what the government has been planning to do. Bukit China is a prime development site in the middle of town—and what could be more economically desirable than to cover it over with steel and concrete?

Yet not everyone sees things that way. Local and national opposition has been mobilised to prevent it happening. And if plans to develop the graveyard go ahead, it could threaten the position of the middle class Chinese party in the government, bring electoral gains to more radical Chinese parties, and destroy the consensus, erected with such difficulty 15 years ago.

For many years, even during the colonial period, the common interest of the elite groups of the various races – Malay, Chinese, Tamil – allowed Malaya to avoid the communal tensions that have afflicted other Third World states with a multi-ethnic population. Only during 'the Emergency' and the period which immediately preceded it was the stability of the country seriously threatened.

In the past two decades an impressive record of economic growth, a diversified export sector, and skilful political management has kept the growing divergence between the various communities from getting out of hand.

But in universities and among the inter-racial intellectual community there is considerable concern about the future. 'We are not predicting an inevitable racial war,' write two university lecturers, Ishak Shari and K. S. Jomo, in an article on development and inequality in post-colonial Malaysia, 'or even a conflagration of the May 13 (1969) variety.' It is quite conceivable, they suggest, 'that ethnic tension and conflict will remain of the "cold war" type, that is, without necessarily erupting.' But present trends, they fear, are not encouraging. 'It is obvious that in such a situation a single spark will be enough to set off an explosion.'

The spark could be ignited by debate over an old Chinese graveyard, or by the turbulent growth of radical Islam.

Sewa plants the seeds of women's rights

Jeremy Seabrook reports on the success of a union of women workers in the Manchester of India

Published 12 April 1985

Dariapur is a district of chawls and hutments, an established slum in the centre of India's spectacular ornate city of Ahmedabad. The dust, in constant movement, creates vivid orange sunsets. Cycles and autorickshaws become locked in traffic jams as people go to and from work in the mills which earned Ahmedabad the inevitable name of the Manchester of India. Open channels of foul indigo water run between the houses; offal and detritus lie in the passageways too narrow to be called streets. Dariapur is far from the current wave of nostalgia in Britain for the Raj.

The women of Ahmedabad are bidi-rollers, chindi makers, charkha workers, ribbon makers, potters, supari makers, blacksmiths, or vegetable sellers. Their lives have been transformed by one of the most inspiring feminist initiatives anywhere. By organising the formerly powerless against the middlemen and monopolists who have always controlled their conditions of work and payment, Ela Bhatt's Self-Employed Women's Association – Sewa means 'service' in several Indian languages – has doubled their income in many cases, and they have been released from their subordination to the male moneylenders and merchants who have traditionally dictated the terms of their employment.

Sewa broke away from the Textile Labour Association in 1981, after Ela Bhatt sided with the harijans in the outbreak of anti-reservation violence; although from 1955 she had been organiser of the women's wing of TLA. She acknowledges her debt to the older union, and has sought to retain its Gandhian inspiration.

In her native Gujerati, she electrifies audiences; and even in English her passion and power are scarcely dinimished: 'Sewa is essentially about trade unionism. It has shown that those believed to be beyond the reach of organisation because there is no direct employer can combine to improve their condition.' Indeed, when one considers the growth of self-employment for women in Britain – homeworkers, stitchers and machinists, toy-makers, card-folders, those doing assembly work, electronics, and soldering – it may be that what Ela Bhatt says has its resonance for much contemporary women's work in the West.

'The purpose of trade unionism is not only for agitation. It is about solidarity and development: 89 per cent of women workers in Ahmedabad are self-employed. If they are excluded from the labour movement, you are cutting off the vast majority of workers, and those who most need protection.'

The three main kinds of female labour – home-based artisans and piece-workers, petty vendors, headloaders, and, increasingly, powerloom workers; and service workers, including manual labourers, agricultural and constructions workers – have traditionally been constrained by their lack of control over their raw materials and means of labour, as well as by the power of those to whom they sell.

The vegetable sellers, for instance, used to borrow 50 rupees each morning from a moneylender, in order to buy their tomatoes, oranges, or onions, and then repay 55 rupees at the end of the day. The cane workers were earning as little as four or five rupees a day. The harijan waste paper pickers would work up to 12 hours a day, and had to sell their pickings to a middleman who made big profits by selling in bulk to factories for re-cycling.

As the traditional marketplace of Manikchowk required more room for bigger stallholders and modern shops and increasing traffic, the vegetable vendors were excluded. It also meant that people were denied the chance to buy cheaper produce, because the women always sold at a lower price than the big dealers. They were refused licences, and their vegetables were trampled underfoot by the police if they failed to bribe them.

One of the early triumphs of Sewa was a petition to the Supreme Court on behalf of the vegetable sellers, some of whom had been in Manikchowk for several generations. They organised a campaign with the slogan 'space for two basketloads' and the right of women to pursue their traditional work was upheld.

But the most important task was to provide cheap credit for women. When the banks were approached, they were appalled by the idea of making loans to poor illiterates with no collateral; their procedures couldn't accommodate crowds of work-stained women with their children besieging the counters. Although the banks did eventually provide loans, this was far from being the end of the problem. Indeed, that was when the real work of Sewa began.

Many women could not repay the loans. The work of organising the different trades began; of getting unofficial slums recognised so they could be provided with electricity and water to make women's lives easier; and of setting up a programme to enhance women's skills and give them opportunities to reach wider markets.

Sewa set up its own bank. It is now autonomous, with over 23,000 members, and a lower rate of default than the commercial banks. The average savings are 400 rupees (£28). Similar difficulties occurred when Sewa tried to organise a group insurance scheme for workers.

The Life Insurance Company of India was prejudiced against women who were seen as a high risk, with childbirth as the most common cause of death; out of 4,100 children born to members in the first few years, 561 died before the age of three or were stillborn. Many women had to be back at work within days, if not hours, of giving birth. A maternity protection scheme is now in operation.

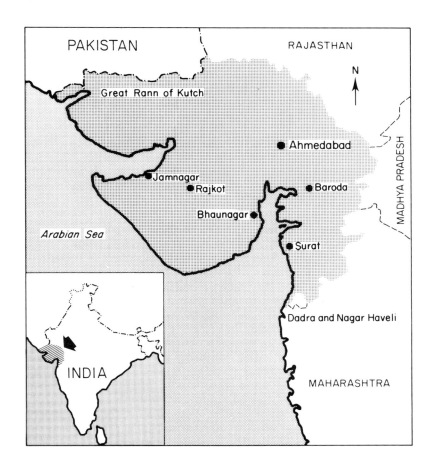

The quilt-makers, who stitch blankets from the waste materials of the mills, formed a cooperative, only to find that the employers would give them only spoilt or oily rags, and even stopped giving work altogether to women who were the sole breadwinners of the family. Sewa now buys the rags in bulk, distributes them to the quilt-makers and helps to market the end product.

The wastepaper pickers couldn't bypass the middle-men, because they had nowhere to store their pickings, while the merchants have big go-downs to accumulate the paper in large quantities.

On the other hand, the cart-pullers have succeeded in modifying the design of the traditional heavy handcarts, the bidi-rollers (the largest group of workers, with over 8,000 members), whose work involves paring away the veins from the tendul-leaves and rolling the tobacco dust inside, have seen a threefold increase in their earnings since they united against the three bidi-owners in the city and the ten contractors from whom they buy the leaves and the tobacco.

The conditions in which many women work are still pitiable. The street-sweepers are at risk from TB from constant inhaling of dust; the fingers of the cotton-pod shellers bleed, the hand-block printers suffer from the chemicals in making their own dyes; the firewood pickers carry loads often greater than their own bodyweight.

The baskets of the head-loaders are reminiscent of the shallows carried by the coster-girls in Mayhew's London, and the carts of the vendors are the identical design. One family of bidi workers I visited included a girl of eight, deftly folding in the ends of the leaves to secure the tobacco inside. Many of them worked 12 hours a day.

The number of women who are the sole supporters of their family varies, according to the different trades, from 29 per cent to 41 per cent. Their men will have deserted or migrated in search of better work.

Ela Bhatt insists on the trade union function of Sewa. Women have not traditionally seen themselves or been acknowledged as workers. Now Sewa has brought together all occupations, many of them caste-based.

Women integrated as workers act as a powerful solvent of differences, create a kind of solidarity quite new in India. 'For instance, a woman will start talking in public for the first time. When a new member joins, she may be unable to speak her own name. She has been so timid and self-effacing, she will cover her mouth when she talks.' One third of Sewa members are rural, a third are muslim, a third harijans.

Ela Bhatt believes that the international labour movement

must be flexible enough to include women and the self-employed, and not see itself only in terms of monolithic blocks confronting big employers.

Fight for recovery in the isolation ward

John Gittings *Published 14 June 1985*

There cannot be many countries where the 1978 Declaration of Alma Ata on primary health care is talked about in the villages and the state constitution has a special section on public health.

For many years Vietnam has had a remarkable health infra-structure reaching down to the local cooperatives, which according to a recent Swedish report 'is matched by few, if any, countries with similar conditions'.

The system helped to sustain basic health standards in the north during years of war. But 1975 brought a whole new area of rural deprivation to be tackled in the south, while nearly half the urban doctors there left the country. For political reasons Vietnam has been denied the rapid transfusion of foreign funds and equipment desperately needed after the war (with a few worthy – mostly Scandinavian and UN agency – exceptions).

An impressive new programme to tackle malnutrition is now under way, but this is a country where there is often a shortage of paper to keep basic medical records. In Marxist terms one might say that the health care structure belongs to a set of production relations which cannot yet be fully sustained by the actual forces of production. But who would argue that the effort should not be made?

A visit to the health clinic at Phung Thuong cooperative, 40 kilometres out of Hanoi, illustrates some of the strengths and weaknesses. It occupies a large clean compound with its own well. The assistant doctor who is in charge has a team of 13 to look after a population of 8,000. One nurse is assigned to each production group in the village.

Clinic treatment is free and patients get a ration of paddy and protein. In the courtyard there are piles of herbs waiting to be ground by a wheeled pestle to make traditional medicine.

The children who mob the foreign visitor are barefoot but cheerful, healthy to the casual glance except for a few eye disorders.

And yet . . . The assistant doctor received his training 20 years ago at a provincial secondary medical school. Only two of his staff have had similar training. A woman looking extremely ill lies on a straw-matted bed, complaining of headache and stomach pains. The doctor says vaguely she has been prescribed penicillin and aspirin and will get well soon.

There is a fine display on the wall, behind a polythene sheet, of IUDs, pills and sheaths including such luxuries as Durex Gossamer. But neither the pills nor the sheaths – all foreign imports – are available. A question about diarrhoea is answered reassuringly: 'We have had very little diarrhoea here for 15 years.'

And the healthy-looking children really need to be examined one by one and asked for their ages. Their median height turns out to be very near the bottom of the WHO international growth curve, which indicates stunting caused by malnutrition.

The fight against malnutrition, says Dr Doang Quynh Hoa, a leading paediatrician in the south, is the key to Vietnam's future health. The ministry of health in Hanoi confirms that between 13 and 20 per cent of children below the age of five (depending on the area) suffer from malnutrition. There are tiny boys and girls in Dr Hoa's hospital with the swollen stomachs, limp limbs and vacant gazes that we now associate with African famine.

How can they survive until the age of two or three when, looking half that age, they are often brought in? Existence is tough and people are so tenacious, Dr Hoa explains, that they hang on to life.

It has been coolly calculated that it will cost the state an average cash equivalent of 28 months' work by the father and mother to bring a child, once suffering from malnutrition, up to normal. It is a further argument for prevention before cure —the slogan of the Vietnamese health service and written into the constitution.

The countryside has enough resources if used properly. These include breast feeding from birth – there is still a cultural prejudice against the first milk – and appropriate diet.

The health structure, long established in the north, is now visible in the south too where well-marked clinics are a frequent roadside sight. The cooperative or commune-level polyclinic is the basic building block. Staffed by an assistant doctor, it should also have one or two nurses with up to three years training, a midwife, and a traditional practitioner. There are 8,000 communes in Vietnam, with a population range usually between two and ten thousand.

One foreign doctor working in the field acknowledges that assistant doctors – like the one at Phung Thuong – often received too little training too long ago during the war. But in general, he says, the doctor's duties 'are clearly defined and he knows what to do though he does not always have the means.'

Local people have confidence too in the delivery system—there should be five maternity beds at the commune clinic. Unlike other Third World countries, there is no recourse to home delivery by witch doctors.

At the district level (over 400 in Vietnam with an average population of 120,000) there should be a hospital with 100 beds which provide free treatment for cases referred from the communes. Curative and preventive branches are clearly separated, and there are separate brigades for hygiene, epidemiology and anti-malarial work.

The system continues through the provincial level to the centre, where most of the research institutes and special hospitals are found. But a regulation that specialists and doctors should spend one month a year working at a lower level helps to diffuse knowledge.

The problems of the north are mostly those of low training, poor equipment and a harsher life style which affects diet and health—although basic rations are guaranteed through the cooperative system. The south is more fertile but the health structure had to be rebuilt after 1975.

- The Socialist Republic of Vietnam was set up in June, 1976, uniting north and south.
- Area: 330,000 sq km, half of it forest
- Population: 1976—49 million (52 per cent female); 1984—60 million. Increasing at 2.4 per cent.
- Doctors: 15,900. Assistant doctors: 33,500
- Major diseases (per 100,000—1983): Malaria 350; dengue fever 250; measles 217. Infant mortality (up to one-year-old) 33.5 per 1,000
- Education: Over 12 million at school, mostly primary; 300,000 in higher education; 25 per cent in pre-school creches
- Estimated GNP per capita: US$175

The figures show clearly how the incorporation of the former free world regime brought its own problems. Health services in the south had been concentrated in the cities – especially Saigon – and focused on therapeutic rather than preventive work.

On the eve of re-unification in 1975, the north had 44 hospital beds per 10,000 head of population. After incorporating the south, that figure went down to 33. The incidence of some contagious diseases went up, particularly with typhoid and haemorrhagic fever. And of course the new Vietnam acquired a million or so cases of venereal disease, plus a drugs problem which has not yet been completely eliminated.

One statistic showed a marked improvement – the number of inhabitants per medical doctor – but not for long as the population grew and many southern doctors left.

One can understand why they left, says one who stayed behind. 'They had two cars, a town house and a beach chalet at Vung Tao, and could earn enough to pay for it with four days work.' Doctors who have remained 'en place' may still do private work, but those trained since 1975 are officially limited to their state employment and salary of 500 dong (less than two black market US dollars). How can they survive? The alternatives seem inevitably to be unofficial moonlighting, or corruption, or theft of state property—medicines.

Family planning is so important that General Giap, in retirement from the revolution, was put in charge of the New National Population Committee last year. In Phung Thuong they say they will reduce the birth rate from 2.4 to 1.7 in the space of a year.

It is an unlikely claim, but the dimension of the problem is smaller in the north where most families only have two children. In the south the average is between five and six. Here, too, adequate nutrition and healthy childhood is the key. Parents must be convinced that fewer children are needed to survive to a productive adulthood.

IUDs are the most common method and ¾ million were fitted last year. (One Western ambassador with a small discretionary fund of money is quietly spending all of it on importing IUDs.) But with no local production of contraceptives, it is doubtful whether the campaign is effective yet outside the urban areas and neighbouring countryside. The Vietnamese calculate that unless checked their population of 60 million will increase more than 25 per cent by the year 2000.

The Vietnamese say they will not follow the Indian method of mass sterilisation – against which there is strong cultural prejudice – nor the Chinese method of fines and penalties.

Vietnam suffers not only from the expected range of health

problems but from its continued isolation. Even the large Swedish programme is now threatened by political opposition at home. The massive foreign aid which a war torn country might reasonably expect has never materialised. Yet with a strong basic primary structure down to the commune level and even the brigade health worker, health in Vietnam is an area where relatively small inputs of equipment and training can produce substantial knock-on effects.

Violence by proxy

John Gittings   *Published 21 June 1985*

To hijack a civilian airliner and hold its passengers hostage is, for most readers of this page, a wholly unacceptable face of violence. Added to the unacknowledged trauma of flying, it conjures up a nightmare where all normality is suspended. We can too easily imagine ourselves there.

But the nightmare of violence for the great majority of the world's population assumes a very different form which is far easier to imagine than the interior of a Boeing 727—especially since most have never flown anyhow. It may be the arrival of soldiers in one's village, or the destruction of one's home by an unexplained bomb, or being taken away by police on the word of an informer and locked up in a notorious camp to suffer torture. Such experiences have been part of the Shi'ite share of violence in recent years, just as they have been familiar to Palestinians for much longer.

The violence in the TWA Boeing 727 on a Beirut runway was, thanks to modern technology, unequivocal. For the first time in such incidents, the Western media could even copy a tape which recorded the suffering of an innocent passenger being beaten before his death.

The evidence of violence in the south Lebanon – where the Shi'ites have been propelled into what is labelled extremism since 1982 by the Israeli invasion – has, of course, never been so electronically evident. The hijackers' principal demand was for the release of the last 700 prisoners from the Ansar prison camp (transported illegally by Israel across the border) which at its peak contained some 10,000 prisoners held without trial. Allegations of torture were described by the Israeli Attorney General as 'distorted' or 'exaggerated', and both versions were duly reported in the Western press. There will be only one version to report in the Western press about the latest hijack incident however it ends, and it is a safe subject for the covers of *Time* and *Newsweek*. Violence at its most brutal will be shown in full colour as it has been in the past.

It is brutal partly because the technology of the hijackers is as backward as that of the television is sophisticated. Knives and grenade pins between the teeth encourage the image of barbarism far more than precision bombardment and surgical strikes.

For the most part the actuality of violence has in the postwar period been confined to the Third World. The excellent series of maps in *The War Atlas* by Kidron and Smith shows North America wholly free from war in contrast to the South. Except for localised unrest in the British and Soviet empires, Europe has also been war-free. The Middle East, Africa and Asia, by contrast have amply borne out George Orwell's prediction that the wars of the future would be fought by proxy outside the imperial heartland.

The same atlas also shows how the Middle East has outstripped every other region in imports of arms from predominantly the US/USSR/Western Europe arms producing complex. It is hardly surprising if Beirut itself is brimming with weapons and the personnel to bring them on board a marooned airliner.

First World violence, since the end of the Vietnam war, has fairly effectively been minimised by the policy of 'letting Xians fight Xians'—the Nixon doctrine where X stands for any continent but North America.

But First World violence of a different kind, optative rather than actual, does frequently feature on the front cover. The most recent issue of *Newsweek* depicted the 'Star Warriors', subtitled 'The People behind the weapons of the future'. Here was no Muslim fanatic brandishing a hand grenade, but a pensive almost wistful Lt. Gen. James Abrahamson, the man in charge of the SDI programme.

There have been plenty of disaster movies about hijacks but none which properly belong to the genre about nuclear war. Athens airport, as commentators were quick to point out, was the starting point for the hijack to Entebbe which inspired no less than three such disaster movies. It is also the title of a poem by the Palestinian poet Mahmoud Darwish which tells us more about the cause of this hijack than any study of airport security.

Rising Sun burns with a new fire

Robert Whymant   *Published 5 July 1985*

'There is nothing Japan really wants to buy from foreign countries,' declared Yoshihiro Inayama, doyen of the nation's business leaders, since all necessary industrial goods are made in Japan. 'Nothing,' he added, 'except, possibly, neckties with unusual designs.' Mr Inayama, 81-year-old president of Keidanren, a highpowered version of the CBI, was commenting on Prime Minister Nakasone's appeal to the Japanese to resolve trade friction by buying more foreign goods.

Japan's businessmen may swap disparaging remarks about foreign goods in their own tight circle, but they seldom are as blunt as Mr Inayama was in this nationalistic way.

Some observers would say that on an individual level, and as a nation, Japan's self confidence is growing, that there is less reticence about asserting Japan's superior attributes and pointing out the weaknesses of the West. Having grown used to winning in business, the Japanese are making their presence felt in other spheres.

In a book published four years ago, prominent sociologist Rokuro Hidaka declared that Japan's economic prowess and worldwide efforts to emulate Japan's industrial policy and management practices were making the Japanese arrogant again. An American writer, Jared Taylor, in a new book, sees the growing self confidence as an overdue corrective to a Japanese inferiority complex, and to a post-war self-loathing after being conquered for the first time in history. But Taylor warns: 'As they begin to swagger, the Japanese will not be as pleasant to deal with.'

For some, the most telling evidence of a changing mood is the government's preoccupation with improving Japan's self-image by putting a new slant on history. School textbooks are being rewritten to downplay Japanese military and colonial atrocities: these moves, like Prime Minister Nakasone's proposals for education reform, stem from a basic desire to instil patriotism in new generations, or what Nakasone calls 'correct-nationalism'.

Nakasone's aim is a renewal of the 'Yamato Damashii', the spirit of Japan the unique country, and the pre-war ethics that required a citizen to put duty to State above individual rights. Until he became Prime Minister two years ago he made little secret of his belief that armed with 'correct nationalism' and devotion to the State, the Japanese could regain their rightful place as lords of Asia, temporarily ceded to the Americans.

As governor of Takushoku University, which before the war trained young men for service in Japan's colonies, Nakasone was fond of reminding students of the 'superiority of the Japanese race' (his words). 'When we go to Europe, we feel the eclipse of European races,' he told them. 'My feeling is that the culture of coloured races will emerge strongly with Japan as a central force.'

His association 1967–1971 with Takushoku (literally: settle and exploit), a breeding ground for the Yamato Damashii, offers useful insights into the attitudes that prevail within the ruling party today. As leader of Japan, Nakasone is more circumspect, but his xenophobia is still apt to get the better of him.

Last year, at a home for A-bomb victims in Hiroshima, Nakasone remarked: 'The Japanese have been doing well for 2,000 years because there are no foreign races (in Japan).'

Nakasone has earned praise from the American press for speaking English, for being 'international-minded', for being the first Japanese leader to achieve first-name status with an American President ('Ron and Yasu'). But it is his alter ego which boasted (to the party faithful) of being among 'those who fought the white man', and asserts Japan's racial superiority and uniqueness that reflects the nation's changing attitudes.

Twice this century Japan has challenged white supremacy, beating the Russians in 1904, being beaten by the Western allies in 1945. Having overtaken Britain and West Germany in the 1960s to become the Free World's second largest economy, the remaining obstacle to economic supremacy is the United States.

Business leaders like Jiro Nishikawa, President of Furu-kawa Mining Co., do not believe that overtaking the United States can be as easily accomplished. But it is safe to say that as long as they remain in second place, the Japanese will be chafing at the bit.

In their strict hierarchical society, Japanese view one another as 'inferior' or 'superior', and they see other nations in the same light. As several commentators have pointed out, there are no equals in this world view. Writing in *Japan Echo*, Yasuaki Onuma, a professor of international law, says that Japan's war on Asia derived from 'a deep-rooted contempt for other Asians', and Japan 'still views Asians condescend-ingly'.

Best-selling author, Akiyuki Nosaka warns that the Americans had better watch out if they want to maintain their pre-eminence. The thrust of Japanese nationalism he says has always been against the United States—ever since American gunboats in the last century forced Japan, then a closed country, to open itself to trade with the world. The American conquest and the occupation, only aggravated what Nosaka calls 'our ongoing vendetta'.

Success is the best revenge, but Japan will not rest until it has surpassed the US in economy and technology. Nosaka predicts intense competition between the two nations for economic influence in China, and resentment at American opposition to Japan having nuclear weapons. 'Japan's urge to dominate is getting stronger,' says the prize-winning author, 'Japan is a very dangerous country'.

Japan's economic prowess has led to a flowering of 'Japanism', pride in the special attributes of the Japanese character, which the West has helped reinforce with lavish flattery, on the lines of Ezra Vogel's ecstatic book, *Japan As Number One*.

It was a sense of Japanese 'specialness and separateness' that stoked the ultranationalism of the 1930s and justified the 'civilising mission' to bring Asia, and eventually the whole world, under the Japanese roof. Today, the sense of uniqueness is being fertilised by a spate of studies on the 'theory of the Japanese' (some by foreigners), analysing what makes them so special, including a treatise on their supposedly unique brain.

But this sense of being special, reappearing when Japan is edging towards a bigger role in world affairs, is unlikely to alleviate the communications problem with other countries. An Australian survey released in October showed that 89 per cent of top businessmen think Japanese are untrustworthy and unethical. Intensive business contacts between two erstwhile enemy countries had clearly done little to improve understanding. Some observers believe that dealing with the Japanese will become more of a strain as their national pride intensifies.

Foreigners who have lived in Japan for several years are acutely aware of the changing attitudes.

'As Europe has declined, the Japanese are less concerned about showing their scorn for us in the West,' says a German professor assigned to a Japanese university. 'I was against chauvinism in any form when I came. Now I shall leave a German chauvinist, or rather a non-Japanese chauvinist.'

Japan's strength, it is commonly observed, was to import Chinese, and later Western learning and techniques, to improve on others' ideas. 'Japan will not be the world's leader in the next century, as some Japanese and foreigners predict, because its arrogance and unwillingness to learn from others will lead to a decline,' says one long-term foreign resident.

The late Herman Kahn, a futurologist who envisioned Japan incorporating its non-communist neighbours into an economic superstate, confided to me once that the idea would almost certainly remain a dream. Japan could never fulfil a leadership role in Asia, he said, because they simply couldn't relate to 'inferior' humans—that is, to non-Japanese.

Having caught up with the West in modernisation – the goal which impelled it forward for more than a century – Japan sees its models in disarray. Europe has fallen prey to the 'advanced nation's illness' which the Japanese employers federation declares must not be allowed to infect Japanese workers. American influence is seen to be declining: 'The United States is not a superpower any more,' declared Prime Minister Masayoshi Ohira in April 1980. These developments, some observers believe underline the rising Japanism, as a way to fill the spiritual vacuum and lend meaning to the next leap forward.

Related to this renewed sense of 'uniqueness', or greatness, is a movement to re-examine recent history, and reject the notion of Japan as sinner, the view promoted by the victorious allies in the Tokyo war crimes trials of 1946–1948.

Criticisms of the 'immoral-Japan' version of recent history are, along with the current preoccupation with the uniqueness of being Japanese, an attempt to re-establish the Japanese sense of national identity, according to Professor Hideo Shimizu, introducing a collection of 'revisionist views', of Japan's recent history.

The challenge to the accepted version of events is from scholars outside the intellectual mainstream: but what makes it significant is that it complements the government's own efforts to heal the 'scars on the Japanese psyche' by refurbishing recent history in school textbooks.

To the fury of Asian neighbours invaded by the Imperial Army, authenticated atrocities are either ignored or downplayed in the books authorised by the Ministry of Education, which applies censorship with the goal of improving the nation's self image so that new generations can be reared on patriotism.

Prime Minister Nakasone is strongly of the opinion that Japan can only command international respect through increased firepower. Not long ago he was obliged to apologise to the Finnish ambassador for a scathing reference to 'Finlandisation'.

Under Nakasone, the campaign for the return of four islands held by the Soviet Union has grown more strident: recently a ruling party mission was dispatched to the USA to request that new maps indicate Japan's claim to the islands.

If 'natural nationalism' were to develop in extreme directions, Professor Hideo Shimizu acknowledges: 'It could become as dangerous as its wartime manifestation was.'

This prompts the question of what direction nationalism might take in an economic crisis. Would it spill over into political confrontation again as happened in the 1930s?

The fangs of militarism were drawn by the 'peace constitution' imposed by the Americans, but Japan is now growing new ones, by flouting the constitution, and with the myopic encouragement of the US. But the most disturbing tendency is the official movement to whitewash recent history.

India's shame

Baljit Malik
Published 12 July 1985

Sikhs in India and the Punjab are now caught in a vice between the terrorism of fringe groups and a floundering, fumbling, not so clean government in Delhi. Coupled with central government's lack of clear policy is Rajiv Gandhi's own lack of political vision and statesmanship. Given the Congress Party's performance in the last general election and culpability in the massacres which followed Indira Gandhi's assassination last November, the Government's behaviour has not been dissimilar to that of groups which believe in a combination of terror and intolerance.

Rajiv Gandhi and the Congress-I have now filled the Indian parliament with a massive, three-fourths majority, and the Opposition is all but wiped out. But Congress's victory followed an electoral campaign in which most of the unwritten rules of parliamentary democracy were discarded.

Indira Gandhi's death was to whip up a Hindu backlash in votes and Sikh lives.

Over 50,000 Sikhs became refugees in Delhi alone, some 1,200 women became widows in a matter of days; more than

3,000 were killed, and property worth millions was looted and destroyed. The police, politicians and civil servants simply looked on, frozen into inaction by dereliction of duty at the highest political level.

Even now, eight months after the massacres, more than 2,000 Sikhs are still living in refugee camps and Sikh temples in Delhi and scores of families have received minimal or no compensation for damage caused to their property. Meanwhile, not a single conviction has gone through the courts as a result of the carnage.

The Government's astonishing policy of turning a blind eye to the worst disturbances to have hit the capital since the partition riots of 1947, was carried to the ridiculous extent of preventing Indians abroad from contributing relief supplies to their people back home. Consignments of woollen clothing were held up by Customs for five months until they were no longer required.

Since last November, New Delhi has acted to set up commissions of inquiry following a number of incidents, such as the murder (by the police) of a member of the opposition in Rajasthan, an outbreak of rioting in Gujerat, and the recent crash of the Air India jumbo in the Irish Sea. In addition, inquiries are under way to investigate Indira Gandhi's assassination, and police in three states are vigorously hunting for those (believed by the authorities to be Sikhs) behind bomb blasts which hit northern India a few weeks ago. This is as it should be, the least that might be expected from a responsible government.

In marked contrast, the Government has gone out of its way to avoid an inquiry into last November's massacre of Sikhs. For nearly six months, the Prime Minister has refused demands from opposition parties, civil liberties organisations, groups of eminent non-Sikhs and the entire Sikh community to investigate the killings. Eventually it was announced that a judge of the Supreme Court would constitute a one-man commission of inquiry. However, this commission has yet to open its proceedings.

Moreover, its terms of reference have been diluted to avoid pinpointing the cause and the course of the disturbances, the adequacy of measures to control them, and the identity of those reponsible. Reasons for government hesitation are perhaps understandable, because three independent investigations so far have clearly placed the stamp of guilt for the November killings on the ruling party and conniving elements in the central Government.

Whether by design or default, sheer cussedness or foolishness, the result is that the Sikhs have been pushed into postures of anger, anguish and alienation. In India today there are two sets of laws and policies: one for Punjab and the Sikhs, the other for the rest of the country. In Punjab all legitimate defiance of unreasonable policies is met with detention under the National Security and Prevention of Terrorism Acts. It is the mailed fist in Punjab, but kid gloves for those responsible for mass killings of Sikhs.

Punjab has been turned into a police-military state, devoid of basic human rights. The law has been tampered with, to put the burden on the accused to prove their innocence rather than the prosecution to prove their guilt. Thousands of Sikhs are under detention, thousands more are still fugitives from army and police terror, while others have been killed in false encounters, and torture has been widespread.

Singapore starts to feel the cold

Nicholas Cumming-Bruce
Published 20 September 1985

Hard times have hit even the hungry ghosts in this island of economic miracles. Chinese Singaporeans are going as usual to the raucous street dinner-auctions where they buy symbolic gifts to help the ghosts of forebears released from purgatory during the seventh moon—and to acquire some good luck for themselves. This year, however, they are spending a fraction of the usual amount on their unhappy ancestors.

It is one symptom of the gloom that has overtaken Singaporeans along with a recession which has plunged the economy from healthy expansion – 8 per cent last year – to negative growth in the second quarter of this one.

Business blues are everywhere, from the former Hill Street Police Station where staff in the official assignee's office say they are winding up 30 or more businesses a month, to the acres of unoccupied space in the gleaming high rise offices or shopping complexes that are the hallmarks of Singapore's recent boom.

Nine months ago the Government was feeding its electorate with the expectation of a living standard equivalent to Switzerland's in the next decade. Now it is telling the public they need to raise productivity drastically and forget about wage increases for two or three years.

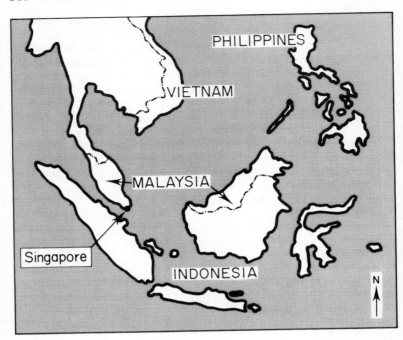

Helping this message across has been the loss of 40,000 jobs in recent months, nearly all among foreign workers. There are still, officials say, around 1.3 jobs for every Singaporean. Some, however, are out of work and jobs available may be at substantially lower pay or of a nature they would not normally accept. Expectations have been painfully dented.

For all the mood of depression, many businessmen and economists express confidence Singapore can ride this downturn and prosper again with the resources built up over the past quarter-century: political stability, a government free of foreign debt, a high level of reserves, efficient services, and educated English-speaking workforce.

Yet it now seems the recession may have profound repercussions for more than the economy. In elections last December, voters showed their irritation with the authoritarian ways of Prime Minister Lee Kuan Yew and his People's Action Party by electing two opposition MPs to Parliament. Mr Lee likes PAP to have all the seats. Government is now concerned that the effects of recession which may be felt for two to three years may erode its hold on the public.

The election result itself posed no threat to party control but it revealed the degree to which the PAP's political sensitivities had become atrophied in the prevailing climate of absolute subservience to party dictates. Some analysts see parallels in the handling of the economy.

Singapore has been hit hard by a sharp downturn in overseas markets, particularly the US, which it could do little to influence the heavy industries in which Singapore has invested most heavily, oil refining, ship building and repair and rig building have suffered from world market decline.

- Population: 2.53 million, of which 75 per cent are Chinese.
- Area: 238 sq. miles, giving a population density of 11,160 per sq. mile.
- Economy: exports S$46,100 million, imports S$59,500 million (1983 figures). The GDP per head of population was S$6,521.

But government agencies played a major part in real estate development which has resulted in a glut of offices and hotels, causing considerable pain to the banks that financed them. A drop in the number of visitors from neighbouring countries is not helping the hotel industry, which in 1983 set about doubling the number of rooms to 30,000. But as one senior official noted, 'I think we'd say we were rather foolish.'

A policy of pushing up wages started in 1979 helped to shift workers from less efficient, low value-added industries to high technology industries but it seems to have gone too far. Wages rose twice as fast as productivity and Singapore lost competitiveness as a manufacturing base.

High costs are identified as the biggest obstacle facing business in Singapore in the interim report of an economic committee under Brigadier-General Lee Hsien Loong, Prime Minister Lee's son and a junior trade minister.

A major component in wage costs is obligatory contributions equivalent to 50 per cent of a worker's salary – half provided by the worker and half by the employer – paid into the Government's central provident fund. Some economists suggest Government could well afford to lower the rate of contributions. But the CPF is a key, and cheap, source of funding for government. It has been willing to discuss different ways of using this enormous pool of capital, which could have far-reaching implications for Singapore's development as a financial market but not, so far, a lower rate.

The message delivered by one of the sub-committees working

for Brigadier-General Lee, according to a participant, was that 'there must be a real partnership' between government and the private sector. If the Government is not responsive to such a significant section of the business community as well as to the general public, he believed, the result would be 'one more nail in the PAP coffin.'

Singapore's 'second generation' leaders such as Brigadier-General Lee say they would like more flexible and responsive government – always in the context of PAP control – but they still have to reckon with the Prime Minister.

Mr Lee responded to the election results by turning over more responsibility to the younger ministers he has been grooming for power. The 'master-pupil' relationship has changed since the election according to Mr Goh Chock Tong, who emerged as first deputy prime minister and heir apparent in the new cabinet. 'We do not regard ourselves merely as pupils.'

Mr Lee seems willing to defer to their judgment on some matters. The Government recently abandoned a controversial scheme offering incentives to graduate women to marry graduate men and reproduce. Mr Lee had been the driving force behind it.

But questions of economic reform show the extent to which Mr Lee is still boss. He shows no willingness to let anyone tamper with what he considers the economic cornerstones of Singapore's security: a high level of foreign reserves, a strong currency and the CPF.

Mr Lee intends to retire in 1988 when he reaches the age of 60 but is preparing to take up the job of an executive president. Constitutional changes to enhance the powers of the largely ceremonial presidency are now in hand. These will include specifically the right of veto over government plans for spending the reserves.

'It's a trade-off,' Mr Lee said earlier this year. 'For going earlier than we need to, we have more say in policies after we are no longer in charge.'

Where there's muck there's yuan

John Gittings *Published 25 October 1985*

Mr Wang's eldest son used to be a projectionist at a country cinema near Changsha. But there is no money in showing films, says Wang, the peasants watch television. So Wang, who runs a private truck business taking pigs to Canton, has sent his son north to buy a load of peanuts.

The publicity given in the Chinese media to the 10,000 yuan (£2,500) a year family with this sort of entrepreneurial talent was criticised at the recent party conference in Peking.

The senior leader, Chen Yun, in a speech which challenged some of the consequences of Deng Xiaoping's agriculture reforms, said propaganda had 'departed from reality'.

● **Population**
rural	800 million
urban	200 million

● **Policies**
1950–53	Land reform
1954–57	Rural co-ops
1958–80	People's communes
1980–	Household contracts

● **Rural Income**
(annual per capita
10 yuan = £2.50)
1980	191.3 yuan
1984	355.3 yuan

● **Income Spread**
(% of peasant households)
above 10,000 yuan	0.2%
above 1,000	1.8%
above 500	18%
below 200	14%

● **Goals**
(7th Five-Year Plan, 1986–90)
6 per cent growth in output value
4–5 per cent growth in living standards

If one digs deeper, the equivocal nature of some rural success statistics is not so hard to unearth. Nearly 10 per cent of the 21,000 peasants in Mr Wang's Chunhuashan township, one is told, still have an annual income of under 100 yuan (£25). That is over 2,000 people and puts into perspective the average income of nearly 400 yuan.

Similar figures for the whole country have been published in an unusually critical article in the government magazine, *Outlook*. About 100 million peasants out of a total rural population of 800 million have an annual income of less than 120 yuan a year, with poverty particularly acute in the less developed north-west and south-west regions.

In Hunan they still present the statistics of rural achievements with little or no qualification. Grain production for the whole province, says an agricultural official, has increased by 25 per cent in the five years to the end of 1983. But in the fields of Chunhuashan one can detect two good reasons for increased yields which have nothing to do with portioning out land to peasant families under the new 'responsibility system'.

One is the new aqueduct which strides across the fields of green paddy. When was it finished? In 1978. And how was it built? With the collective labour of three adjacent communes, plus a state grant of 3 million yuan. Productivity and income have clearly benefited from state sector investment – itself partly based on the extraction of rural surpluses under the commune system – and from the investment of human labour which might not be so easily organised today.

The second reason rests in the ears of rice which hang ripely. A high-yield species was introduced progressively from 1976 onwards.

Recently the State Statistical Bureau issued a report saying that the rural economy was now 'on a balanced track'. The proportion of arable land sown with grain, it reported, had fallen by 3.7 per cent between 1980 and 1984, but output had still increased.

Chen Yun saw it rather differently. In his speech, he lamented the tendency among peasants to shift away from grain on the grounds that they 'only get rich from industrial crops'. In Hunan province officials say cautiously that such a tendency does exist, although it is not a big problem.

Some peasants, they admit, do prefer to plant lotus roots instead of rice in the irrigated fields, or they claim that their granaries are full this year, and ask to shift to another crop.

Chen Yun, it must be emphasised, was never in favour of the people's communes as they were speedily developed by Mao Tsetung. But neither, apparently, is he happy about the equally headlong rate at which the new 'rural responsibility' system has grown. His concern is shared to some extent by Mr Deng's reformists as well.

In Chunhuashan the reform was only completed in 1983— perhaps an indication (although denied) of continuing leftist opposition in the province containing Mao's birthplace. Like any reform which gives the land back to the peasant, it is likely to be most popular in its earliest years. At least one possible cause of future friction is already apparent in this community.

All the available land has been divided among the existing peasant households in the 'township' (as the commune must now be called although in popular speech the old term is still retained). But what happens when families grow larger or smaller?

When the system was first introduced elsewhere the answer was that there would be a 're-adjustment' at the end of five years. But it was then decided by Peking to encourage peasants to invest properly in the land, and not exploit it for short-term gains, by promising them that 'nothing will change for 15 years'.

The Chunhuashan township leader has a novel answer to the conundrum: 'We took it all into account when we divided the land. For example, if you have three growing boys, you will get more land because they are expected to marry, bring a wife home and have one child each. That makes six more people.'

Provincial officials – perhaps reflecting disquiet at recent trends – do spend time asserting the new system is still based on socialist ownership. The land is collectively owned, and cannot be bought or sold. Some assets are still run collectively – such as irrigation canals and water pumps – although others are contracted out by tender to small 'specialised groups'.

There is a welfare system based on the dues which must be still paid into a collective fund. The cooperative medical scheme still exists in the poorer areas, though 'not where they have money' and prefer self-reliance. Households still contribute to collective endeavours, but they can now commute their services with a cash payment.

Meanwhile, new forms of collective production are emerging around specialised activities. There is, for example, a large pig-farm, involving over 700 peasant families. But they do not all clean out the sties. Some contribute with technical skills, others with their labour—and some let their capital do the work for them.

Political usurper at the helm of a country in fear

Safdar Shah   *Published 8 November 1985*

General Zia ul Haq, after the National Assembly passed the indemnity bill on 2 March this year, went to the assembly in person, thanked the members, and said that the bill was a victory for 'wisdom, reason and patriotism' and a defeat for 'egoism and the negative thinking of those outside the assembly who had been trying to sabotage democracy'. Sadly, that was not true. The passing of the bill has made no difference to martial law. If anything, it has institutionalised as well as anointed martial law, by making it a part of the Zia Constitution.

Understandably, General Zia has not restored the 1973 Constitution; it would be restored, he said, in 1988. The Constitution that he gave Pakistan is of his own liking. In fact, it was a part of the indemnity bill, and he had made clear to the assembly members that if they wanted him to lift martial law by the end of the year, then the bill must be passed unanimously.

The euphoria of the members, as if they had achieved some kind of a victory, was indeed misplaced. Quite apart from the fact that General Zia emerged as the most powerful President under his own Constitution, naturally he was careful to ensure that no loophole was left for anyone to exploit against him, as long as he ruled. In Article 279A(I) of his Constitution, for example, it says 'The Proclamation of the fifth day of July, 1977, all President's Orders, Martial Law Regulations, Martial Law Orders and all other laws made between 5 July, 1977, and the date on which this Article comes into force, are hereby declared, notwithstanding the judgment of any court, to have been validly made ... And notwithstanding anything contained in the Constitution, shall not be called in question in any court on any ground whatever.'

Clearly the Article provides a blanket cover to whatever Orders were made during martial law, including Orders which curtailed the independence of the judiciary, proscribed political parties, banned all kind of political activity, banned the holding of elections under the 1973 Constitution, validated the imposition of martial law from 5 July, 1977, suspended the fundamental rights chapter of the Constitution, and voided the Begum Nusrat Bhutto judgment of the Supreme Court retroactively, which had allowed General Zia to rule for a limited period in order for him to hold elections and hand over power to the elected representatives of the people.

Moreover, under Article 270A(6) of the Constitution, none of the Orders/Regulations can be altered, repealed or amended without the previous sanction of the President. The result is that the people of Pakistan are denied basic human rights, and their judicial and political institutions continue to remain atrophied.

What kind of democracy has the indemnity bill given to the people of Pakistan? The truth is that the political parties in the country are too weak and disorganised to remove General Zia, and restore the 1973 Constitution. Therefore, the assembly members settled on the only possible alternative: to pass the bill.

- 1947 Independence. Prime Minister Liaquat Ali Khan (assassinated 1951).
- 1958 Martial law. General Mohamed Ayub Khan.
- 1971 East Pakistan became the separate country of Bangladesh.
- 1971–77 Prime Minister Zulfiqar Ali Bhutto of Pakistan People's Party.
- 1973 Third Constitution provided for Parliamentary government.
- 1977 Martial law imposed by General Zia ul Haq.
- 1981 Announcement of transition from martial law to 'Islamic Democratic' government.

Why, one may ask, is General Zia bent upon damaging the Pakistani political structure, irreparably? Even in the US, for example, a President can be elected only for two terms, so why must General Zia feel tempted to rule as long as possible? Quite honestly, fear more tham ambition seems to be determining his priorities. On 5 July, 1977, General Zia was under the double threat of being charged for high treason: under Article 6 of the 1973 Constitution; and under the Asma Jilani judgment of the Supreme Court, reported on page 139 of the 1972 Pakistan-Legal Decisions.

In the case which arose in the wake of the dismemberment of Pakistan, the Supreme Court upturned its previous judgments The State v Dosso, in which it was held that a victorious revolution furnished its own justification. In other words, since 'nothing succeeds like success' was said to be law by the highest court of the country, it was no wonder that General Ayub Khan removed President Iskander Mirza the day the judgment was handed down, and sent him into exile.

The Dosso judgment occupied the constitutional field in Pakistan for 14 long years. There is no doubt that it opened the door to adventurism that eventually led to the break-up of Pakistan. In the Asma Jilani case, the Supreme Court therefore administered a warning to those who might be harbouring an ambition to usurp the legal order of Pakistan: 'Maybe, that on account of their holding the coercive apparatus of the State, the people and the courts are silenced temporarily but as soon as the coercive apparatus falls from the hands of the usurper, he should be tried for high treason and suitably punished.'

That was the law in Pakistan, when General Zia toppled the Bhutto government, and imposed martial law in the country. His self-effacing and conciliatory public broadcast of 5 July, 1977, must be seen in context. What he said on that occasion was that he had no political ambition; his sole aim was to organise free and fair elections which would be held in October this year (1977); and 'I give solemn assurance that I will not deviate from this schedule.' Moreover, in answer to the petition filed by the Begum Nusrat Bhutto, wife of the executed Prime Minister, the Attorney General toed the Zia line. The Constitution, he said, had not been abrogated, the judiciary continued to possess complete jurisdiction under the Constitution, General Zia had stepped in to save the country from plunging into civil war and his only aim was to hold elections and hand over power to the elected representatives of the people.

The Supreme Court, which was largely influenced by the charge of the March elections rigging by the Bhutto government, held, among other things, that General Zia's takeover was justified by the requirements of the State necessity; however, his rule was only 'for a temporary period and specified and limited purpose', and that 'during this period all his energies shall be directed towards creating conditions conducive to the holding of free and fair elections leading to the restoration of democratic rule in accordance with the dictates of the Constitution.'

Clearly, the court's judgment was conditional. But instead of 'creating conditions conducive to the holding of elections', General Zia prolonged his personal rule on one untenable excuse or another. During that time, however, he continued to pay lip service to the Supreme Court judgment because it suited his strategy. After consolidating his position, however, he issued, among other orders/regulations, Presidential Order No. I of 1980, through which he curtailed the writ jurisdiction of the high courts with respect to anything done by the martial law authorities; and he also validated his takeover of the country's administration from 5 July, 1977.

Implicitly, therefore, this order did away with the Supreme Court judgment. But the open assault on it had to wait for another year. On 24 March, 1981, General Zia promulgated the Provisional Constitutional Order, which claimed to validate everything done by the military government since 1977; it abrogated the fundamental provisions of the 1973 Constitutions; under its Article 16 General Zia assumed the power to amend the Constitution at will; the order proscribed all political parties; and it voided the Begum Bhutto judgment of the Supreme Court, at a time when the court was about to hear petitions challenging the legality of the continuing military rule.

Clearly, the kind of steps Zia took made him lose the protection of the Begum Bhutto judgment, with the result that he reverted to the position of a usurper with effect from 5 July, 1977.

Can a usurper give to Pakistan a constitution of his own liking? There is no known constitutional principle to support any such hypothesis. Unless of course the majority of the people of Pakistan were to agree voluntarily, in a free and totally impartial referendum. In fact that has not happened. The present assembly was elected on the basis of laws made by a usurper. Evidently then the whole exercise beginning with the December 1984 referendum, which 'elected' General Zia president for a term of five years, and the passing of the indemnity bill by the national assembly is illegal and of no constitutional effect.

If General Zia had been properly advised, he should have respected the Begum Bhutto judgment of the Supreme Court and held the promised elections under the 1973 Constitution many years ago and handed over power to the elected representatives of the people. In doing so he would have brought lasting credit to himself and some measure of stability to Pakistan. Sadly, he chose the course of his own liking instead, which as a result involved him as well as the institutional life of Pakistan in deeper complications.

As it stands today, Pakistan is in an unenviable position. General Zia, because of the fear of Article 6 of the 1973 Constitution, as well as of the Asma Jilani case, has turned Pakistan politically and constitutionally on its head. Today all the country's institutions are mongrelised.

Company becomes cosmos

Jeremy Seabrook   *Published 7 February 1986*

Tata Sons Ltd and Tata Industries Ltd together form the largest private company in India; and as such, are under constant scrutiny, always open to (generally favourable) comparison with a vast unwieldy public sector. It is a particular kind of private enterprise—81 per cent of the profits are held in philanthropic trusts, a fair approximation of the Gandhian idea that wealth is a social trust, and that every individual is entitled to benefit from its proper use for the common good.

Founded as a trading company in 1868 by Jamsetji Tata, who was born into a Gujarat family of Parsi priests, the enterprises that have grown from it now touch every aspect of Indian life. It is impossible not to use the products and services of the company every day—buses and trucks, steel, cotton goods, soap, refrigerators, magazines, air-conditioning, hotels, chemicals, cosmetics. It has created whole cities, notably Jamshedpur in Bihar, site of the steelworks; and its influence extends far beyond India, with interests in Singapore, Malaysia, USA and Britain; indeed, Tata has just acquired two prestigious hotels in London—Bailey's and the St James.

The total assets of Tata are now about £1.3bn, and there are a quarter of a million employees. In those places dominated by the company, Tata ensures a lifetime's job security, high wages and welfare provision unequalled in India. In a country where 40 per cent of the people are estimated to be below the official poverty line, to be employed by Tata is to be set apart; one is tempted to say it is to belong to a separate (and superior) caste. Tata readily becomes an object of veneration to those who benefit from it. At times, it seems, the company has become cosmos.

Telco Engineering Works at Pune is the largest in India, and a Tata showplace. It has the most extensive design and development facility in the Indian automotive industry, with a growing export market in commercial vehicles, especially in Third World countries, whose roads require robust and durable trucks. The factory on the outskirts of Pune, is entered through a modernistic triumphal arch, which leads to a wide boulevard, where harijan women beat back the dust and blossoms that fall from the cerise bougainvillaeas.

The pay is high—between 1800 and 2000 Rs (up to £140) a month. Forty thousand people are directly employed by Telco, many of them bussed in from surrounding villages. The company has just entered the car market, in association with Honda, to build the Accord. Telco, say the management, is the flagship of India's modern sector. It is the Taj Mahal of industry.

There is a fiercely competitive apprenticeship and graduate training scheme. And in the re-cycling of waste products, the factory has created a number of co-operatives; scrap wood made into packing-cases, boxes, furniture; waste metal turned into gates and cycle-stands. The women's co-operatives make uniforms, cable harnesses, toolbags and prepare spices, papad and chappatis for the canteen. Women are allowed to work no more than four hours a day, 'so that their work does not interfere with their family responsibilities'.

But the influence of the company does not stop there: it reaches far into the hinterland, where a rural development programme is under way in 10 villages of the Bhama River basin. A dam was built at Pimpri Budnik in 1981, financed jointly by Telco and the State government, and has brought 500 hectares of arid land into cultivation.

When I visited, the potatoes were being harvested. A bullock-plough was turning the soil; women followed sieving the potatoes and storing them in cream-coloured pyramids. The workers are from 13 harijan families who, between them, owned only 35 acres of land, more than a quarter of which had not been cultivated for generations. They were persuaded by one of Telco's community development officers to pool the land and farm it co-operatively. They now grow onions, groundnuts, maize, wheat, chillies, coriander and toor, all of which are guaranteed a market by Telco canteens.

Telco has provided a new secondary school, opened on Independence Day this year. For the first time in Pimpri, girls can now get a secondary education.

Other benefits are tangible and lasting too. Six latrines have been built close to the harijan dwellings. These drain into a biogas plant, which provides gas for cooking for nine families. The houses are clean and prosperous. Biogas saves firewood, and makes more practicable Teleco's commitment to social forestry: more than 6,000 subabul trees have been distributed in the area. These help replenish nitrogen, while the agave plantations limit soil erosion.

In the centre of Pune is the Tata Management Training Centre. Its director, Mr Menzes, speaks enthusiastically of Rajiv Gandhi's aim of liberalising the economy. He has recently returned from the USA, where he has been trying to encourage highly qualified Indians to return. India has some of the most effective technical manpower in the world, but there has been little opportunity for them until now to practise their skills.

3 LATIN AMERICA AND THE CARIBBEAN

Fallen Comet

John La Rose pays tribute to Michael Smith
Published 2 September 1983

'He came across our sky like a comet. And vanished.' That was
the thought that came to me after the first shock of hearing
about Michael Smith's death.

I had first heard of Michael Smith from Edward Kamau
Brathwaite, the poet, literary critic, and historian. Then others
told me of him. When the poet Linton Kwesi Johnson went to
Carifesta in Barbados in the summer of 1981, he was presenter
in a film made for the Arena television programme about the
Carifesta. It was then I saw Michael Smith in the flesh.

He came to the First International Book Fair of Radical
Black and Third World Books in London in April, 1982, and
electrified the international poetry reading, which was the best
I had ever experienced. He found an audience for his words
prepared by that television programme.

His reputation in Europe soared from that moment. It was an
audience of people, including writers and artists from Britain,
Africa, Asia, and other parts of Europe, the Caribbean, and the
US. He made his long-playing record, *Mi Cyaan Believe It*, with
Island Records in London, and later toured with Gregory Isaacs.
He performed at Unesco in Paris in November, 1982, then in
Amsterdam and Milan. There was later another television
programme with that magnificent performance of a Shelley
poem in Westminster Abbey.

The circumstances of his death highlight what seldom strikes
us, except when someone as talented and outstanding as he
dies: the brutalisation of everyday life in Jamaica and most
other modern societies.

Michael Smith had attended a public meeting in Stony Hill,
St Andrews, Jamaica, on Tuesday, 16 August, the night before

he died. He had confronted the main speaker at that meeting, the Minister of Education in the Jamaican Government. The next day, as he was passing the ruling Jamaica Labour Party local office in Stony Hill he was stopped by four men who wanted to know what he was doing there. He was chased, stoned, and robbed. The attackers were seen by witnesses to enter the JLP constituency party office. Michael Smith became unconscious from the battering and was taken to the local clinic and then to the public hospital. He was dead on arrival. It was a case of sheer barbarism.

He belonged to none of the parties in Jamaica. And he scorned the partisan politics there.

Michael Smith performed his poetry; he did not read it. And he was a considerable performer of his work. He had studied drama on a scholarship to the Jamaica School of Drama. He was in a revived and renewed tradition of orality which preceded poetry in Caribbean standard English and had been held in contempt until recently. But this tradition has survived and developed and is now storming the arts in the Caribbean.

Michael Smith was a dub poet, a poet using the rhythms of reggae and the resources of the common language. His poetic expression was not in the standard English but in the national language, the patois of Jamaica, the 'nation language'.

Derek Walcott, the Caribbean poet and playwright, has a line in his book *The Castaway* where he says: 'To change your language you must change your life.' With Michael Smith his language was his life. And the poetry was his language and his life.

The man whose new jewel was shattered

Victoria Brittain   *Published 4 November 1983*

Grenada's New Jewel Movement, which brought the first social revolution to the English-speaking Caribbean, has had an impact in the Third World which goes far beyond its size or its achievements over four years. And the violent American attempt to crush this mildest of revolutions has ensured that the legacy of Grenada, and its Marxist Prime Minister, Maurice Bishop, will have enduring effects in the Caribbean, the Third World, and in the Caribbean diaspora in Britain and America.

Bishop had a vision of Pan-Caribbean unity of regimes based on social justice, a vision of equal rights for 'the ant and the elephant' as he called Grenada and the United States. This vision captured the imagination of Caribbean people and brought the best of West Indian intellectuals to Grenada to work in education, health and economic planning.

Bishop: equal rights for the ant and the elephant

The achievement of the New Jewel Movement was, in Bishop's words, 'to have given pride and dignity to Grenadians – no longer is underdevelopment and powerlessness inevitable – growth, investment, schooling, health care, housing repairs are seen to be possible. Grenada is a stunning contrast to the other societies in the Caribbean, the Reagan models, which are collapsing under escalating unemployment and debt-ratios.'

The long-standing open hostility to Grenada of Eugenia Charles of Dominica, 'Uncle' Tom Adams of Barbados and other Caribbean leaders who joined the US invasion came, Bishop believed, from fear of their own people's enthusiasm for Grenada's example, an enthusiasm demonstrated at every public appearance by the Grenadian leaders in the region.

Grenada's determination to change Caribbean history from its traditional economic and political dependence on the West brought an unrelenting US hostility, much of it channelled through the conservative Caribbean governments and their press which the government faced openly.

In an interview in September, shortly before he died, Bishop said: 'It is difficult to say how immediate the threat of the US, and especially the CIA, is today, but I think it is always going to be there in the sense that this US administration, particularly this one, is very hostile to any progressive of revolutionary regimes.

'Their approach is to invest the stamp of legality only on regimes which fully support them. Therefore, for a government like ours which is so determined to maintain an independent non-aligned path, obviously we are going to have problems with them at all turns.

'In 1979 I disclosed a CIA plot against us . . . the CIA pyramid plan. It was the usual kind of thing. At the bottom was propaganda, in the middle was economic aggression, at the top was the military threat, the terrorism, the assassinations. In 1980 the bomb blast in Queens Park was an attempt to wipe out the entire leadership. From the interrogations of those arrested the US link is clear.

'In 1981 the US mounted a mock invasion exercise. Earlier this year, linked to the US proxies' invasion of Nicaragua, I had to warn Grenadians that the same threat faced us, and that sending in contras is no different from sending in the marines.'

The Prime Minister's words were prophetic. 'This particular period, the Central America crisis, obviously makes our own situation much more dangerous. You have these thousands and thousands of troops, hundreds of ships, planes and manoeuvres off Nicaragua, bases built inside Honduras, an atmosphere of instability where aggressors thrive.'

Earlier this year Bishop spoke in London to a packed hall of enthusiastic West Indians of the threat Reagan's America posed to world peace. 'Reagan's dream is that he can construct a new Pax Americana to destroy the socialist world. But why should we be dragged into his geo-political game? Reagan is the great-

est disaster to hit mankind since Hitler. He has a total dis-
honesty and is unscrupulous enough to unloose another World
War. His contempt and disrespect for all other nations' own
choices even extends to his friends in the industrialised world.
He doesn't want Mitterrand to have Communists in his government, or Western companies to work on a pipeline to the Soviet
Union.'

Grenada's growing status as a spokesman for the smallest,
poorest and weakest countries of the Third World came from
the clarity and consistency with which Bishop, like Mrs Gandhi
and Fidel Castro, linked the arms race to the horrifying statistics of underdevelopment, and demanded change from the
West.

'Half the resources at present allocated to military expendi-
tures in one day will finance a programme for the total worldwide eradication of malaria,' Bishop told delegates at the Delhi
conference of the non-aligned.

Foreign Minister Unison Whiteman, who was killed with
Bishop, was the co-founder and joint leader of the New Jewel
Movement. In September he said: 'Sometimes it feels like a
race against time. But I believe Grenada is demonstrating what
the US would have us believe is impossible . . . the achievement
of prosperity without them. We have fought for the world's
acceptance of our right to build a society according to our ideals
and to reject domination. Our sincerity and careful adherence
to principle are paying off—we have won support from countries
like Canada and Saudi Arabia, from the EEC. No one who looks
at us firsthand buys the blustering accusations of Reagan or
the propaganda against us.'

Serene confidence in the triumph of rationality was the hall-
mark of both Bishop and Whiteman, both young lawyers of
around 40 who had spent the last 10 years on political work
among the poor. Behind their calm, relaxed manner, the lurk-
ing threat of the CIA to their lives meant bodyguards, darkened
car windows as they drove around the island—a jarring note
in the atmosphere of Grenada before its double disaster.

Cuba, Vietnam, and Mozambique have become the god-
fathers of this particular revolution. Grenada's brother was
Nicaragua, which wrought a revolution of the same vintage
against another despised dictator who was supported by the
West.

Not long ago Bishop talked about the high price of defying
America being paid by these countries, by Angola, Chile, and
even his neighbour, Michael Manley in Jamaica.

'No price is too high for freedom. It took several hundred
years for feudalism to be finally wiped out and capitalism to
emerge as the dominant mode of production, and it will take

several hundred years more for capitalism to be replaced by socialism. Meanwhile, our message, as I said over and over again on my recent trip to America, is that our socialism poses no threat to anyone. We are not interested in toppling governments but in struggling, not just for Grenada's interest, but for the whole Caribbean.'

As the Grenada High Commissioner in London, Mr Fennis Augustine, said in reference to Grenada's many warnings of US intentions, 'some believed us, some did not'.

Enter the era of banana-skin republics

Michael Manley   *Published 11 November 1983*

The invasion and occupation of Grenada by US troops will prove to be a watershed in Caribbean history. The popular support which the invasion now enjoys cannot conceal the grave, underlying implications of what has taken place.

Like so many other parts of the Third World, the Caribbean is the scene of a fundamental struggle involving two inter-related questions. All these English-speaking territories which make up the Caribbean community are the products of an extended colonial experience, within the matrix of modern imperialism. This left societies which were profoundly elitist in class terms, since colonialism divided each society within the European empires into a minority of beneficiaries, who were the traders and the plantation owners, along with the appended groups which attended to their professional needs, and owed their success to the external authority which the imperialist system represented.

The nationalism, which united elements of the minority and the majority groups in the successful demand for independence, is an uncertain force in the post-independence period because each society came to independence with its social and economic structures fashioned by the colonial experience.

Accordingly, newly independent nations face two issues: what to do about their elitist class structure with its heavily-loaded advantages and disadvantages; and what to do about an economic structure which underpins the social arrangement and is deeply dependent on the world economic structure which imperialism built.

Michael Manley, former prime minister of Jamaica, sees sovereignty as the real casualty of the US invasion of Grenada

Throughout the Third World, those political parties and movements which seek to address the problems of social injustice, the mal-distribution of wealth and over-concentration of economic power, find it is not possible to separate the internal struggle to achieve change from an external struggle involving the direction and control of the national economy. Hence, progressive parties are as much concerned with the problem of economic dependence as with the struggle to re-arrange society.

Equally, the old class of local beneficiaries of the colonial system regard the defence of their internal position as irrevocably bound up with the maintenance of present arrangements.

It is against that background that we must look at the invasion of Grenada, its reception and its implications for the future. The revolutionary Government of Maurice Bishop had built up a good record of sound economic management, laying the basis for participatory democracy in tackling many problems. Its performance in land reform, education, health and literacy was widely accepted as positive. On the other hand, spurned by the United States, it had sought increasingly close relations with Cuba and the Socialist group of countries, and amongst the West European democracies.

Convinced that the US was considering an invasion, the Government built up a substantial arsenal, a tough little army and insisted on basic military training for most of the adult population. Its foreign policy was aggressively non-aligned and anti-imperialist.

When, therefore, the leaders of the New Jewel Movement committed the crass blunder of detaining Maurice Bishop despite his overwhelmingly mass popularity, they invited the disaster which quickly followed. The brutal execution of Bishop and his loyal colleagues set the stage for the US invasion at the invitation of elements of the democratically elected political leadership of the Caribbean.

The invitation to invade was issued because Edward Seaga of Jamaica, Tom Adams of Barbados and Ronald Reagan of the US have an identical political aim for the Caribbean. Seaga and Adams want no truck with progressive political processes which they see as posing a threat to the flow of private US investment and North American tourists to the region. In this, both have the support of the classes who were the beneficiaries of the old colonial system. Although both lead parties that bear the label 'Labour', both are Conservatives in reality.

The invasion itself is popular in the Eastern Caribbean which was appalled by the slaying of Bishop and generally frightened by the turn of events. In Grenada itself, three factors combined to produce a warm welcome for the US invaders. All the old conservatives, small a minority as they were, were overjoyed to feel that a dangerous socialist experiment was being decisively eliminated. The great majority, who genuinely loved Bishop, were pleased to feel his death was being avenged. In any event, the great majority must have been terrified by the whole experience of the Army firing upon the crowd that had released Bishop.

What of the future?

The events in Grenada have thrown into sharp relief the second part of the double question which informs the Caribbean political process. As second thoughts begin to occupy the recesses of the mind, the question is being asked: What was the Caribbean independence all about? What were the struggles which won independence for if it can be so lightly swept aside by 2,000 US Marines, a handful of rangers and less than one-half of the 82nd Airborne Division? That question is followed by its logical corollary. Now that the precedent is set, who will the next target be, should anyone be so imprudent as to provoke Washington's disfavour? This is followed by the final question: What do some of our own leaders make of our sovereignty, so hard to win and so difficult to defend, if they can suspend its meaning with such reckless cynicism in pursuit of their neo-colonial agenda?

Efforts are being made to pass off the invasion as an example of statesman-like magnanimity aimed solely, at bringing succour to a beleagured people. To the more discerning, this won't 'wash'. The Revolutionary Military Council was vulnerable, isolated and scared after the death of Bishop. The Cuban Government had told them in no uncertain terms not to look for reinforcements or other kinds of help from them.

Furthermore, they had underlined the message by saying that they felt neither politically nor morally capable of coming to their defence because of the events surrounding and including Bishop's death.

There was firm reason to believe the crisis had been resolved and the population relieved without the firing of a shot. Yet Seaga and Adams contrived the invasion behind the backs of their senior Caribbean colleagues with a haste so indecent as to suggest that the real agenda had nothing to do with relief but everything to do with wiping out a political process.

As the emotions of the moment recede, yielding as they must the hard realities of scarce foreign exchange, soaring unemployment, foundering programmes of economic development, the stark questions will re-assert their claim for answers. When will the social structure of the countries of the Caribbean respond to the change from colonial to independent status? As the young jobless stare at the blank wall of poverty, they ask increasingly: From whence is relief coming?

The invasion of Grenada supplies no answer to either question. It is a victory for the neo-colonialists, the defenders of the status quo ante. But the problem, they will find, is that it is a victory against the wrong end. In the meantime, to the extent that events have revealed the essential fragility of Caribbean nationalism, so too do they set in train second thoughts about independence.

I believe there will arise new political alliances in the Caribbean binding together those who see our independence as the essential condition to be preserved if we are to have a future at all. As this unfolds, I believe that Grenada may yet prove a pyrrhic victory at best. The very ease with which the battle was won is beckoning new defenders to the battlefield. Because in the end, the real casualty of the invasion was neither Socialism nor the process which Bishop started. The real casualty was the sovereignty of Grenada and by extension the sovereignty of the entire English-speaking Caribbean.

Michael Manley was Prime Minister of Jamaica from 1972 to 1980.

Death at the door in the land of the Saviour

This testimony of a Salvadorean woman was given at a seminar for visiting and European academics organised by the Catholic Church in Mexico   *Published 2 March 1984*

Nearly 10 years ago Base Christian Communities began in El Salvador and the people in the cities and the peasants began to think differently and to organise themselves against injustice.

Any of you that go to El Salvador without even asking them could easily observe the misery in which the people in rural areas live. In the faces of the peasants you can see the hunger and the misery.

The people in the city may live a little differently but this doesn't mean that there isn't any misery. Their salaries are low and 60 per cent of the factories have closed. They live on the sides of the ravines because they don't have a chance of living in decent houses. There may be up to eight people living in each one of these cardboard shacks. People search for work but they don't find it, and when the people decided to form trade unions, the Government considered it a crime. People known to belong to a union have been captured and have simply disappeared. The majority of them have been murdered.

In 1964 I started work in a maternity hospital. At the time, I was making 40 colonis a month (about £10 a month). The salaries were very low. There were many young people who worked in the hospital doing cleaning etc. These young men made ten colonis. None of our salaries covered our real needs, much less those that made ten colonis, so we began to organise ourselves in a union in order to ask for a pay increase. We struggled for a year and achieved an increase in salaries by ten colonis. Because we had organised the union we were demanding more equitable wages and this led 104 nurses to be killed, and 504 nurses were fired from their jobs because they belonged to the union. Many of the young cleaners were also fired and 52 of them were murdered also because they belonged to the union and were asking for more wages.

Because I was in the union I was threatened and was forced to leave because I was clearly in danger. Eight days after having left my work I saw suspicious people close to my home. I discovered that one of the young men who was working on the telephone in the hospital was working as a spy for the government. He was a member of one of the para-military groups.

I have been participating since 1975 in the Base Christian Community. My sons were catechists and also leaders of the Christian community. They began to be persecuted and so were forced to go into exile in Mexico. They went to the Mexican embassy to ask for asylum. While there they heard that Father Antonio, the pastor of San Antoniobad, had been murdered by the military. There was another priest from Belgium who was captured by the National Guard. They kept him for 20 hours, blindfolded, bound, and naked. In this state they applied electric shocks to him. Twenty-four hours later they abandoned him on the Guatemalan border.

In Guatemala he was taken to prison until finally the Belgian consul heard of this situation and went to liberate him.

In 1981 we had to leave our homes also. Twenty strongly armed men came to us. They identified themselves clearly as the death squad. They asked us, 'Who were the people who used to meet together with Father Antonio?' My husband and I were both tortured by the group. They did very nasty things to all of us including my 12-year-old daughter. Many other young people who belonged to the Base Christian Community were victims of these attacks. Five young people from the Christian community were captured in Santa Lucia. The next morning their bodies were found in the park having suffered very cruel tortures. One had his skin peeled off his back and face. One body was scattered over a large piece of ground.

In Celetry they captured three catechists. Their bodies were found three days later. That day we were in that area because the son of another woman of the Christian community had disappeared so, though this place was a little far away, we decided to go. We found the three bodies tied to the trunk of a tree completely without skin. They had left the skin of these people hanging from some bushes close by. They had scalped them and left the hair hanging from the bushes. They do these things to terrorise people so that they don't have the courage to continue in the community.

In La Pango the priest had a lot of Base Christian Communities in his parish. He had formed many communities among the peasants and by forming these communities he was awakening the people and creating co-operatives to help the people economically. The peasants could buy consumer articles cheaper. He was also murdered. Many priests and seminarians have been killed.

There is another case I saw personally, involving a young fellow who was a Protestant pastor. He would gather the people of his church at a place called Allwahh. This young fellow was captured and then assassinated. The only crime that he was accused of was carrying the Bible under his arm. This young Protestant pastor's body appeared in Apulpa. He had been assassinated after very cruel torture. They left the Bible laying on his breast with a sign which said, 'This man was assassinated because he was a Communist.'

I came to participate in the Committee of Mothers of the Disappeared when my son, aged 13, was captured. I went around the prisons looking for him and everyone said, 'No, No.' At none of the prisons and barracks would they give any information. I decided to go to Bishop Romero. With his support I was finally able to locate my son at a place called La Libertad. Three months later they finally gave him to me.

In 1981 my two brothers were captured, aged 17 and 18. The older one was found dead. We found three pieces of his body in different locations. The younger one is still missing. Because of this I continue to denounce the lack of human rights and I help other mothers who have suffered. Thousands of families in rural areas have been brutally murdered. Women have been raped, both mothers and daughters.

All these killings, kidnappings, and disappearances have created the tense situation that we have today. We have tried to find all kinds of peaceful ways to bring about change, but we have not been heard. The voice of the people is not heard. The Salvadorean people are tired of so much injustice.

Now, as the Committee of Mothers, we struggle for the liberation of many political prisoners and thousands of the disappeared. We also have responsibility for hundreds of orphan children, because the parents have been assassinated. As brothers we feel the responsibility to help these children who have been completely abandoned. Beside this there are thousands of families whose homes have been burned. The Committee of Mothers with a little help that has arrived now try to help those families to protect themselves.

The sinking of Burnham's Guyana

James Dunkerley   *Published 18 May 1984*

Last week a delegation of leading opponents of Forbes Burnham's regime in Guyana visited London. If its members had come from Grenada or El Salvador their visit would have been the object of widespread public attention. As it was, a couple of hundred people had the rare opportunity to learn about the increasingly critical condition of the people of Guyana under the 'democratic' and 'cooperative socialist' regime of Burnham's People's National Congress (PNC) which removed Cheddi Jagan's People's Progressive Party in 1964 with the considerable assistance of the CIA and the British government.

Burnham's retention of power through parliamentary elections, the nationalisation of 80 per cent of the economy, and the fact that he occasionally adopts anti-US positions in international affairs have obscured the other side of his rule: the blatant rigging of the polls of 1973 and 1980; the assassination of Walter Rodney and other members of the Working People's Alliance (WPA); the Jonestown massacre; the doctrine of PNC 'paramountcy' over all public affairs and institutions; the increasingly vicious repression of the opposition parties and independent trade unions.

Moreover, under PNC 'socialism', Guyana has for the last seven years suffered an unparalleled economic crisis that has taken it from being the second richest country in the Caribbean to the second poorest, next to Haiti, in the space of a decade.

Leading last week's mission was Clive Y. Thomas, the young Director of the Institute of Development Studies and Professor of Economics at the University of Guyana. Popularly known as 'C.Y.', Thomas belongs to the same generation of radical Caribbean intellectuals as did Rodney, Maurice Bishop, and Bernard Coard. His critical works on the political economy of underdevelopment have acquired an international reputation, but this latest visit was tied to the launching of a modest publication by the Latin America bureau entitled *Guyana: The Fraudulent Revolution*, which outlines the story of Burnham's adoption of dictatorial means, and lays bare the economic reality behind the rhetoric of 'cooperative socialism'.

Admitting that he has engaged in politics with great reluctance but as an inescapable result of his intellectual work, Thomas speaks in the measured tones of a professor but unveils his message with a clarity and precision that has encouraged many Guyanese to see in him a successor to his slain colleague Walter Rodney.

Although he rejects such an accolade, Clive Thomas now plays a leading part in the WPA, formed in 1979 after Rodney was arrested on a trumped-up charge of arson. This recent visit was also marked by clear political objectives: to denounce Burnham's management of the economy and to alert public opinion to PNC preparations to rig the elections due in 1985 as part of a broader adoption of authoritarian methods.

Alerting opinion – Clive Thomas

Thomas denies that the nationalisation of the key sugar and bauxite industries in the mid-70s and the incorporation of the majority of the economy into the state sector should be seen as socialism. The population has no say in its management. The ruling party, on the other hand, is absolutely dependent upon the funds of the nationalised sector for its political survival, managing the state industries with minimal concern for increased production or the reallocation of wealth rather than to preserve its privileges in an increasingly polarised and impoverished society. Thus, for Clive Thomas, 'Burnham likes capitalism. He just doesn't like capitalism he can't control.'

According to Thomas, the PNC cannot possibly concede to the IMF's demands for deregulation and the opening up of the market because this would rapidly erode the party's economic power in the face of superior competition. Equally, the Government resists the WPA's demands for the democratisation of the nationalised sector because this would open it up to an unassailable political challenge from the independent unions, particularly the sugar and bauxite workers.

The remarkable drop in productivity in the key sectors of the economy – bauxite, sugar and rice – is not, as might be expected, simply another case of a Third World country entering into crisis as a result of the world recession.

Privileged by protected markets for sugar and rice and possessing the best bauxite in the world, Guyana enjoyed favourable terms of trade until the end of the 1970s and still has exceptional export potential. Yet, none of the main sectors is currently producing anywhere near the levels of the early seventies or even at 50 per cent of capacity. The sugar and rice market quotas have not been met for years and Guyana's bauxite has been outsold by poorer ore from China.

As a result, Thomas estimates that there are now more Guyanese living outside the country than in it. Even according to the 1980 census – a classified document inside Guyana – the population has grown by a mere 7,000 since 1970.

Those Guyanese that remain must subsist on an average daily wage of £1.80, roughly the equivalent of the local cost of a cake of Soviet soap. A worker in full-time employment – some 50 per cent of the economically active population – has to work a fortnight to buy two kilos of powdered milk but will be unable to obtain liquid milk, bread (wheat imports are prohibited) or even rice and sugar, cultivated exclusively for export and foreign exchange.

The collapse of the economic infrastructure is manifest everywhere. Public transport is so poor that many people spend over four hours a day travelling to work. Schools which were once prized as the finest in the Commonwealth now lack books and desks, and hospital beds are frequently shared, even in maternity wards.

There are no longer any functioning telephone or post boxes in the country. Electricity is frequently limited to two hours a day; typhus is once again a threat because of unpurified water; the university has not purchased a single book since 1980.

Thomas sees Burnham's foreign policy as opportunist but also a necessity founded upon the widespread acceptance of socialism as a motif in a country which had, in Jagan's PPP, an avowedly Marxist government as long ago as 1953. The much-vaunted recognition of Cuba was only part of a uniform move throughout the English-speaking Caribbean, and Guyana's offer of facilities for the transport of Cuban troops to Angola was by no means unique: Barbados made the same offer.

The absence of strong anti-communist forces within the country also explains why the bulk of the opposition lays such great stress on democratic demands and is mobilising around the popular slogans 'bread and justice' and 'free and fair elections; elections free from fear'. One in 35 of the population now serves in the security forces, which are increasingly being used in a Latin American manner. The official TUC leadership numbers several cabinet ministers who effectively negotiate with themselves and, as ministers, have just tabled a bill for a retroactive wage cut. In line with the doctrine of PNC paramountcy, independent journals are frequently denied newsprint and ink and often raided by members of the House of Israel religious sect that enjoys close relations with Burnham, as did Jim Jones.

The President himself has taken to an ostentatious imperial style, dressing entirely in purple and riding a white charger, fully in keeping with his power to dictate all state and party policy.

Drawing attention to Lord Avebury's international observer's report on the 1980 elections as so fraudulent that it was difficult to conceive that the rigging had been planned to dupe anybody, Thomas fears that the 1985 poll will be even worse and complete the consolidation of a one-party state.

Clive Thomas in particular and the WPA in general have for some time emphasised the importance of political democracy for socialism and believe that it has been critically undervalued by the Left, which has often given its backing to one-party states in the post-colonial era. The WPA is known to have expressed its reservations on this score to the NJM in Grenada well before the final debacle in October 1983. Next month sees the publication of Thomas's *The Rise of the Authoritarian State in Peripheral Countries*, which criticises the general tendency towards state-based autocracy by national liberation forces. Although the book makes scant reference to Guyana, many of its passages are clearly informed by a remarkable decomposition from one of the most politically advanced countries in the western hemisphere into a corrupt and irrational autocracy that has cut the income of the population by a third and threatens its opponents with the same fate that met Walter Rodney. This week Clive Thomas and his colleagues return to Georgetown far from certain when they will be able to make another trip abroad.

A dream of Pinochet's fall

Adrian Mitchell   *Published 21 December 1984*

When it rains in Santiago, the water knows its way—the gutter, the drain, the Mapocho river, the ocean. But when it rains on the campamento Cardinal Silva Henriques, a huge shanty town not far outside the Santiago city limits, the water finds its resting place in the woolly fraying sweaters of the kids, in the mudways between the wooden shacks, in the stoves, in the food, and in the beds.

I recently spent five days in Chile, in the rich streets and in the campamento. Pity that it rained.

It was a strange visit. Earlier, I had had a phone call from a Chilean political exile in England. Would I go to Chile to celebrate what would have been Pablo Neruda's eightieth birthday?

When Salvador Allende was elected I wanted to go to Chile. Since that time I've had plenty of Chilean friends and when the fascist coup came, Chilean refugees arrived at my house. Over the years I've written poems about Chileans and taken part in pro-Chile concerts. I wasn't too keen on visiting Chile until Pinochet went down the gutter, the drain, the Mapocho, and into the ocean. But I couldn't say no to these friends who ask for so little.

I put tourism as my visa reason for visiting, bought a convincing camera and slung it round my neck. Luckily I wasn't on the airport list of undesirables.

'Chile progresses in peace and order', said the sign in front of Santiago airport; well, half the sign said that. The other half advertised Viceroy cigarettes.

My friends weren't there to meet me so I caught a cab, found a hotel, made some phone calls and switched on the TV. Rain was pouring down outside as I watched Chile's Independence Day parade on the box.

It was some parade. The goosestep. Boots smashing hell out of the tarmac. A big show of military might with cauliflower ear music favoured by armies from Washington to Moscow and all stops in between. But precious few people were watching, mostly women, mostly middle-class. An arrowhead of jets zapped through the air across the screen.

I went out into a main avenue in Santiago, which was drying off after the rain, suddenly full of stalls of all kinds. Remnants of the big parade—sailors marching along whistling in unison, clapped by three very old men. Pedestrians were watched by soldiers with automatic rifles plus a machine-gun mounted on an armoured car. I decided not to take a tourist snap of this group.

In the music shops I saw tapes by Victor Jara, Violetta Parra, and Inti-Illimani—all of them among the regime's unfavourite musicians. Some shops feature them in their windows, others confine them to the back racks. I saw a plaque celebrating Pablo Neruda in a window dedicated mostly to tourist gunk.

Then I rounded a corner and the last days of Allende came into my mind. There was the Moneda Palace. It has been repaired since the fighters zoomed down on it and President Allende was murdered there. But I did spot a crack in the Palace's stonework. I put my hand on that crack and laid a tourist's curse.

A friend told me of the popular chant—'He is falling, he is falling.' Who's he? Pinochet, of course. They say that every night he has the dream of falling.

I took flowers to Neruda's tomb, where his widow Matilde, frail and beautiful, was surrounded by friends. And flowers for Victor Jara in his tomb only a few yards away. The rain thickened. It became a deluge. 'Only a fool or a Communist would be out on a day like this,' said a friend.

At the last moment the concert had to be moved indoors, to a room about the size of a small pub. A table was converted into a small stage with a Chilean flag behind it and a swiftly improvised bank of three lights.

I read a few poems which a Chilean actor translated for me. A smiling young woman sang a song called *I Want To Be Minister for the Impossible*. She gave the first verse like a child giving a bouquet. She gave the second verse like a mother giving milk. She gave the third verse like a mugger giving the knife.

A Dutch guitarist, big as a garage, played very delicately and spoke in relaxed Spanish. The Chileans laughed like an avalanche.

A tall woman with a fist like a loaf strode straight out of the French Revolution and sang Venceremos and other revolutionary songs. When she spat out the word 'Pinochet' a couple of members of the audience looked at each other for a second. Insulting Pinochet even among friends is a dangerous act.

That night I had dinner with a group of former exiles. They've returned to Chile now, not because it's safe to do so but because they want to be home, especially now when anything may happen.

Returning after ten or eleven years they find that their days are full of sweet collisions, reunions with people in the streets.

There was a glow of affection between these ex-exiles which was good to share.

These former exiles, when they talk of Allende's time, speak of Our Government. Speaking of the present regime, one said: 'The Government is very scared. It's a dangerous moment. In Argentina they passed a law that if you are proved to have practised torture you may be sentenced to death.'

LA COPIA FELIZ   ©PMOMR

THE NEW WINDS IN HAITI AND THE FILIPINO HURRICANES HAVE NOT GONE UNNOTICED BY THE MAN IN THE STREET, STILL LESS BY THE MAN IN THE MERCEDES, OR THE MAN IN THE JET SET, OR THE MAN IN THE PALACE

WE ALREADY KNOW THAT, THROUGH FORESIGHT, OR PERHAPS EXCESSIVE CAUTION, PINOCHET'S SUPPORTERS BEGAN BACK IN THE SEVENTIES TO PUT THEIR 'ALMA MATER' INTO SAFE-KEEPING

BUT NOW THERE ARE STATISTICS, STILL UNCONFIRMED, SHOWING AN UNPRECEDENTED INCREASE IN THE SALE OF MAPS, COMPASSES, AND ROUTE-CHARTS FOR TRAVEL BY AIR, LAND & SEA

WHAT'S THAT YOU'RE SELLING LIKE HOT CAKES? HASBUN'S BOOK?

NO! A HANDBOOK ON EMIGRATION PROCEDURES!

PLASTIC SURGEONS FIND THEIR SERVICES IN EXTRAORDINARILY HIGH DEMAND

DOCTOR, I'VE GOT TO CHANGE MY NOSE ... FOR ONE THAT SMELLS BETTER!

AND WITH A DEMOCRATIC PROFILE

I'LL PAY WHATEVER IT COSTS!

LET'S SEE WHAT CAN BE DONE

TAKE OFF YOUR HELMET!

OTHERS WATCH THE PASSAGE OF EVENTS PHILOSOPHICALLY. PERIPATETIC, OR JUST PATHETIC, THEY WANDER THE PALACE PATHS, NO LONGER ASKING 'WHAT ARE WE?', OR 'WHERE DO WE COME FROM?' BUT SIMPLY SPECULATING -

WHERE ARE WE GOING?

©PMOMR

So Pinochet, trying to tackle roaring inflation and an increasingly angry people, twists and turns unpredictably. He is falling, they said. Maybe three months, maybe three years. He is falling.

But the most important event was when I visited the campamento Cardinal Silva Henriques. 'Welcome to the Territory of Free Chile,' said the banner at the entrance. I'd been caught up in the celebration of the first anniversary of the day when the people of the campamento marched on to this bleak patch of land in the shadow of the Andes, pitched their tents, and refused to budge.

The term shanty town gives a false impression of the campamento—conjuring up chaos and random squalor. This is a very ordered, self-governing collection of about 22,000 people—minus those who have been arrested.

It's divided into 24 sectors, block after block of wooden huts, mud-packed paths between them treacherous ditches, rubbish holes, and primitive sanitation.

Each sector elects its own leaders, appoints its own guards. Last June they held elections, amid some excitement. Many of the election slogans haven't yet been washed off the wooden walls.

'It was the first election in Chile since we elected Allende,' one man told me. He grinned.

Of course there's some delinquency in the campamento, but the place polices itself. The two main threats are the Army and disease.

There is a pharmacia—just another wooden hut with a bed and shelf of medicines. Outside it two girls examined the colour photographs of people with vile skin complaints. Charts showed the progress of diseases in each sector. Dysentry is endemic. Bronchitis, rats, malnutrition, lice, and tonsilitis are entries which occur in most of the 24 squares.

A children's doctor calls once a week. A 28-year-old man, trained as a male nurse, is in charge of health. Already he's had to deliver seven babies.

Rain is one curse. Fire is another. The only two-storey building on the whole campamento is the blue-painted fire station. Kites fly everywhere. A kite's about the cheapest toy you can make for a child. The kids are poor but not neglected.

In one of the schoolhouses—another wooden hut decorated with paper chains and children's paintings, we celebrated the first anniversary. The kids had painted pictures of Smurfs and there was a child's drawing of Victor Jara singing *Luchin*, his famous song about a slum kid playing in the gutter.

The band from the campamento's Pablo Neruda Cultural

Centre packed itself against a wall to sing a Parra song—*The Absent Dove*.

The audience, visitors from many countries, packed the floor. More and more people crowded round outside the windows to hear the songs. When a song by Victor Jara – *Prayer to a Labourer* – was sung, everybody knew the words, everyone joined in.

I was asked to take part so I said I would read the poem I wrote about Victor Jara, with a translation. Immediately a young musician offered me his guitar. I said: Sorry, I can't play. He nodded sympathetically and, although he'd never heard the poem before, improvised a gentle and subtle accompaniment to the words.

I felt safe there, walking the earth paths between the huts, greeted at every step by woolly-hatted kids longing to be photographed. A damn sight safer than in the posh avenues of Santiago, with their omnipresent soldiers.

But I suppose that poor people who organise themselves, who run their own medical programmes, and hold their own elections must be frightening for a dictator, especially for a dictator like Pinochet, who is falling.

The day Grenada's leader went to the wall

Morris S. Thompson   *Published 24 May 1985*

The day had dawned clear and bright. Redhead, then 23, said that members of Coard's faction of the party began to gather at Fort Rupert as early as 1.45 am. That day businesses were closed and schoolchildren went out on strike in support of a pro-Bishop demonstration led by foreign minister Unison Whiteman and other government ministers who resigned in protest of the anti-Bishop moves. Bishop had been confined to his house a week earlier by a faction of his ruling New Jewel Movement party, under the leadership of Bernard Coard.

At about 8 am, a crowd of 6,000 to 10,000 people unusual on this island-nation of about 92,000, marched from Market Square, near Fort Tupert, up the hill to Bishop's house. The central committee had gathered at Bernard Coard's house next door and as the first 300 or so protesters arrived at Bishop's gate, one of the committee members, Lt. Col. Ewart Layne,

25, ordered – according to his statement – three armoured personnel carriers to come and deal with the crowd.

But the full crowd at Bishop's residence overwhelmed the soldiers, who fired into the air. Abdullah (First Lieutenant Callistus Bernard) said: 'The crowd continued booing and saying, "Shoot us". Then they burst into Maurice's house and brought him out holding him high in the air and went down the road with him. The armoured cars then left and went back to Fort Frederick.'

The crowd swarmed down the hill with Bishop and Jacqueline Creft, minister of education and Bishop's lover – who later told her executioner that she was three months' pregnant with their second child – and some of the other former cabinet ministers and labour leaders who had organised the demonstration. Most of the crowd backed off, but about 2,000 people overran Fort Rupert without arms and did not meet armed resistance.

Lt. Col. Ewart Layne said that on his recommendation, the central committee went to Fort Frederick. Major Leon Cornwall arrived at Camp Fedon on Point Calavigny, south-east of the city, and dispatched two truck-loads of soldiers in full combat gear to Fort Frederick, Pvt. Cosmos Richardson said in his statement.

Meanwhile, Major Christopher Stroude, then 26, who was in command of Fort Rupert, said that Fitzroy Bain, a pro-Bishop member of the central committee who had helped lead the demonstration, told him that pro-Coard members already had surrendered to the crowd and so Stroude ordered the soldiers to lay down their weapons.

Layne said he saw the crowd far below take Fort Rupert and telephoned Stroude. Layne claimed that Stroude told him the crowd 'had destroyed military documents and had abused the female soldiers, that the situation was one of fatal chaos and that they were afraid for their lives.'

Layne said he also spoke with foreign minister Whiteman on the phone, and he said Whiteman refused more negotiations. Stroude said Bishop told him that he wanted negotiations to take place 'right here in the operations room' and that he wanted Coard gaoled immediately.

Bishop added, Stroude said, that the army could continue but that Layne and Cornwall must surrender. According to Stroude, Bishop said that Layne 'was a bloodthirsty maniac, since in a party meeting he was calling for Comrade Maurice to be expelled from the party and also to be court-martialled. He said that there will be a new type of army. When I asked about the party, he told me that it will continue as usual.'

Redhead said that he had gone from Fort Rupert to Coard's house when he saw the crowd approach Bishop's house, found

the central committee there and was sent in search of tear gas
to defend Fort Rupert. He said that by the time he got back to
Fort Rupert with the tear gas, the crowd had already overrun
it. He said he laid down his rifle on Stroude's order and that he
and Stroude went, on Fitzroy Bain's request, to talk with Bishop
in the operations room.

Bernard Coard

Bishop, Redhead said, 'came over and asked me, "What is
the position?" I told him that it was time to compromise and
put an end to the situation and let the army remain as an army
and let us try and get all of the people off the fort. Maurice said
no. So I asked him if I could report the situation to Lt. Col.
Layne or Major Cornwall and he said no . . . he wanted them
arrested immediately.'

Layne said 'we' got a message that weapons were being
handed out at Fort Rupert and that Bishop and labour leader
Vincent Noel had issued orders 'to eliminate the whole central
committee, in particular myself, General Austin and Comrade
Coard.' Layne said he called Austin (General Hudson Austin,
the Grenada army chief) outside and 'put it to him that the
only way to save the revolution and the party was to move to
recapture Fort Rupert and for the military to take control for
a short period.'

Austin disagreed, Layne said, but 'he allowed me to have my

way, recognising the tremendous respect I have amongst the men and that even he was paralysed in this situation. It was from there on I could say that I took over the situation completely.'

Then Layne said, he called Officer Cadet Connie Mayers and told him whom he wanted on the mission and to dispatch the three armoured personnel carriers to retake Fort Rupert. 'If there was resistance, then them was to battle it out and the leaders were to be liquidated.'

Maurice Bishop: 'liquidated'

Inside Fort Rupert, some weapons were being handed out. Osborne Alexander, who shortly after the 1979 revolution had been one of Bishop's bodyguards, has said this was for the protection of Bishop when the group went down to Market Square to speak to the crowd.

Outside, the armoured personnel carriers arrived. Abdullah said: 'As soon as we reached the bottom of the hill to go to Fort Rupert, some civilian opened fire from the direction of the fort and shot and killed one of the soldiers on the armoured car which O.C. Mayers was in charge of. Immediately a rocket was fired from O.C. Mayers' armoured car and machine gunners opened fire towards the crowd.

'I jumped off my car and fired some rounds,' Abdullah continued. 'We advanced towards Fort Rupert and the crowds started dispersing. Vehicles started burning; this was caused by the rocket launcher. I told Major Stroude to take charge of the fort and restore order . . .'

Said Abdullah, 'I remained at Fort Rupert because we had instructions that Maurice Bishop and the other members of the party with him were to be executed by gunfire. I knew that they were to be executed before I left Fort Frederick . . . When I was at Fort Frederick, I knew that the central committee had met and Lt. Col. Headache Layne told me that the decision was to execute Bishop and the people with him.'

Central committee member McBarnette said that he was present at a meeting in which 'the central committee decided that the army should retake Fort Rupert. The armoured cars left and about 25 minutes later, Iman Abdullah returned to Fort Frederick and spoke to Ewart Layne. The central committee then held a meeting, and it was agreed by all the committee members there that Comrade Bishop and his clique must be executed. All of the army officers – Ewart Layne, Leon Cornwall – left the room. I do not know whom they spoke to. Iman Abdullah had left also.'

At Fort Rupert, Redhead said: 'A lot of people were leaving the compound and I joined other people in telling the people to leave the compound with their hands in the air. At the same time, I saw Jacqueline Creft, Maurice Bishop, Unison Whiteman and Norris Bain walking away from the fort, so I said, "Halt" and they halted. I directed them up the steps and they came. Abdullah told them to turn against the wall and take off their shirts. Jacqueline Creft was taking off her shirt and I said, "No, let the sister keep on her jersey" . . . Abdullah told me that the chief say that they must be executed.'

Stroude said that as Redhead was marching people up the steps, he 'was stating "is execution time". I responded, "Cool," knowing that it was only the central committee that can take that decision and that he was in contact with them the same morning.'

Abdullah said: 'I lined them up facing the wall. Major Stroude and Captain Redhead were behind me and we all had weapons. Stroude and Redhead had AKs and I had an M-3 submachine-gun. Captain Redhead then told (pro-Bishop central committee members) Brat Bulleen and (Evelyn) Maitland (a man) to go, and join Maurice and the others on the square, and he went and lined up facing the wall. Some person also sent (Bishop supporter) Keith Hayling, and he joined them.'

Stroude said: 'Sister Creft said that she was three months' pregnant, but Vincent Joseph responded with some terrible remarks such as "Wha' the—you doing up here," and "is bullet for you".'

A few moments later, after Creft had asked in vain for the soldiers to wait, the shooting started. Gabriel said: 'Abdullah had a small piece of paper in his hand, he said, "The central committee has made the final decision" . . . he said to the two machine-gunners (almost certainly Andy Mitchell and Vincent Joseph) "Prepare to fire." They lift the machine gun off the ground up to their chest, Abdullah cocked his SMC gun and reckoned . . . "One, two, three, fire".'

The bullet-riddled bodies were wrapped in blankets, placed in a dump truck and driven to an army camp south of the capital, St George's. They were piled up in a common grave, doused with petrol and burned.

- Population 90,000
- Maurice Bishop's People's Revolutionary Government in power, March 1979, to October, 1983
- Head of State: Queen Elizabeth II represented by Governor-General Sir Paul Scoon
- Armed Forces 1,800
- People's Militia 3,500
- Election, December 1984, brought to power Mr Herbert Blaize, of the New National Party
- US troops occupying Grenada due to leave in October on the second anniversary of invasion

Abyss of fear

Paulo Evaristo Arns   *Published 2 August 1985*

It is not a secret to anyone that riots and loss of life have spread through the Third World in relation to the policies of the International Monetary Fund. These policies have led in the past and may lead again to military dictatorships. An elected president can go only so far in cutting off the means for his peoples to survive.

If we are determined to face the problem of world poverty we have to work together on the most concrete of levels, that is the economic and the political.

On the economic level the greatest problem is the debt of the Third World to the First World. There is a real debt and there is also a manufactured debt.

In 1976 the Third World paid 5 per cent in interest. But in 1980 the interest had risen to 21 per cent. Last year, the Third World owed a trillion dollars and paid interest of more than $100 billion. Every time the United States raises its interest rates thousands die in the Third World because money that would be used for health care and food is sent outside these countries to pay the debt.

United States capitalism has become so dependent on sales financed by the expansion of credit that it is hardly exaggerated to say that its very survival is in question.

Every school of economics has one or more answers to the international debt problem. We must choose an answer that not only alleviates the crisis at this moment, but that prevents it from happening again. Connected with the problem of the debt is that of the multinationals.

These companies have, for several decades, expanded in all the main branches of our industry. We have paid dearly in royalties and profits that have left the Third World for the First. But now the multinationals have expanded their presence in agriculture. Agribusiness is interested, in the first place, in exports. Food is exported from countries where the majority are undernourished to the countries of the First World.

In Brazil, for example, 21 per cent of the land is in the hand of small farmers and 43 per cent is owned by agribusiness (government data in 1975). But the small farmers produce 73 per cent of the food consumed in Brazil and agribusiness produces 6 per cent! If Brazil were a country of small farmers there would be no more hunger. The national priorities of the Third World must be determined by the basic needs of the majority in each country.

On the political level our criteria must be the defence of the life of the poor majority. We have to acto so that the people have food. When Pope John Paul II visited Brazil, the poor in the north of the country held up signs that said: 'Holy Father, the people are hungry!' This is the first and greatest problem: the great international political powers must work to see that the poor have food.

The problem of the Third World is not between capitalism and communism. We are not in an ideological struggle between East and West. We are hungry. We are ill. We are homeless. We are illiterate. We want to live. We want our children to be nourished in mind and body.

And this leads to a second point on the political level. The fear the First World has of political alternatives in the Third World.

Alternatives must be identified; must be given legitimacy and must be set in motion. Political and economic alternatives are the hope of the Third World and the salvation of the First World.

We have an old political joke in Brazil: We were at the brink of an abyss and now we have taken a great step forward.

International poverty is an abyss. And the fear of national alternatives in the Third World is exactly this great step forward.

Cardinal Arns is Archbishop of Sao Paulo.

A life after the torture chamber

Carlos Sanabria   *Published 29 November 1985*

I was born in a small Argentine city called Bahia Blanca. At the time of my abduction I was 23 years-old and in my fifth year of civil engineering studies. I also worked full-time as a tyre salesman. I was also an active member of the Peronist Party, which was ousted from power during the military coup of 1976. I have never used violence to further my political beliefs nor have I ever been charged with a crime.

I was attacked by a group of soldiers at noon while I was at work on 12 January, 1977. I was hooded, beaten, thrown into a truck and taken away.

Hours later, still blindfolded, and now naked with my arms tied to my back, I was sent to the torture chamber. At first the place was silent, but once on the metallic torture bed with electricity applied to my skin and genitals, electrodes on my head and scrotum, the shocks of the cattle prods running through my body, people screaming and beating me, the noise and pain were like hell. I was terrorised. I realised that pain can always increase without end. To have that feeling is devastating for the mind. There are not enough words to describe it. There was only one thing left: my mind and my will to live.

During my three months in the concentration camp, I was dirty, starved, and frequently tortured. For the entire 3½-month period I was tied, blindfolded, and prohibited from talking with other prisoners. In that condition one day felt like an eternity. There was nothing to hear, nothing to see, and no one to talk with. I lack the words to communicate how I felt.

Absolute loneliness and endless time are abstract ideas that a human being can think about, but when experiencing them, the desperation is hard to describe. The pain in my shoulders caused by being in the same position on the floor with my arms tied to my back, the pain in each of my wounds, on the tongue, the nose, kidneys, eyes, seemed to be my only physical company. I was always waiting for another session of torture. Once in a room with another blindfolded prisoner, we secretly communicated by clicking fingernails. The communication has one single meaning: You are not alone.

As much as they tortured me I still have the vision of my daughter and parents. I wanted to see them again. I frequently fell deep into terror and depression, but it was never enough to make me forget them. For others what motivated their survival may have been an ideology: their political or religious beliefs.

While at La Escuelita I received medical attention on two occasions. One time during a torture session and while still blindfolded, someone listened to my heart and lungs with a stethoscope. Later samples of my urine were collected, because one of my kidneys had been injured. I felt like an animal in a laboratory experiment with a professional taking care of my vital functions but not of me as a human being.

After three and a half months in the camp, I was sent to a gaol. I was kept in isolation for an additional one and a half months as a 'disappeared' person until my name was published. I was then publicly acknowledged as a prisoner in administrative detention at the disposition of the executive branch. When I finally gained contact with other political prisoners, I felt the warmth of all the inmates who gave me the advice and consolation of brothers. The commitment of the prisoners to each other was very strong.

Finally, on 24 October, 1979, I was taken by soldiers to the international airport in Buenos Aires, placed on a plane, and flown to exile in Seattle, Washington. Freedom was a shock. Initially, my main problem was lack of initiative. I was depressed about how difficult it was to restart my life. The language and cultural change were difficult. But the hardest part for me was to realise that the human warmth of fellow prisoners that I had experienced in jail was not always a part of the real world—the world outside.

Extracted from: The Breaking of Minds and Bodies edited by Eric Stover and Elena O. Nightingale MD, sponsored by the American Association for the Advancement of Science.

Innocents in the crossfire

Letter to the editor   *Published 3 January 1986*

Sir, After less than a month in Nicaragua, I find myself in Cristo Redentor parish, in a small town called Muelle de Los Bueyes (which means Oxford, but there are no university spires) on the chief link road between the Pacific and Atlantic oceans.

In the last month this area has become the main focus of combat between the local Sandinista army and the US-backed 'Contras'. This parish house may well be turned into a casualty hospital within a day or so.

One Sunday I was scheduled to say Mass at 2 pm in the village of Cara de Mono, but the Contras got there first. At 12.30 about 100 heavily armed mercenaries burst out of the tropical rain-forest and tried to capture the village. There was heavy cross-fire immediately behind the Catholic chapel, and the first to die was Ivan Torres, a 17-year-old villager fighting with the Sandinistas.

From the parish house here in Muelle, only 10 km from Cara de Mono, we clearly heard the machine-gun fire. Father Jose Curcio (the parish priest) and myself reached the village at 3.30 pm and discovered that the mercenaries had been driven off; 19 of them had been killed, and many others severely wounded.

The Sandinista Air Force had sent in three small reconnaissance planes and two troop carrier helicopters, and the village resembled an outsize wasp nest. My most poignant memory of that Sunday afternoon was the horrified grief of the young brothers of Ivan Torres, whose head had been blown off by a grenade.

The village catechist ('delegate of the Word' is the official title here in Central America) is a woman who also belongs to the Sandinista police. She described how her house was surrounded by a group of Contras, and how she repelled the attack singlehanded with a sub-machine gun. Her prompt action must have saved the village from a blood-bath.

Since the Contra attack that Sunday afternoon there have been reports of a build-up of forces on both sides. One of the six parish deacons came in yesterday to the parish house; 80 mercenaries had passed within a few yards of his smallholding. His fear was all the more understandable when I learned that his teenage daughter was taken hostage to Costa Rica a few months ago, where she was repeatedly raped before eventually escaping.

Not everybody here supports the Sandinista Government, of course. Most of the shop-keepers and commercial travellers have seen their living standards eroded, and would welcome a change at the top. It is not difficult however, to discern that a large majority of the population supports the present leadership.

In many ways we are living from one day to the next, without a clear vision of the way things will work out. The massive involvement of the US in trying to destroy what it regards as communism is yet another major error on the part of the Reagan Administration.

The silence and compliance of most of the Nicaraguan Bishops is perhaps no worse than the performance of the German Bishops when faced with Nazism 50 years ago, but it is equally unpalatable.

Who is to condemn our Deacons and Catechists for taking up arms to defend their families and their freedom? Does 61-year-old Father Curcio act wrongly by publicly declaring his readiness to fight alongside the youths of his parish against the American invaders?

I don't think so. And I'm sure that in war-torn Nicaragua, and in all Central America, God has taken sides, just as he took the side of the enslaved Hebrews in Ancient Egypt. God is visible in the faces of the poor who are struggling for a better life, a life without fear and hunger.

Please give these people the support they deserve, by making known the justice of their cause.

God bless you.

Padre Juan Luis
(John Medcalf)

No end of trouble for the general

Malcolm Coad   *Published 10 January 1986*

After a year in which Chile reached the top of the Latin American unemployment league, political bombings became an almost daily event, and opposition parties formed a political pact broader than any in the country's history, President Augusto Pinochet ended 1985 in characteristic style—by flatly rejecting Church attempts at mediation between his government and an increasingly threatening opposition.

His decision was delivered personally to the Archbishop of Santiago, Cardinal Juan Francisco Fresno, at a brief audience granted to the Cardinal on Christmas Eve. The media razzamatazz laid on for the event – Pinochet's embrace of the Cardinal, television focus on the General's smiles, the gift to the prelate of a lapis lazuli cross – belied its tensions. Msgr Fresno wanted rapprochement over the 'national accord for a return to full democracy', the pact he sponsored in August between 11 parties ranging from socialists to right-wing government supporters.

When General Pinochet dismissed the accord with a curt, 'Let's change the subject', the Cardinal was, said his advisers later, 'desolate'.

Erstwhile government supporters were furious. 'Pinochet will be to blame for the polarisation that will come now,' said Pedro Correa, a leader of the right-wing National Party. Former military junta member, air force General Gustavo Leigh, said: 'Pinochet has thrown away the only lifebelt on offer. He'll have to be dragged by force to the negotiating table, and mass mobilisation is the only way to do it.'

Such mobilisation is what the Opposition is now planning. By rejecting any dialogue over the accord – which proposes elections and the lifting of emergency measures, but without explicitly rejecting the military's controversial constitution – Pinochet removed at a stroke the main point of difference between those in the Opposition who favour intensifying such action against the regime, and others who have succeeded recently in holding it back in the hope of talks. Parties from centre-right to revolutionary left are now talking of a General Strike 'at the latest by April or May'.

General Pinochet's stance will also cause problems in his main remaining base of support—the military. The accord was viewed sympathetically by a significant group of generals as signalling a way out of a situation which they know threatens to become unmanageable. In December military junta member and air force Commander General Fernando Matthei said, 'If the accord didn't exist, perhaps we would have to help creat it.' In November President Pinochet sacked his own representative on the junta, army General Raul Benavides in part, it is thought, for harbouring similar views.

General Benavide's departure was the second blow to the junta since August, when police chief General Cesar Mendoza went, after evidence of involvement by his men in death-squad activity. That affair brought the military face-to-face with the public revulsion of often brutal military rule, and triggered inter-service friction which led to the first coup rumours since the 1973 'pronunciamiento'.

High among the fears of both the military and the political Right is the increased presence of the Left, blamed by many on General Pinochet's intransigence. The semi-clandestine Popular Democratic Movement (MDP), made up of Communists, Socialists and the Cuban-orientated Movement of the Revolutionary Left (MIR) is riding high in many student and trade unions, generally behind the country's main political force, the centrist Christian Democrats, but first in many of the former.

In city slums, now experiencing poverty unknown in decades, the MDP is the main organised political force—though its leaders admit that the slums' thousands of militant youth are finally an explosive law unto themselves. Through the Communists and the MIR the MDP is also linked to the armed groups responsible for hundreds of bombings last year, the deaths of several police, sabotage of power lines and even propaganda raids on military and secret police targets.

According to sources close to the military, an increasing number of generals now favour isolating the left through an opening to othe parties. The national accord was seen as offering this, and damaged General Pinochet's rhetoric of 'me or chaos' by proving that the much-maligned 'politicos' were capable of agreement.

Further encouragement comes from the overt support of the accord shown by the US, EEC, and regional governments, and the Vatican—which wants progress to democracy before the Papal visit planned for March, 1987. In particular, the Pentagon, formerly a Pinochet mainstay, now supports the view of George Shultz's State Department that regional security requires a change in Chile, and is making this clear to its Chilean allies. President Alfonsin, fearful for Argentina's stability if tensions continue in its neighbour, is also believed to have made soundings aimed at a truce between Pinochet and the opposition.

Sources also say that studies carried out by individual services have raised technical doubts over aspects of the planned 'protected democracy', in which Marxism would be banned and the military would maintain a powerful overseeing role. There is particular concern over the practicality of the procedure by which Pinochet could be ratified in power for a further eight years, prior to the opening of a partially elected congress in 1990. His current term ends in 1989.

- 1964–70 Eduardo Frei (Christian Democrat) 1970–73, Salvador Allende (Popular Unity leftwing coalition), September, 1973, onwards, General Augusto Pinochet, backed by four-man junta of military chiefs, after coup in which President Allende died in bombing of presidential palace. Congress closed, parties technically illegal.

- Population: 12 million. Unemployment officially 13 per cent, and 17 per cent in cities.

- Main exports: Copper (50 per cent of total, and world's largest exporter), fruit, fishmeal, forestry products.

- Economy: extreme Chicago school neo-liberalism. Foreign debt—$20 billion. Interest and principal payments due this year—$2.25 billion. Growth per capita—nil. Export earnings—$3.65 billion (estimate). Trade surplus—$710 million (estimate). Balance of payments deficit—$1.35 billion (estimate). Inflation—26 per cent.

It is impossible to know how far such doubts have spread in Chile's rigidly hierarchical armed forces. But right-wing parties hope that, in spite of Pinochet's intransigence, the military can be persuaded to drop formal support for him in 1989, back open elections and return definitively to barracks. Other aspects of the current Constitution, such parties either agree with or would leave for later negotiation.

But it is here that other groups, from the MDP to most Christian Democrats, violently disagree. 'The problem is not just Pinochet, but his Constitution and everything he stands for,' says Luis Maira, leader of the Christian Left Party, which supports the accord but also has close links with the MDP. 'You can't have democracy in Chile with most of the Left excluded. Nor can we wait four more years.'

After General Pinochet's rebuff to Cardinal Fresno, such groups are even more determined not to be 'blackmailed' by the Right into holding back the mass mobilisation which, says Socialist MDP leader German Correa, 'is the only way to break this regime's legitimacy once and for all and oblige the armed forces to fulfil their duty and restore our democracy.' The Christian Democrat-dominated Democratic Alliance coalition has said it will now campaign for 'an elected congress in 1986'.

And what of General Pinochet himself? So far he seems determined to stay on until after 1989.

Mystic and Marxist

Jenny Morgan   *Published 17 January 1986*

A book – entitled *Fidel and Religion* – of conversations between Fidel Castro and a Brazilian priest, Frei Betto, sold out in Cuba within days of publication.

The publication of the book says a lot about how much weight the Cuban leadership gives to Liberation Theology, particularly since the involvement of believers in the Nicaraguan and El Salvadoran struggles. The Minister of Culture, Armando Hart, says in his introduction that, 'This marks the start, not just at the tactical and political level, but also at the strategic and moral one, of a profound exchange of ideas between forces that until recently seemed incapable of understanding each other.'

Hart's comment reflects the tension that existed for many years in Cuba between the revolution and the Catholic Church, whose hierarchy condemned the Marxist-Leninist nature of the revolution. Yet it was in fact Cuba's manifest success in tackling the injustices that still afflict much of Latin America that produced a ferment in the Catholic Church in the 1960s, out of which grew Liberation Theology.

Frei Betto based his book on 23 hours of conversation with Fidel Castro, conducted over four days last May. The urgency of the situation in Latin America is, he says, what prompted him to do the book.

'The problems of the Caribbean and Latin America threaten believers and non-believers alike, both Christians and Marxists. The foreign debt, imperialist aggression, oppression, military dictatorship, lack of housing, of health care, of education, threaten all of us equally, and the only way to change this state of things is to apply in liberation practice the fundamental criterion of our coming together and our unity.'

Frei Betto himself is an example of the kind of priest the Church in Latin America is producing. In 1964, when he was 20, he was imprisoned for student activities; a year later he became a Dominican priest, though he continued to work as a journalist. In 1969 he was arrested again, and imprisoned until 1973. 'I can say that, thanks to the dictatorship, I was able to do a complete course on Marxism, because in prison we had many books, among them *Capital*, and *The State and Revolution*, hidden in the jackets of cowboy stories.'

Now he works in an iron-mining region near Sao Paulo. 'The contradiction between believers and atheists is not significant. I'm a Christian and yet I don't believe in the god of capitalism, in the god of exploitation, in Reagan's or Pinochet's god.

'Incredible as it may sound, I feel that Cuba is more conducive to cultivating one's Christian faith than those countries that call themselves Christian. Here, I feel more in tune with the Gospel, and I have no doubt as to the existence here of a society of cooperation, of internationalist spirit, and all the other values of socialism that are essentially Christian.'

There's no doubting the seriousness of Cuba's engagement with Liberation Theology.

But the interest of the Cuban people is particularly striking. Walfredo Pinero, university professor, cinema critic, and Catholic, who over the years has lost neither his faith nor his commitment to the revolution, says that many believers in Cuba suffered a 'trauma' because of the Church's hostility to the revolution. People had felt they had to choose between the revolution and their faith, and many had left the Church. Now changes in the Church were gradually healing the wounds. Next month the Catholic Church in Cuba will hold a major congress to revise its position with regard to the revolution.

But how to explain the keenness of the young to read *Fidel And Religion*? 'You have to realise that Cuba is still part of a profoundly religious continent. Spirituality is rooted deep in people—even among the young who have had a scientific education.'

A momentary flash of scepticism passed at this point across the face of our young translator. But the same thought is in Frei Betto's description of Fidel Castro:

'I'd say that it's a godsend for the history of this continent to have a man like Fidel, a man fortunate enough to have a revolutionary view combined with Marxist coherence and a Christian upbringing.'

Vote farce

Andaiye *Published 17 January 1986*

The conduct of the elections in Guyana last month was no surprise, since in free and fair elections, the ruling People's National Congress (PNC) would have lost the power to which it has clung for 21 years. The surprise for many was that the elections were again blatantly rigged in conditions where it would have been better for the PNC if they had seemed credible.

The final report of the fact-finding mission into political freedom in Guyana, headed by Lord Chitnis, documented 'the historical record of the Guyanese electoral system, showing how, since 1964, that system has been undermined and brought under the control of the ruling PNC.' It was this undermined system into which Desmond Hoyte introduced minor reforms when he became President following the death of Forbes Burnham last August.

If the December elections were to be credible, those minor reforms had to be followed by the appearance of fairness during the voting, with the fraud being carried out discreetly between the vote and the count; to facilitate this, Mr Hoyte had refused to consider the main demand of the Working People's Alliance and other forces that a preliminary count of ballots be made at individual polling stations. In the event, the PNC dispensed with the need to appear fair: instead, in the full view of all, the military wing of the civilian/military regime hijacked the ballot boxes and bore them away for the 'count'. The result: PNC, 42 seats; People's Progressive Party, 8 seats; the pro-business United Force, 2 seats; and the WPA, 1 seat.

During 1979–80, Walter Rodney often spoke of what he called the 'Haitianisation' of Guyana—a process of economic, social, and political degeneration of a country that is both product and producer of a massive alienation and dispersal of the working people. In Guyana that process is well-advanced.

According to a Caribbean development bank report, Guyana has the highest inflation rate, and the highest mortality rate in the English-speaking Caribbean; in the region as a whole, only Haiti's per capita income is lower, Guyanese working people are being dispersed from jobs into hustling and out of Guyana everywhere: out of a total population of 800,000, 100,000 Guyanese are estimated to be in Canada. In 1984, Guyanese made more applications for refugee status in Canada than did the citizens of any other country, including Haiti.

The PNC seems to believe this situation can be reversed if the economy is fixed, and that the economy can be fixed by large-scale external economic aid. It is reported to be working for better relations with the US, negotiating 'reasonable rescheduling terms' with the IMF, and to have accepted a World Bank proposal for 'economic liberalisation' to bring $730m (US) into the economy.

But in Guyana as in the Philippines, donors and investors want a guarantee of a stable climate; they want workers who are not alienated; they want workers to be pacified. And in Guyana as in the Philippines, it is an error to disconnect the economic and social from the political conditions as products and producers of workers' alienation.

During the pre-election period in Guyana, Mr Hoyte, for his own purposes, offered a brief, minor relaxation of the normal conditions of the dictatorship which the WPA was able to use to work among the people in a way that is not usually possible. Those 'normal conditions' were fully restored on election day and within eight days the homes of leading members of the WPA, the PPP and the Church were being searched for arms and ammunition in the context of renewed threats of 'containment'. The Burnham peace has already been succeeded by the Hoyte peace.

In a recent TV programme in the UK, the South African Ambassador to the UK tried to deflect Sir Shridath Ramphal's criticisms of South Africa by reminding him that the US State Department had defined both South Africa and Guyana as 'partly free'; as he knew, the Commonwealth Secretary-General is a former Minister in a PNC Government in Guyana.

But Guyana is not South Africa; apartheid is a uniquely anti-human system. The Guyanese people have the same right to a Government of their choice; the same duty to struggle until they win it.

Andaiye is a Guyanese teacher. She was the local editor of Walter Rodney's History of the Guyanese Working People.

4 MIDDLE EAST AND ISLAM

An Egyptian intellectual's view of Sadat

Andrew Graham-Yooll talks to the Egyptian poet, Lotfi El Khouli, banned from publishing in his own country
Published 16 September 1981

Lotfi El Khouli, by the doubtful grace of a heart attack, is not in a Cairo prison today. One of the luminaries of Egypt's intelligentsia, he regrets that President Sadat's decision to run a security bulldozer through the Egyptian intellectual community last week will put the cultural clock back several years with an effect throughout the Arab world.

El Khouli, one-time trade union lawyer, former *Al Ahram* columnist, active member of the liberal-leftist-Marxist front known as the Progressive Nationalist Unionist Party of Egypt, publisher, filmwriter, playwright, short-story writer, is in Paris for a medical check-up. He is also making political contacts and trying to coordinate financial and filming arrangements for a forthcoming documentary on the Middle East. So he missed the raids, though his name was on the lists of those recommended for arrest.

Before Paris, in an interview in London, he said he expected a crackdown by President Sadat, but did not seem to imagine it would be so widespread.

He rattled off a list of names of right-wing and left-wing writers, all of them, like himself, banned from publishing in Egypt. However, he put considerable hope in a younger movement of writers, journalists, and artists who were working in small semi-clandestine groups and 'café-concerts'.

'Sadat bans everybody. He cannot bear criticism. But the kind of agreement he seeks is impossible. Even if you support the Government 99 per cent you are considered part of the opposition; if you agree 100 per cent you are suspect. You have to be 101 per cent in favour of Sadat to be seen as sympathetic. Naturally, that does not make for a very large group of supporters.'

El Khouli is an articulate spokesman for the Egyptian intelligentsia. He explains the concern that President Sadat's obsession with his own image, with the Camp David programme, and with the encouragement of Egypt's new entrepreneurial class has shut out a realistic view of Arab affairs.

'Farouk's police threw me into prison five times before the July, 1952 coup. I was arrested seven times under Nasser.' And he was in prison in 1970 when Nasser died. 'But Sadat bans, and hopes the problem will go away.'

Lofti El Khouli

El Khouli started the magazine *Al-Talia* in 1965. An avant-garde publication with a print run of 32,000 on the arts and politics, it was banned in January, 1977, after supporting a series of public demonstrations against President Sadat. 'I read in *Al Ahram* that the magazine was to be banned. And it was.'

Since then he has written three plays, three collections of short stories – from which Heinemann, in London, took one for an anthology – and the script of five films.

He is working on a film about Egyptian emigration. There are three million abroad, from a country of 43 million. Egypt's loss, he says. He is also working on a play about the new merchant 'non-productive' class, 'a result of the oil and of the fictitious peace of Camp David.'

'In Egypt there are two cultures: that of the ruling class, now allied to the middle class merchants who care little about local expression; and a youthful movement which is to be found operating in a semi-clandestine manner.'

El Khouli's plays are staged outside Egypt. To keep people like him in check there is the Law of Shame, which forbids publication abroad without permission. If authorisation is not sought and Cairo considers a publication offensive, there is a trial by what Egyptians call the Court of Shame.

Asked if he did not think that President Sadat deserved some credit for allowing him to keep a job at *Al Ahram*, even if not writing, he said: 'It is their justification and my prison. They know where I am and I can only go away with their permission.'

Much of his criticism of Mr Sadat concerns the Camp David agreement. 'Egypt's bourgeoisie has always been the cultural backbone of the Arab world. Since Camp David, the body has lacked a backbone. President Sadat said that only a few people, mere intellectuals, opposed the Camp David peace. But that handful, even if puny, has not been allowed to express any views, which leads me to believe it is not so small. Camp David has benefited an uncultured middle class, not interested in any of the problems of the Arab world. And this break in Egyptian society is beginning to hurt Egypt.'

Anguish and venom from a poet on the run

Michael Simmons talks to the Palestinian poet, Mahmoud Darwish
Published 25 November 1983

Few people have articulated the anguish of the Palestinian cause with as much force as the poet Mahmoud Darwish. A grim and relentless anger pervades much of his verse, which he has declaimed before crowds of thousands at sittings throughout the Arab world.

For year he has been a senior lieutenant and close friend of Yasser Arafat and until recently was director of the PLO Research Centre in Beirut. But always, he says, he has had the ability, or the facility, to drop what he is doing to write. At 42, he is now probably the foremost 'poet of the occupied land', regularly producing work which goes beyond what Wilfred Owen called 'the pity of war' into the realms of unending pain. For years too he has been on the Israelis' hit list, a constant thorn in their side though he was born near Galilee and cherishes images of his father, a peasant, scooping up the soil with his hands. Now, according to his friends, he is on an Arab hit-list for speaking out against what he sees as an Arab conspiracy with the Israelis to discredit the Palestinian cause. He rarely sleeps more than two nights in the same place.

Mahmoud Darwish

Until this time last year, he survived in Beirut, but left in protest soon after the Sabra and Chattila massacre, vowing not to live again in an Arab country – any Arab country – that could sit by and allow such things to happen. Unattached and apparently unencumbered, except with his work and his verse, he commutes between London, Paris, Moscow or wherever people will give him a hearing. At the moment, he says, he is in 'long transit' in Paris.

This week he was in London for a reading before friends and supporters and next week will be here again. He talked for a while in an anonymous West End hotel before moving on to Heathrow.

For a man who produces such painstaking and intricate work, it is disarming to hear somewhat staccato sentences from a mind that is apparently not easily distracted. When the hotel manager said he wanted to have the lounge cleaned where the interview was taking place, it was the interviewer and not the interviewee who was put out. A fresh cup of coffee was calmly ordered and the conversation went on as before.

'We are being killed by Arab hands,' he said, speaking of Tripoli. Arab regimes, and particularly the regimes of Assad (Syria) and Gadaffi (Libya), had 'a common interest' with the Israelis. 'But I see no defeat in Tripoli. This conflict is not between the PLO and Syria, but between the PLO message and the Arab situation.'

Most of his venom is reserved for President Assad of Syria. 'The Syrians,' he said, 'have no ears. The Syrians have no policy; there is only Assad's policy. The Soviets are using moral and political pressure to stop him, but he will not listen.'

Darwish says he has been writing verse since the age of six, and that when he was 12 he 'dreamed' that poetry would be his destiny. 'Now it is the only way I can express my existence and my spiritual power. Poetry justifies my life.'

To understand the verse the reader needs a certain sympathy with the writer's cause and a recognition that his work fits in with a long Arab tradition. 'But Palestinian poetry,' he has said, 'is not a substitute for, nor a rival to, modern Arabic poetry; it is an indivisible part of it, one of the tributaries of the main stream.'

He insists, though his imagery to a Western reader may appear deeply complex, on accessibility in his work. 'Poetry,' he wrote in an early poem, 'is the blood of the heart. Salt to bread. The eye's water. As such it is too important to be allowed to remain divorced from life.' In another, he has written that if simple people do not understand the meaning of the poems, 'It were best we scatter them to the winds. And abide for ever in silence.'

The complexity of the imagery marries Arab beliefs and customs with contemporary political demands. To understand a wry and poignant piece called *The Wandering Guitar Player* one has to know that it is popular Arab belief that when the moon is in eclipse it will be eaten by a whale. To get near to almost any of his work, one has to see Palestine as a lost and all-embracing love, a bride, a mother, to whom the suitor, or the son, pours out an endless stream of dreams and hopes and regrets. But the loved one is also the land, the soil scooped up by his father, and not the cold intellectual concept, even the hope that it is for a wandering Jew.

Darwish is fluent in Hebrew and speaks with unguarded respect of some very great Israeli poets. He holds the country that has hounded and persecuted him and his cause with respect also. One suspects that if he were not constantly on the run, he would co-exist.

He has been for years an active Communist, though not currently a paid up member of any party. He speaks some Russian and readily relays the names of some 'real' Soviet poets of his acquaintance. Earlier this year he was awarded the Lenin Prize in Moscow, the Russians' highest accolade for a writer. He does not like to speak of censorship.

The Palestinian and the Marxist causes are a constant pre-occupation. 'I am afraid,' he says quietly, 'that people will stop believing. The battle between Arab regimes and the Arab people is a serious one.'

He prepares to go. Where, one asks, does he expect to finish up? He brushes down his immaculate suit before preparing to leave, and smiles wistfully. 'I would like to die in my village,' he says, 'in any Palestinian village.'

Widow makers

Leila Sayigh   *Published 6 January 1984*

If you are an adult Palestinian in Beirut today, you are almost certainly a woman, and probably a widow. If your husband is not dead he is either in prison or has left the country. If he was not resident in Lebanon since 1948 (even though you were) your children have no legal existence – no right to either a residence permit or a passport – and your family cannot be registered with the UN Relief and Works Agency (UNRWA). This means exclusion both from 'hardship case' benefits and from ordinary UNRWA services like schooling and medical care.

Take Hamideh, for instance. She is 25 and had four children. Her husband has been missing since the Sabra-Shatila massacre—one of 950 men who were driven away in trucks and never seen since. Her home was destroyed. She is now living in a classroom in an abandoned school. Her youngest child, aged 18 months, is blind and brain damaged, but because she is not registered she has been denied medical treatment.

Hamideh's husband came to Lebanon from Jordan, so by Lebanese law her children should be Jordanian. But Hamideh never had the chance to get to know her husband's family, and the Jordanian authorities do not want to know about her. There are said to be 257 widows in the same situation in the Sidon area, and there must be as many in Beirut, and in the Dekaa valley.

Um Nabil, another Palestinian widow, had four sons killed in 1976 at Tell Zaater, the refugee camp overrun by Phalangists. Two years ago her fifth son was kidnapped by them. As is the custom, someone claiming influence with the Phalangists approached her and offered to secure his release for a consideration—£8,000.

On 4 September, while the fighting raged in Beirut's southern suburbs between the Army and Amal (the Shi'ite militia), Um Nabil set off to Sidon with, as she thought, the last instalment of the ransom, taking with her a teenage daughter and an eight-year-old, orphaned grandson. Two days later, alone, she started back to Beirut to get more money, but between Damour and Naimeh Phalangist militiamen ordered her out of the taxi, stripped her, and killed her in front of the helpless taxi-driver.

In spite of incidents like this, women still brave the road to the south. In September, many took their children that way to escape the fighting in Beirut. In October, with UNRWA school reopening, many risked Phalangist roadblocks to return. It is like Russian roulette, for the Phalangists do not check the occupants of every car. 'It's you and your luck,' as the Palestinians say. Every time they approach a checkpoint, women's knees turn to jelly.

The school in Sabra where Hamideh lives is full of homeless families. If one goes, another immediately moves in. Throughout Beirut there are 3,000 Palestinian families under threat of eviction from buildings they have been occupying since their expulsion by the 'Lebanese Forces' (Phalangists and allies) from Eastern Beirut and the mountains behind. The government has frozen mass evictions, but individual ones occur daily. Housing is desperately short, and landlords will not let houses or flats to Palestinians. Evicted families have to crowd into already overcrowded refugee buildings, or rent garages or shops. Palestinians threatened by the Phalangists in the Sidon area are still trickling back into Beirut.

Many people in today's Lebanon are defenceless, the victims of militiamen and armies having every conceivable religious and political hue. But of them all, the Palestinians are the most vulnerable. Most other categories still have some armed force purporting to represent their interest on the battlefield or at the negotiating table. Many defenceless civilians have been killed during the fighting or been the target of atrocities in the wake of conflict, as in the Shouf.

Many refugees repaired their shelters after the Israeli invasion when the Lebanese government told UNRWA that camps could be reinstated. But last August, 12 families in Shatila were taken to court for illegal reconstruction, and instructed to smash the shelters they had rebuilt with their own hands. Permission to reconstruct the camps, they were told, referred merely to UNRWA installations, not to human habitations. It is difficult not to conclude that the permission originally given to reinstate the camps, which received wide publicity, was a political act to assuage international opinion. The reality on the ground seems to have been different.

Fanning the flame

Noam Chomsky examines the relationship between Israel and the United States
Published 13 January 1984

In the war of words that has been waged since Israel invaded Lebanon on 6 June, 1982, critics of Israeli actions have frequently been accused of hypocrisy. While the reasons advanced are spurious, the charge itself has some merit.

It is surely hypocritical to condemn Israel for founding settlements in the occupied territories while we pay for establishing and expanding them. Or to condemn Israel for attacking civilian targets with cluster and phosphorous bombs 'to get the maximum kill per hit', when we provide them gratis or at bargain rates, knowing that they will be used for just this purpose. Or to criticise Israel's 'indiscriminate' bombardment of heavily-settled civilian areas or its other military adventures, while we not only provide the means in abundance but welcome

Israel's assistance in testing the latest weaponry under live battlefield conditions—to be sure, against a vastly outmatched enemy including completely undefended targets, always the safest way to carry out experiments of this sort.

In general, it is pure hypocrisy to criticise the exercise of Israeli power while welcoming Israel's contribution towards realising the US aim of eliminating possible threats, largely indigenous, to American domination of the Middle East region.

Clearly as long as the United States provides the wherewithal Israel will use it for its purposes. These purposes are clear enough today, and have been clear to those who chose to understand for many years: to integrate the bulk of the occupied territories within Israel in some fashion while finding a way to reduce the Arab population; to disperse the scattered refugees and crush any manifestation of Palestinian nationalism or Palestinian culture; to gain control over Southern Lebanon.

Since these goals have long been obvious and have been shared in fundamental respects by the two major political groupings in Israel, there is little basis for condemning Israel when it exploits the position of regional power afforded it by the phenomenal quantities of US aid in exactly the ways that would be anticipated by any person whose head is not buried in the sand.

Complaints and accusations are indeed hypocritical as long as material assistance is provided in an unending and ever-expanding flow, along with diplomatic and ideological support, the latter, by shaping the facts of history in a convenient form. Even if the occasional tempered criticisms from Washington or in editorial commentary are seriously intended, there is little reason for any Israeli government to pay any attention to them.

The historical practice over many years has trained Israeli leaders to assume that US 'opinion makers' and political elites will stand behind them whatever they do, and that even if direct reporting is accurate, as it generally is, its import will gradually be lost as the custodians of history carry out their tasks.

The point seems simple enough. Some years ago it was in fact as simple as it seems. It would then have been possible to influence Israel to join in the international consensus – which has long included the major Arab states, the population of the occupied territories, and the mainstream of the PLO – in support of a two-state political settlement that would include recognised borders, security guarantees, and reasonable prospects for a peaceful resolution of the conflict. The precondition, of course, was for the US itself to join this consensus and increase its support for the adamant rejectionism of the Labour Party and then Menachem Begin's Likud coalition.

What seemed simple several years ago, however, has become considerably more complex today. By now it is not at all clear what the effect would be if US policy were to shift towards the international consensus, abandoning the commitment to a Greater Israel that will dominate the region in the interests of American power.

This book is not intended as a comprehensive review or analysis of the network of relations among the United States, Israel and the Palestinians. Rather, its more modest aims are to bring out certain elements of the 'special relationship' between the United States and Israel, and of their relationships to the original inhabitants of the world, which I think have been insufficiently appreciated, or addressed and often seriously misrepresented, with the consequence that we have pursued policies that are both disgraceful and extremely dangerous, increasingly so.

These remarks will be critical of Israel's policies, its consistent rejection of any political settlement that accommodates the national rights of the indigenous population; its repression and state terrorism over many years; its propaganda efforts, which have been remarkably successful – much to Israel's detriment in my view – in the United States.

But this presentation may be misleading, in two respects. In the first place, this is not an attempt at a general history; the focus is on what I think is and has been wrong and what should be changed, not on what I think has been right. Secondly, the focus on Israeli actions and initiatives may obscure the fact that my real concern is the policies that have been pursued by the US government and our responsibility in shaping or tolerating these policies.

To a remarkable extent, articulate opinion and attitudes in the US have been dominated by people who describe themselves as 'supporters of Israel', a term that I will also adopt though with much reluctance, since I think they should more properly be called 'supporters of the moral degeneration and ultimate destruction of Israel', and not Israel alone.

The essential features of the US contribution towards the creation of a Greater Israel were revealed in a stark and brutal form in the September 1982 massacre of Palestinians in Beirut, which finally did elicit widespread outrage, temporarily at least. The Israeli invasion of Lebanon was supported by the US and by editorial comment generally, though qualms were raised when it seemed to be going too far (perhaps threatening US interests) or to involve too many civilian casualties.

It would be salutary, for the US to abandon hypocrisy. Either we provide the support for the establishment of a Greater Israel with all that it entails and refrain from condemning the grim consequences of this decision, or we withdraw the means and the licence for the pursuit of these programmes and act to ensure that the valid demands of Israelis and Palestinians be satisfied.

These extracts are from The Fateful Triangle, The United States, Israel and the Palestinians, by Noam Chomsky, published by Pluto Press.

Turkey's intellectuals sign up for a trial of strength

Dr Can Ege   *Published 3 August 1984*

In the next week or two, the Ankara Martial Law Prosecutor will open court proceedings against 56 cultural and academic figures in Turkey. Unlike many of the trials which have moved slowly and painfully through the courts since the Army took power in 1980, this one does not concern activities undertaken before that coup. On the contrary, it is an official response to something new and unexpected, something which may yet prove to be a turning point in the political trajectory of General, now President, Kenan Evren.

In mid-May Husnu Goksel, a world famous cancer specialist, led a delegation to the gates of the presidential palace at Ankara. With him were Aziz Nesin, well-known humorist, and Bahri Savei, a prime mover of Turkey's 1961 constitution (repealed by the military after September, 1980) and the popular singer, Esin Afsar. Their purpose was to present a petition signed by 1,256 intellectuals and cultural figures calling for a thaw in the ideological permafrost which has settled over post-coup Turkey.

Careful to remain within the limits of the restricted constitutional rights recognised under the present regime, the signatories nonetheless touched a very raw nerve. The claim that Turkey is moving toward real civilian democracy is a vital part of the generals' campaign to secure approval for their regime not only in Nato but in wider Western public opinion.

In perhaps the most forthright public statement since the coup, signatories demanded the total eradication of torture. Its existence, they said, had been proved by court decisions. 'A fundamental feature of statehood is respect for the law in the struggle against terror. The existence of terror can never justify the state resorting to the same methods as the perpetrators of terror.'

Significantly the declaration has been endorsed by retired officers, former MPs, and Cabinet ministers, as well as academics, writers, media celebrities and the like. The tenor of their five-page appeal was set by the statement that the Turkish people are entitled to enjoy the full range of human rights and freedoms which exist in 'contemporary societies'. Pluralist democracy, they added, cannot be blamed for the acute terror experienced in Turkey during the late 1970s. The country has not overcome the social and economic crises so frequently cited to justify the military coup and the subsequent reorganisation of Turkish society along the lines of a 'dictated democracy'.

For President Evren this identified all the 1,256 signatories as 'traitors who want to bring the days of the terror back'. The authorities used their powers of censorship to keep news of the petition quiet for as long as possible. Even so, the Prime Minister, Turgut Ozal, had his chief adviser, Adnan Kahveci, give a 'categorical assurance' at the time that no measures would be taken against those who had signed what has come to be called in Turkey 'the intellectuals' declaration'.

Interrogations began on 21 May, when a group of film-directors and artists were detained after seeing Ozal himself and the Speaker of Parliament to lobby them over the state of their industry. They were taken to the Ankara Martial Law Prosecutor's office. Interrogations rapidly followed in other cities with groups of up to 50 being called in at any one time. While this was happening another 150 public figures signed the petition. So far 56 have been actually charged with publishing an 'unlicensed document'. They face up to one year in prison, if found guilty; the case opens on 13 August.

The head of the Higher Education Council, Professor Ihsan Dogramaci, gave an assurance of no moves against academic signatories, that turned out to be as short-lived as Ozal's. With 1,200 university teachers sacked since the coup, the academics involved have now been told to prepare defence statements on the charge of having breached the council's disciplinary code.

Such measures have stimulated a now widely circulated petition of support in Western Europe and North America similar to those who put their names to the original Turkish document. But in a country where the rulers claim to be crafting a return to democracy, why has there been such a harsh reaction to so modest a political act? After all, Turkey managed earlier this summer to slip back into the 'democratic club' of the Council of Europe on the basis of the supposed progress made —and that its supporters' claim is yet to come. In fact, the 'intellectuals' declaration' takes as its starting point the very

European Convention on Human Rights the council is deputed to defend.

There is no doubt that many Turkish people, sickened by the terror of the late 1970s, did accept the military's argument over the need to root out violence. The generals, however, took that acceptance to be a mandate for the imposition of a complete restructuring of political life, entrenching themselves in the country's government and State apparatus.

Unlike the follow-up to the previous military coups of 1960 and 1971, this time the military have shown no inclination to retire to their barracks. One of the main features of the current situation is the way in which the new military rulers have dispensed with the traditional triple alliance within Turkish governments dating back to the Young Turks: that of the army officers, State bureaucrats, and 'aydin' or intellectuals.

The word 'aydin' literally means 'enlightened one' and denotes a social group which has exercised considerable power and influence in Turkish life. It began to lose its position of prestige in the eyes of the military after the 1971 coup. The generals and senior bureaucrats have increasingly turned to company boardrooms instead.

Even for those intellectuals not already numbered among the 33,000 'ideological offenders', the past four years have been ones in which their environment has become increasingly intolerable. Hence the breadth of the challenge to the generals' plans for 'disciplined democracy'.

Beginning with the declaration in May, important cracks have begun to open in Turkish politics. Lawyers have denounced the prison regime and the holding of political prisoners. Members of the legal trade union federation, Turk-Is, used a mass rally as the opportunity to call for the right to strike—and to embarrass their officials in the process. The Opposition party outside parliament, Sodep, quickly gave its political endorsement to the petition. But there have also been repercussions within the ruling alliance of the authoritarian right.

Sections of the military are said to have tried to free Colonel Alpaslan Turkes, the gaoled leader of the old Nationalist Action Party involved in extensive Right-wing terror before the coup. Within the ruling Motherland Party of Mr Ozal, there is now a power struggle between the former supporters of Turkes' neo-fascist movement and Islamic Fundamentalists.

Amid all this movement there are at least two things that have not changed—the regime's use of repression and its cynicism over the exercise. 'That only 56 people have been charged,' Ozal declared, 'is a concrete step in the transition to democracy.'

The art of challenge in Turkey

**Michael Simmons talks to Yilmaz Guney
and to Oguz Aral**
Published 17 August 1984

While the Turkish director, Yilmaz Guney, was making his latest film in a converted old abbey in northern France, the most recent phase of military rule was ostensibly coming to an end in Turkey itself. Ostensibly—because the generals still hold effective power and martial law still prevails in 41 of the country's 67 provinces and in all the major cities.

This latest film, called *The Wall*, is, like its predecessor, *Yol*, a prison film. It centres on the atrocious conditions in Dormitory Four, where the prison's child inmates, some barely teenagers, seek to survive in an environment of brutish deprivation and violence. If they cannot survive, they try to escape – for which they are viciously punished – and when that fails, they plan revolution.

The end of the film brings a sequence of police mug shots, full face and profile, all stamped with the date, 7.11.82. On that date, Turkey voted for the generals' constitution and General Evren became President Evren. But, according to Guney, nothing changes: the film is intended as 'a slap in the face of the Fascist military dictatorship.'

Guney, a film-maker of international distinction and an actor with the reputation of stardom at home, is currently in hiding in Paris, on the run from extradition requests. The Turkish authorities want him for murder – for which friends say he was framed – but he says it is his revolutionary zeal which upsets them.

There is an incongruity about the setting as this tall, gaunt figure whose origins are in the remote Kurdish hills of south-eastern Turkey sits in an elegant Parisian drawing-room talking of radical change. In conversation he is undemonstrative, doodling on a pad as he talks. But angry and uncompromising references to Fascism and anti-democracy are frequent. Turkey, he declares, has never been democratic, drawing what looks like a flower on his pad.

His roots are deep in today's Turkey. His preoccupations are such that he will not somehow cosmopolitanise himself as, say, Roman Polanski or Omar Sharif have done. 'Certainly,' he says, 'I want to go back. One day, I shall. But that day has to be one of success. I go back a winner, not a loser.'

Dignity, he insists, comes first. He has never surrendered his dignity. The measured tone is a far cry from the violence and the torture which he has come to know, and to depict, so incisively.

He speaks 'as an artist' and strenuously qualifies his socialism. 'Revolution,' he argues, 'is not something I seek personally —but objectively it is required. The long-term aim is democracy.'

Yilmaz Guney

His political views are anathema to the present Turkish regime, and he himself, while he acknowledges that he has Marxist convictions, rejects socialism as practised in the Soviet Union, China, and Albania. The Russians he describes as 'revisionist, decadent and imperialist.' Not a single country, he claims, deserves to be called socialist; Turkey, on the other hand, has yet to cut its links with feudalism.

The Ataturk legacy, which remains inviolable and sacrosanct in official Ankara thinking, he divides into two. 'He freed the country from Ottoman rule, belongs to us and we have pride. But immediately after settling up the republic (in 1923) he became a dictator. Our anti-democratic traditions date from this period.'

His films, according to critics, are permeated by a certain bleak fatalism, but Guney says his heroes are 'smashed' because they have chosen the 'wrong' way. In *The Wall*, they struggle and are defeated. 'But it is not that there is no hope. It is that there is no hope in this situation. The outside world thinks there has been a transition in Turkey towards democracy; all the facts and the reality suggest it is just a show.'

Inevitably, when asked whether he is an optimist or a pessimist about his country's future, he replies – with a twisted smile – that he is a realist. He tries not to be subjective and through his many contacts in the country admits that his 'conception' at the moment has little chance. Thus he now seeks through his films to mobilise international opinion.

'My aim now,' he adds, 'is to succeed in organising a broad alliance of all those forces who proclaim themselves for democracy and against Fascism. Today, they are divided and it seems hard to coalesce. But they have common goals—and the groups are coming together.'

His own role, outside the world of films made for minority if discerning audiences, remains difficult. He moves from safe house to safe house in various West European countries, accessible only by devious routes and through trusted contacts. 'In a way,' he agrees – with another twisted smile, 'it is changing one prison for another—but security is not my main concern.

'I miss my people, their ordeal, their pains, and I want to share their hardship.' But, he says finally, he has no immediate plans.

This was one of the last interviews given by Guney before he died in Paris on 9 September, 1984.

Interviewing Oguz Aral can be totally disarming. First, there are whole areas of conversation – mainly political – that are *sub judice* because of Turkey's extraordinary political situation. Second, he is likely to get into animated discussion with his translator. Third, he is apt to seize the interviewer's pen and start drawing a satirical cartoon to underline his point.

'I want,' he says, 'to change the spoons.' This, having drawn a little man with a very big spoon (the capitalist) and a big man with a very small spoon (the worker) trying to get their fill from a shared bowl of soup. Turkey and all its resources are that bowl of soup, but the real trouble is that there are others who get in the way of both. Progress is a series of interruptions.

Oguz Aral

Aral is unashamedly one of the signatories of the May petition. He is the founder and editor of *Gir-Gir*, the country's leading satirical humour magazine, with a circulation approaching 500,000. His brother, Tekin Aral, edits another comic journal called *Firt*.

He seems to enjoy provoking and being provoked. A couple of military regimes, interspersed with hyper-sensitive civil administrations of would-be democratic persuasion, have led to nearly 20 prosecutions in a dozen years, usually because the people he caricatures have not liked his way of seeing them. 'Life,' he says, 'has always been fun.'

The latest military takeover in Turkey – in September, 1980 – is likened by Aral to open-heart surgery. The complication is that the country has been both patient and surgeon. The patient, in a sense, has lost and is weaker; the surgeon has gained. Now is the time for therapy and convalescence; the Army is going very carefully.

Aral's situation is clearly unique—prosecution and official castigation are routine to him, but he also counts some of the country's leading politicians among his friends. The present Prime Minister, Turgut Ozal, with thick horn-rimmed glasses, a heavy-jowled chin that is covered in stubble, and a short, stocky figure is a gift for his cartoonists—but he has been to *Gir-Gir* offices for a chat several times. A framed caricature, not all that kind, is on the Prime Ministerial desk in Ankara.

In the last three years or so, the magazine was stopped just once—for offending with a drawing, in the 'wrong' context, of the national flag. For four weeks it was off the streets, but readers responded by sending in the cover price just the same. Their Turkish lira notes were initially hung on the wall of the editor's office; then they were used to give a decent burial to a colleague who died suddenly. That is Aral's way.

He argues that Ozal becoming Prime Minister, as a gesture towards full democracy, has been the magazine's 'biggest loss'. During the preceding period, when Ozal was a chief economic adviser, he drew the man frequently in all sorts of quandaries. Now he can be drawn in every publication that appears—and, Aral claims ironically, his ideas are being filched.

The magazine, which gets its bizarre title from the noise made when cranking up an engine to make it work (or laugh), is his life and he gets restive if kept away, even on holiday in London, for too long a period. Perhaps this is why he draws the answers to some questions.

It started 13 years ago with three people – Aral, his brother, and a friend – and a circulation of just 40,000. Today it is ten times higher with 50 professional contributors, all drawn originally from the readership, and some of whom send their offerings from prison. A prime qualification to draw from the magazine is to be one of its regular 'natural' readers. Aral's greatest joy is to pass someone in the streets of Istanbul or Ankara and hear them laughing out loud at its humour. 'That rarely happens in any other country,' he says.

Aral reached his position on the magazine after a career in the theatre and in cinema. He had also done a spell teaching amateur boxers—something which gives him some pride, as if fighting had always been essential to him, Occasionally he sighs heavily. Asked his age, he answers: 'I am 49. But I was tired when I was born, and I have been 49 all my life.'

This pen is mightier . . .

Haifaa Khalafallah
Published 21 September 1984

Satire like this has made Naji Al-Ali the highest paid cartoonist
in the Arab world. It also made him a wanted man during the
worst of the fighting in the Lebanon during 1982. Almost every
major faction was after him for the comments his work made
about them every day in the Beirut daily newspaper, *al-Safir*,
and other Arab publications. Ask him why he never came to
harm and he replies, scratching his silver hair, 'They were
looking for tough guys. Who would suspect that someone who
looks like me could be harmful?'

Al-Ali is a Palestinian and the nearest thing there is to an
Arab public opinion. Deeply concerned at the lack of political
expression and participation across the whole Middle East
region he has assigned himself the role of spokesman for the
mute majority and uses political cartoons instead of words, for
they are not easily censored. It also helps, of course, that it is
not necessary to have a political vocabulary or even the ability
to read to understand them.

His work, published daily in Cairo, Beirut, Kuwait, Tunis,
Abu Dhabi, London, and Paris in publications ranging from
far Right to far Left, expresses opinions about almost every
sensitive subject in the Middle East.

He has made enemies and has been deported from a number of
countries, denounced by different social groups, and physically
threatened. Yet, he emphatically refuses to speak about his
oppressors and those who try to censor his work. He draws
them instead.

One reason is that he draws more easily than he talks. But
he also believes the lack of democracy and freedom of speech is
universal in the region and at the root of every problem.

Al-Ali has no political affiliations, and it is the absence of
slogans and dogma in his caricatures that has brought him
both success and criticism. Some say he sees the world only
through political eyes; others that he is not political enough.

Political cartoonists are a recent innovation in the region,
except in Egypt. Apart from illuminating political crisis in
the Middle East, al-Ali's accomplishment lies in taking Arab
artistic appreciation on from words and poetry to drawing and
illustration.

He sees the period in Beirut as the best part of his career and
says the affluence in the Gulf, where he now lives, has restricted

his creativeness in ways he does not understand. Perhaps this is because he feels that refugees (he was brought up in a refugee camp in South Lebanon), and poor people in general are his kith and kin and his inspiration.

Lifted by the Winds of Paradise

Yasser Arafat　*Published 7 December 1984*

Democracy is not just a political slogan. It is a way of life. In a democracy the people must be free to say what they think and what they want—which is why I insisted that all of the liberation fronts and groups should be included in the PLO. And I have always believed that this freedom was essential to our struggle. My own slogan is that *only free men will fight*. Now let me tell you what I mean.

From the beginning I knew that our struggle would be a very long one and that it would have to continue for many years, perhaps even beyond the lifetime of my generation. I also knew that we would be the defenders and the Israelis would be the attackers once we had demonstrated that the Palestinian problem could not be swept under the carpet. And this is where my slogan is important.

Do you think my people would have continued this struggle for so long, and would have suffered so much pain and misery, if the only reason for continuing was the fact that I was dictating to them at gunpoint? Of course not. Our resistance continues because it is the will of our people freely expressed.

To tell you the truth it is not by our guns that we have survived against such impossible odds. If it was a question of guns and military technology we would have been finished many years ago. Israel is the superpower of the region and we are resisting it with the equivalent of bows and arrows. We have survived because of our democracy.

If you are an ordinary Arab and you live in a dictatorship under a regime which you know doesn't care what happens to you, why should you give your life for such a regime? This was the lesson the Arab regimes ought to have learned after the 1967 war. So I repeat, we have survived because of our democracy.

A delegation of leaders and notables representing the whole Muslim community came to see me [in Beirut]. They came to plead with me to give up the fighting because, they said, the PLO's position was hopeless and there was no point in causing more casualties.

Yasser Arafat – we have survived because of our democracy

They said to me: 'Why are you going on? The Arab regimes are not going to help you. The governments of the world are not going to help you. Has anybody promised you anything? No. If you had evidence that something was coming to help you, we would continue to support your struggle. But nothing is coming. There are no miracles . . . So please, Abu Amar, we ask you to give up the fighting now.'

I said to them: 'My dear friends, if that is what you really want I am ready now, this moment, to give the order to stop the fighting. You have the right to ask me to stop and I will respect your wishes. But first, please, listen to what I have to say.' And then I spoke to them about the lessons of Arab history. It was a long talk and I made many points.

In the end I said we owed it to future generations to stand and die if necessary. I said that if we gave up our struggle now, the spirit of Arab resistance would be crushed for ever. And finally I spoke of the sickness in our existing Arab world. I said the sickness existed because each new generation had been betrayed by its fathers. And I asked them a question. I said: 'Are we going to be just like all the other generations and betray our children, or are we going to be the first generation to set an example of how to be steadfast?'

When I had finished they came close to me and their tears were flowing. They said: 'Abu Amar, we are ashamed of what we said. You must fight on and we will die with you.'

In August, Israeli tanks completed their encirclement of West Beirut and seemed to be closing in for the kill.

Although I didn't tell my colleagues at the time, I was completely upside down – confused – for some hours. I couldn't understand how the Israelis had completed their encirclement in just six hours. So I went and I prayed for 30 minutes. And when I finished my prayers, I said to my colleagues, 'I feel the winds of paradise are blowing . . .'

According to our religion and our traditions I was saying two things. First, that I was ready to fight and die as a martyr and so to enter paradise. Second, that I expected to die. Then I issued my final battle order with that slogan: 'The Winds of Paradise Are Blowing'. The change in the morale of our fighters was unbelievable, incredible. I can't tell you how things changed. If the Israelis were really coming all the way into Beirut, we were ready for them.

Alan Hart: 'You really were expecting to die?'

'Oh yes,' said Arafat. 'No doubts. No doubts at all.'

These views were expressed by Yasser Arafat to Alan Hart while he was writing Arafat—Terrorist or Peacemaker? published by Sidgwick and Jackson.

The long march of the Kurds

Christiane More   *Published 17 January 1986*

Two hours north-west of Sulaymaniyah on the way to the
Iranian border, you pass the last Iraqi army post. From there
on, you are in a sort of Kurdish Wild West, a barren country,
where villages and springs are few and far between. The Patriotic Union of Kurdistan (PUK) has its own checkpoint here, in
the 'Liberated Zone'. Since 1983, this has been the refuge of
the armed opposition groups to the Khomeini regime; from here
they conduct their operations with Baghdad's blessing.

Each of these groups has set up its headquarters here—
mudwalled, earth-roofed houses for the top brass, tented villages for the rest. These settlements have been set up alongside
the scattered villages in the area, which are built into the
mountainside, giving it the appearance of a gigantic stairway.
Smuggled goods are openly on sale here—Adidas trainers
(made in Iran), samovars, Iraqi cigarettes and Kalashnikovs
side by side with crates of Pepsi and blocks of ice. Radio trans-
mitters have been installed, field hospitals, training camps,
primary schools and even prisons (for Iranian captives) have
been set up.

There is fierce rivalry between the two main factions competing for public sympathy in the area; the Kurdish Democratic
Party of Iran (KDPI) brings in medical volunteers from abroad
and organises mass vaccination campaigns, while the Komala
(Kurdish Communist Party of Iran) relies on the dynamism
and commitment of its fighters. A large number of young people,
including a high proportion of women, are attracted by their
revolutionary and egalitarian fervour.

A dozen 'peshmergas' (Kurdish freedom fighters—'those who
precede death') conduct us to Alan, near Sardasht inside Iran,
at the foot of Mount Nori, which is patrolled by 500–600 Iranian
soldiers. We pass the Komala checkpoint where smugglers
exact customs duties, issuing an official looking 'receipt'. The
political groups share control of the crossing points between
Iran and Iraq and the dues are one of their main sources of
income.

We are now in territory controlled by the Komala. Gunfire
can be heard in the distance. A few days before these villages
had been heavily bombarded by Iranian cannon and mortar
fire. On this side of the mountains, the villages are much richer,
set amid lush gardens and orchards. Local people offer the
peshmergas bed and board for the night.

● Kurds: 10 million people in Iran, Iraq, Turkey, Syria and Soviet Armenia.

● Kurdistan is the homeland claimed since the late nineteenth century in northern Iraq, north-western Iran and southern Turkey.

● Main groups based in Iraq: Kurdish Democratic Party of Iran (KDPI), allied with Iraqi government; Patriotic Union of Kurdistan (PUK), shaky recent alliance with KDPI.
Based on Iranian border: Kurdish Democratic Party (KDP), allied with Iranian government; Kurdish Communist Party of Iran (Komala), opposed to KDP and KDPI.

● 1975 Algiers accord between Iran and Iraq threatened all Kurdish movements.

● 1975 KDP almost wiped out.

● 1979 Khomeini took over in Tehran, KDPI briefly hoped for autonomy under new regime.

● 1980 Gulf War began.

● 1982 KDP sent back into Iraq from Iran.

● 1983 Iranian government offensive against Kurds began new phase.

At nightfall the peshmergas take over control of the territory from the Iranian pasdaran (revolutionary guards), who retreat into their bases. We are invited to supper in a house where the main room serves as a dining room-cum-bedroom. A plastic sheet is spread on the floor and a supper of rice and yoghurt appears. On the draining board stands a samovar which has been brewing all day, and tea will be served continuously until bedtime. Weak tea is swallowed with a lump of sugar held between the teeth here in Iranian Kurdistan—in Iraqi Kurdistan they drink it strong and sweet from the glass. The mountains unite the Kurds – they belong to them – but they also divide them. This detail is one of many that illustrate how the Kurds adapt to the customs of the country where they live. The alphabet, of necessity, is another: Iraqi and Iranian Kurds use Arabo-Persian script, Turkish Kurds use the Roman alphabet and the Kurds in the Soviet Union use the Cyrillic.

Whichever group one belongs to, listening to the radio is an important part of the evening—one's own station, the opposition's, the broadcasts from the Islamic Republic, all foreign stations broadcasting in Iranian or Kurdish, especially the Voice of Israel.

A woman fighter with Komala: 'free and invincible'

With the KDPI, the evening discussions touch on the current political situation in Iran, on the murderous armed conflict in which they have been engaged since January with the Komala and on the recent Iraqi bombing of nearby villages. With the Komala, organised evening meetings are compulsory. They spend their time questioning, convincing, explaining, educating . . . Parwin, 22, is a student and a committee member of Komala in Alan. After our five-hour trek, she takes off her Kalashnikov and ammunition belt and helps prepare a meal.

Then she organises a meeting to discuss the Khomeini regime's decision to evacuate the 66 villages in the Sardasht region.

Nearby, in a tented village, Shaikh Ezzedin Husseini, a respected Kurdish Sunni religious leader and opponent of Khomeini pleaded with us: 'In the name of God, tell the world that the Iranian Government is trying to evacuate the areas where the Kurds are living to establish its sovereignty, that it is harassing the Kurdish people to try and cut them off from the peshmergas. Khomeini is destroying all life in the Alan and Seusni region. Tell them that there is a people here suffering injustice and resisting to win the right to self-determination.'

Another three-hour trek from the Komala HQ takes us to the HQ of the KDPI, which is considered to be a class enemy by the Komala. The general secretary of the KDPI, Ar Qasemlu, tells us: 'The Komala have always refused to cooperate with us in any real sense. We proposed a single military command structure, but they refused. For four years there were clashes between us and the Komala but only of a localised nature and we collaborated when the situation became militarily dangerous. But now they are waging all-out war against us.' During the evening conversation Khomeini is forgotten, as is the economic blockade and the Iran–Iraq war—all they can talk about is getting their revenge on the Komala.

Qasemlu explains the presence of his party and that of the other Iranian opposition groups in this border area. He says that he does not consider himself a hostage of the Baghdad Government. 'If you look at the map of Kurdistan, you'll realise that we are surrounded, geopolitically speaking. Geographically we have no access to the sea. Politically we are surrounded by more or less hostile countries (which is the least that can be said of the Turkish government). If any country offers us unconditional freedom of movement, then we will cooperate with them, as we are doing with the Iraqi Government. We – Kurds and Iraqis – are both fighting the Khomeini regime. Although we are effectively fighting on the same side of the barricade, we are not fighting on behalf of the Iraqi government; our struggle began long before the Iran–Iraq war, which is useful for them. We consider this *de facto* cooperation to be legitimate since it helps the liberation movement of the Iranian Kurds.

'We would never do what Mustafa Barzani did, and what his sons in Teheran are now doing, that is to say, form an alliance with a foreign government which would be harmful to the Kurdish people. Thus, our alliance with the Iraqi Government is in no way directed against the Iraqi Kurds.' In any case, the physical support which these Kurds receive from the Iraqi government is minimal—the peshmergas rely largely on the vast Middle East 'Kalashnikov market' for their supply of individual weapons.

The KDPI have come a long way since the party was founded in 1945 with the creation of the Mahabad Republic (this Kurdish Republic was set up by the Soviets and British allies to offset the political void caused by their occupation and lasted only a year). Last August, in this no man's land, an important meeting took place to mark the fortieth anniversary of the party's foundation. It brought together the leading figures of the Iranian Kurdish parties (apart from the Komala) and Jalal Talabani, leader of the Iraqi PUK. Talabani had spent the best part of a year negotiating with the Baghdad Government for an improvement in the status of the autonomous region, but no agreement was signed and between February and December, 1985, his committee had engineered the kidnapping of more than 30 foreign hostages in Kurdistan to bring the Kurdish problem to world attention and to force foreign companies working in Kurdistan to pay a tax to finance the revolution.

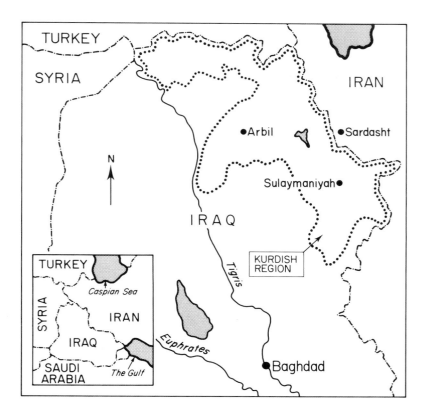

The Iranian Kurds seem to be well-entrenched in their rebellion and there seems to be little likelihood of the situation changing as long as the Iran–Iraq war continues and as long as Khomeini, who refuses to discuss autonomy, remains in power. But the hope born of the 1979 revolution is still very much alive and the Kurds feel themselves to be essentially free and invincible in their mountain strongholds.

Trekking through the mountains with the peshmergas, in their trainers and plastic shoes (no robust mountaineering boots here), one feels that this Kurdish optimism about the future must sometimes wear a little thin. They travel light and lightheartedly—they carry only a Kalashnikov, a radio, and some sticky tape (to secure the tightly folded messages which every Kurd carries to and fro for relatives and friends). They laugh, they sing and joke. But their cheerfulness alternates with sadness; their songs are mournful, the songs of homeless men, dreaming constantly of love but for ever making war.

5 INTERNATIONAL AID – THEORY AND PRACTICE

Wanted—a new map of the world

Dudley Seers *Published 28 May 1982*

It is high time to take a hard look at European attitudes to the South (or Third World) in the light of developments both here and overseas. Most of us have shared a sort of liberal consensus: the Third World countries need capital and technology, which we should provide at low or zero cost; also we should allow their exports of industrial products to enter our markets at cheap or preferential rates.

Now this all seems very obvious, part of our map of the world. I am going to suggest that we need a new and very different map that corresponds better to the realities of the Eighties.

Our attitudes to the South had their origins in the colonial period. The economic pattern of empires was highly profitable. Minerals and crops were secured for European economies, while simultaneously investment opportunities were provided, and markets opened for our industrial products.

The economic benefits were not only enough to finance the armies and navies that protected the colonial system, the bureaucracy that administered it, and the capital and technical progress to strengthen it—they also facilitated raising wages and salaries in Britain and other metropolitan countries and expanding social services so the suffrage could be broadened without danger of far-reaching political change.

Those responsible for colonial administration claimed, however (and apparently believed), that they were helping to civilise the people in the colonies. This meant exporting our institution—educational, social, economic, and political. Schools modelled on those of the metropolis were set up, at first by religious missions. (Many Africans, in particular, had to join a number of churches in turn in order to climb up the educational ladder.) These were followed by technical colleges and universities.

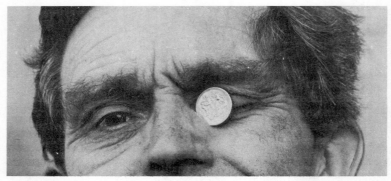

It's time for the industrial powers to look beyond simple gain and old-style relationships

Political participation was gradually increased in colonies as part of the process of 'education for self-government', which involved passing power by stages to those identified as 'responsible' leaders.

Now the point is that it was always the imperial centre that defined progress and decided which leaders were responsible and what the pace of decolonisation should be. Some, like those in the Fabian Colonial Bureau, used to argue for greater confidence in national leaders, even those with a radical rhetoric. But there was little appreciation of the absurdity, indeed the arrogance, of anyone in Europe taking up positions about helping people overseas whose languages and cultures were barely understood. The assumption on all sides – that we knew what is good for them – is the essence of paternalism.

By 1945, the colonial powers had been greatly weakened by the two world wars and the system was ceasing to be so advantageous. In due course, independence was conceded to virtually every colony, not because of a series of considered judgments that they were all suddenly 'ready' for it (there had actually been little 'progress', especially in Africa), but simply because of a realisation of the rising costs and falling benefits of holding on to them in the face of increasing nationalism. Metropolitan Governments that were slow in seeing this (e.g. the French in Algeria, the Portuguese in Angola and Mozambique) paid a high price.

But in general the breakup of the colonial system was by no means a disaster for its masters. The basic pattern of exchanging industrial for primary products did not change much or rapidly: indeed, new investment opportunities were opened up. The industrial countries still dominated the world politically, financially, culturally, and in military might. Their living standards became even more distant from those of the millions of landless labourers, peasants, and urban slum-dwellers in the tropics. So it is not doctrinaire to call the new system that has emerged 'neo-colonial'.

Although leaders in the former colonies have, of course, more political power at home now, their use of it has in many cases been limited by economic difficulties especially in the past few years. This has made many of them highly dependent on support from the governments of the main industrial countries, including aid provided bilaterally or through multilateral agencies which these governments dominate, such as the World Bank and the IMF.

But aid is only one component in the package. Approved governments are allowed trade concessions. They are given political support, e.g. *vis-à-vis* neighbours. They are provided with military training programmes and arms.

Actually it does not really matter – any more than in colonial times – what rhetoric political leaders use (they can call themselves 'socialists' or even 'Marxists'), provided they do not adopt policies hurtful to foreign companies, default on debts, or provide military bases to the Soviet Union. Those that have erred in these respects, such as Castro, Ho Chi Minh, Allende, and Michael Manley have been punished, if not by military action or overt destabilisation then by trade sanctions, and the abrupt withdrawal of aid.

Just as humanitarian motives were not entirely absent in the colonial system, so they also enter into policy towards the South. But this clearly reflects in the main commercial and political interests. Otherwise support would go mostly to governments of the 'least developed countries', which showed some willingness to allow the poor to mobilise politically and responded to their needs.

In reality, the governments that are given the greatest support are mostly the ones that are in 'strategic positions' (like Turkey) or deeply in debt to private banks (again like Turkey), whatever their resources and however repressive their regimes.

Elites overseas who cooperate in running the neo-colonial system do so because it provides them with a lifestyle consistent with their self-respect. As mass social and political awareness increases with literacy, etc. the only way that this highly privileged lifestyle can be maintained is by keeping at bay those who would claim a share in the benefits of economic growth. This implies repression of those advocating change or even making political criticisms. In much of the Third World many people 'disappear' each year, not merely in Argentina, Chile, Guatemala, and El Salvador. A new technique of government is emerging. There is little need to bother with due process of law; those who are suspected of being dangerous are mugged, tortured, or killed by security officials in plain clothes.

Some aid goes directly or indirectly to buying interrogation equipment, tanks, and jet fighters. An increasing part is used to finance the interest payments on debts to private banks. Much is used to buy Mercedes cars for the big landowners, contractors, officials, and ministers who take their cuts on aid projects.

So aid is one of the links that bind the system together, and propaganda like the Brandt Report that treats it as just a sort of international welfare benefit is dangerously misleading. Increasing aid would doubtless ease the conscience of the aid lobby—but only so long as they do not worry much about its social damage overseas.

No doubt a member of the aid lobby will say that this need not happen. Aid could be provided only to the 'good' democratic governments that urgently require it and would spend it responsibly, without too much corruption. But in the first place most of the aid agencies do not in fact provide aid only, or even mainly, to such governments. And even those donors, such as the Swedes, who concentrate aid on a few 'good' governments, are, through that very policy, deeply paternalistic. Some of the forms of paternalism have changed since colonial times—though there is an even bigger emphasis on population control. On top of the old aims based on exported European feminism and fears of political instability overseas, there are fresh concerns now arising out of the declining proportion of Europeans in world population and the danger of the shortages of world supplies of oil, metals, and crops needed by the European economy.

It is less implausible in fact to argue that benevolent policies towards the Third World are in *our* interest. The neo-colonial system has been benefiting practically everyone in the North. It has made possible a further development of the welfare services that started in the colonial period.

However, buttressing the system often turns out to be a bad investment for the donors, notably what was provided to Idi Amin by the British and Israeli governments to help him replace Milton Obote—who was considered (then) politically unreliable.

It is sometimes argued by those on the right that concessions to the Third World are nevertheless necessary to contain Soviet expansion. But in the first place, Soviet influence, like our own, often turns out to have results quite different from what was intended—Egypt was once a big recipient of Soviet aid. Moreover, it is now clear that the Soviet Union lacks the economic resources and the technological leadership it would need to run a big, colonial system of its own in the South.

The Russians have enough of a problem controlling and developing the Asian colonies inherited from the Czar and new ones such as Cuba: they could not afford, for example, to save the Allende Government in Chile.

Basically, a pro-South policy is hardly in 'our' interest any more because the neo-colonial system is becoming less beneficial to us. It will be a liability, in time, if it is not already, just as the colonial system became a liability after the Second World War. The main fundamental reason is the same, rising nationalism in the South.

The programmes of industrialisation in the South are cutting into our export markets. Moreover, in several countries tax-free and subsidised industrial zones are being established (in some cases, made possible by aid) to promote the penetration of our domestic markets too. It is true that many of the firms which benefit from such subsidies (and from a docile labour force) are 'ours'. Much of the exports of Singapore, e.g. are really made by foreign companies. But is this the best use of European capital in view of our own unemployment problem, especially since much of the profits are not repatriated.

Anyway, really large profits cannot so easily be made any longer by European firms that invest in the South. The governments there are becoming less inept at bargaining and at monitoring foreign investment. And as they buy more arms (often with loans) and as political cooperation in the South grows, Northern military intervention to protect investments becomes more expensive, and less likely to succeed, as has become clear in the Falklands. In fact, the danger of major wars is implicit in the neo-colonial system, as in its forerunner.

Furthermore, only the US Government has the resources now to police the system: at least its acquiescence is needed if Britain or another industrial power plans military intervention in the South. This is not automatically available nor is it politically costless.

The aid required to run the system looks increasingly expensive when our own economic and social infrastructure is starved of capital, and it is no longer clear that our institutions are what we need ourselves let alone suitable for export. The relatively weaker technological capacity of Britain now also means that many economic concessions to the South promote the exports of other industrial countries as well as our own. In addition, the rules of the system require us to keep our doors open to imports of Japanese cars, televisions, etc.

The diminishing value of the neo-colonial system (to Britain especially) does not imply that we should completely and rapidly cut our links with the South. Eliminating aid to Bangladesh, for example, or refusing trade concessions, would not only hurt the local elite, it would also have some impact on the poor there who are in a very precarious position as it is. Moreover, as long as democratic institutions survive in Europe we can provide facilities for education vastly superior to what is available abroad, not in the sense that our techniques are suitable abroad, but because we can make available opportunities for discussion and study impossible now in most of the world. We also still have a role as a haven for political refugees.

In addition, suddenly delinking from the South would shake our own economic structure, which is still heavily dependent on imports of food and industrial materials.

Breaking with the South would mean, quite apart from its effect overseas, politically unacceptable rates of unemployment and inflation. As long as the governments of the United States and Japan use aid for promoting their exports, we are bound to do the same.

But the emerging world system will be, I hope, less asymmetrical. I am not talking about the 'New International Economic Order', which is essentially a programme for the elite of the South to get a bigger share of the benefits of the neo-colonial system. What is required, I believe, is a considerable reduction in economic links with the South and thus much less need for political intervention, military support, private investment and aid (which always go together). We could then give up trying to spot 'responsible' leaders and shape policy overseas.

But how would this help people in the Third World? One possible answer is that it would be a response to their increasing emphasis on 'self-reliance'. It would lessen the pressure of outside advice, and the cacophony of ideologies, theories and techniques we emit, which is so loud and persistent that those in the Third World can hardly hear themselves think.

But the real reply is that we no longer rule the world. The sooner we realise this the better—for almost everyone.

Dudley Seers was the former director of the Institute of Development Studies at the University of Sussex. He died on 21 March, 1983.

The world we are handing to our children

Fidel Castro *Published 25 March 1983*

The world is undergoing one of the worst economic crises in its history. This crisis has most severely affected underdeveloped countries and indeed, its effects have been worse in these countries than in any other area in the world. This holds true particularly for those oil-importing underdeveloped countries whose growth rates, which had averaged 5.6 per cent from 1970 to 1980, dropped to 1.4 per cent in 1981 and probably lower in 1982.

A decisive factor has been the drop in commodity prices since late 1980. The prices for sugar, coffee, cocoa, tea, palm oil, coconut oil, sisal, cotton, alumina and practically all commodities have dropped significantly. Even oil prices, which started to decline in late 1981 as a result of the crisis, have fallen faster in recent weeks, due among other things to the policies of British and Norwegian firms which have started a price war.

It has been estimated that the losses experienced by oil importing underdeveloped countries in two years alone – 1981 and 1982 – amount to some $29 billions. With the decline in commodity prices and the continuing high prices for manufactures and oil, the inevitable result is the worsening of unequal exchange affecting most of the Third World.

To illustrate this phenomenon, here are some examples:

In 1960, 6.3 tons of oil could be purchased with the sale of a ton of sugar. In 1982 only 0.7 tons of oil could be bought with the same amount of sugar.

In 1960, 37.3 tons of fertilizers could be bought for a ton of coffee. In 1982 only 15.8 tons could be bought.

In 1959, the sale of 6 tons of jute fibre could buy a 7-8 ton truck. By late 1982, 26 tons of jute fibre were needed to buy the same truck.

In 1959, one ton of copper wire could buy 39 X-ray tubes for medical purposes. By late 1982, only three X-ray tubes could be bought with that same ton.

These terms of trade are repeated in most of our export commodities, and this situation is coupled with the growing protectionism in Western markets against exports from the

Third World. Added to the traditional tariff barriers there is now a wide range of non-tariff barriers.

It is not surprising under these conditions to see the extraordinary increase in the Third World's external debt, which last year passed the $600 billions figure and according to econometric projections, will reach an incredible $1.473 billions by 1990.

The situation is now such that underdeveloped countries are forced to incur new debts with the sole purpose of meeting the obligations of the debt itself. This huge debt drains the underdeveloped countries' export earnings, without the countervailing flow of real resources for development. It is in itself a denunciation and conclusive evidence of the irrationality and inequity of the present international economic order.

The underdeveloped world's agricultural output is also facing a serious crisis today. Accelerated population growth, coupled with the growing deterioration in soil, fertility and losses resulting from erosion, desertification and other forms of degradation, suggest even greater difficulties by the end of the century.

Though the current average of less than 0.4 hectares – about one acre – of agricultural land per Third World inhabitant is insufficient, by the year 2000 this ratio will be less than 0.2 hectares.

Between 1975 and 1980, world food production per head grew at the very low rate of 0.3 per cent a year. In the developed capitalist countries it grew 8 per cent in 10 years. More than 70 underdeveloped countries have seen a net decline in food production. To maintain the already minimal food availability, underdeveloped countries have had to increase their imports. In 1980 alone, import values amounted to $52.3 billions.

Industrialisation is a decisive process in the Third World's economic development. It means in strategic terms, laying the main technological and material base for progress. The model that postulates agriculture and raw materials as specialised enough for the underdeveloped countries, leaving industrial production in the hands of developed countries, serves only to perpetuate the model which our countries firmly reject as irrational, unequal and unjust.

UNIDO has predicted that, if present trends continue, the underdeveloped countries – with over 80 per cent of the world's population – will be contributing only 13.5 per cent of world production in the year 2000.

Claims about the supposedly positive contribution transnationals may make toward the development of the Third World countries are not new. The underdeveloped countries are offered a transnationalised development model, which would turn them into 'export platforms' of manufactured products for the world market.

But the results of such transnational industrial development are proven by the fact that, for instance, in the 1970s, for every new dollar invested in all the underdeveloped countries, transnationals repatriated approximately $2.2 to their home countries. So far as US transnationals are concerned, during 1970–1979 they invested $11,446 million and repatriated profits amounting to $48,663 million, which means a $4.25 return from the Third World for every new dollar invested in that period.

Obviously, then, the industrialisation of the Third World must not amount to the sorry left-overs of the transnationals after the brutal exploitation of the underdeveloped countries' labour resources, the depletion of their natural resources, and the pollution of their territories.

It has been rightly said that true development should be measured, not by growth rates but rather by what has been termed the 'quality of life'. But when we attempt to measure factors that indicate the quality of life, considering not only its dramatic present, the picture we see regarding the future of the underdeveloped countries appears even more impressive.

In 1980, three out of every four of the world's population lived in the underdeveloped world. On present growth trends, from 1990 onwards, there will be 95 million additional inhabitants in the underdeveloped countries every year. From now until the year 2000, the underdeveloped world's population will grow three times faster than the developed world. That is, more than 90 per cent of the total population growth in the period up to the year 2000 will occur in our countries.

Until recently, the year 2000 seemed an indicator of a distant and unforseeable future. But two-thirds of the world population in the year 2000 are already living today; the infant population born each day in our countries will comprise the overwhelming majority of the adults by that time; the children who will be 15 in the year 2000 will be born just two years from now.

Whatever measures are taken today to protect them, to prevent death and illness, to provide food, housing, medicine, clothing and education, they will shape the lives of a decisive percentage of the world's future population.

But, looking at present trends, what sort of world will we hand over to those children? What sort of life lies ahead for those five billion mouths that will have to be fed in *our* underdeveloped world, those five billion bodies that have to be clothed, shod and sheltered, those five billion minds that will strive for knowledge, those five billion human beings who will struggle for a decent life, worthy of the human condition? What will *their* quality of life be like?

By the year 2000, in the developed countries as a whole, the annual GNP per head will amount to almost $8,500, while in the underdeveloped countries it will remain under $590. The value of gross production, which in 1975 was 11 times lower for the underdeveloped world than for the developed world will be 14 times lower by the year 2000, thereby increasing the inferiority gap. Our countries will be poorer.

At current growth rates, the poorest countries would need two to four thousand years to bridge the gap separating them from the present level of the most developed capitalist countries.

Food is another index of the quality of life with the greatest negative impact on underdeveloped countries. According to recent FAO data, 40 million people – half of whom are children – die every year from hunger and malnutrition. If we were to keep a minute of silence for every person who died in 1982 because of hunger, we would not be able to celebrate the coming of the twenty-first century because we would still have to remain silent.

In 1975, in 80 underdeveloped countries, more than 10 per cent of the population suffered from undernourishment. In 49 of them, this figure was over 15 per cent. While tens of millions of people literally starve to death in the poorest countries every year, health statistics from the developed countries reveal a continuous growth among the highest-income population strata in the incidence of illness resulting from an excessive food intake.

Future projections are not similar, but are equally grim. FAO, for example, estimates that 10 years from now 150 million human beings will join those who are currently suffering from hunger and malnutrition.

For its part, the World Bank estimates that the number of undernourished will rise from 600 million in the mid-1970s to an impressive 1.3 billion in the year 2000. UNICEF anticipates that in the year 2000, one out of every five children in the world will be malnourished.

While in the developed countries life expectancy ranges from 72 to 74 years, in the underdeveloped world this rate does not pass 55 years. In Central and Western Africa, life expectancy fluctuates from 42 to 44 years.

According to the World Health Organisation, infant mortality – fluctuating from 10 to 20 deaths per 1,000 live births in the developed countries as a whole in 1981 – amounted in the poorest countries to a figure ten times higher.

UNICEF has stated this reality graphically and dramatically: of the 122 million children born in 1980, 12 million (one out of ten) died before the end of 1981, 95 per cent of them in underdeveloped countries.

During their first year of life, nine out of 10 children in the poorest countries are never given the most elementary health services, much less are they vaccinated against the most common childhood diseases.

The executive director of UNICEF has said that in 1981 the life of a child would be worth less than $100. If such a sum were judiciously spent on every single one of the 500 million poorest children of the world, it would cover basic health assistance, elementary education, care during pregnancy and dietary imrpovement, and would ensure hygienic conditions and a water supply. In practice, it has turned out too high a price for the world community. That is why, in 1981, every two seconds a child paid that price with its life.

Malaria kills one million children a year in the African continent. Nevertheless, it is estimated that the world cost of malaria campaigns would only amount to $2 billion a year—a sum equivalent to what mankind invests in military expenditures every 36 hours.

This is an edited extract from President Fidel Castro's speech to the non-aligned summit. The issues are treated at length in The World Economic and Social Crisis by Fidel Castro, published in Havana, 1983.

Alibis for playing the bad Samaritan

Robert Cassen   *Published 9 September 1983*

The developing countries today have suffered the worst setback since the 1950s. They grew rapidly in the 1950s; less so in the 1970s but still making progress. Now at the start of the 1980s their growth has fallen off drastically. Gross domestic product in Latin America has *fallen* by 3.6 per cent between 1980-82. Developing countries' exports fell in 1981 and 1982 to a point 7 per cent below what they were in 1980. Low-income African countries are the worst affected: according to the World Bank (1983 Report), it is quite possible that their income per head will be lower at the end of the 1980s than it was in 1960.

The record of North–South cooperation in recent years is not wholly empty. But protection is still advancing rather than retreating, and there is no sign of action on measures to assist the trade of the poorer developing countries. The only areas in which some gleams of hope remain are on Special Drawing Rights, where the proposal of a new allocation is not yet dead, and some areas of World Bank assistance.

Why is the North so negative? Let us look at some of the most commonly offered alibis:

'The recovery which has started in the world economy will take care of the developing countries' problems.' In fact we do not yet know how firmly based this 'recovery' is, and whether it will prove any more lasting than previous glimmers of anticipation in 1981 and 1982. The current OECD forecast is for 2 per cent growth in the industrial West in 1983 and 3¼ per cent in 1984. Such expectations could be defeated if interest rates fail to fall, or any of a number of other things go wrong.

However, even under scenarios more optimistic than this, two important Third World problems will not be resolved. The countries with major commercial debts, especially Brazil, Mexico and other Latin American countries, need export growth more rapid than such a modest recovery will provide if their debts are to become manageable without additional international support. As it is they are beginning to cut into living standards, with dangerous political consequences—in Brazil, for example, where the first fragile efforts at democracy in many years are seriously threatened by the austere economic regime imposed by external events. A recent assessment by economists of the Morgan Guaranty Trust Company, in a projection with OECD growth averaging 3½ per cent to 1985, 3 per cent thereafter, and a number of other favourable assumptions, suggests that debt burdens in such countries will not be reduced to the point where they can borrow freely again in the market till at least the end of the decade, even with rigorously austere policies.

Also, a recovery of such modest dimensions will have little effect on the poorest countries whose foreign earnings mainly depend on exports of primary commodities. While the average of commodity prices began to climb off the floor in November 1982, the rise has mainly been for metals and other industrial inputs; tropical beverages in particular are still struggling, and with past over-production and substantial stocks, together with slowly rising demand in the main (industrial country) markets, prospects are poor. The World Bank's surmise already referred to, that low-income Africa may be worse off by the end of the 1980s than it was in 1960 (in per capita terms) is, again, based on a fairly optimistic scenario of world growth; even in its most optimistic scenario (or 'high case') 'by 1995 low-income sub-Saharan Africa still fails to regain its 1970 per capita income'. Plainly, 'recovery' by itself is not enough.

Now for 'aid does not work'. Aid is attacked from several ideological quarters, both left and right, and often in ways that are mutually contradictory. One thing on which they are agreed is that aid does not 'reach the poor' in the Third World, or that, in an excessively fashionable taunt, aid is a transfer from the poor in rich countries to the rich in poor countries. In fact there are two questions, whether aid assists growth that in turn helps the poor; or whether aid reaches the poor directly.

On the latter question, it is only in the last decade or so that aid donors have made major attempts to initiate directly 'poverty-orientated' projects. The evidence for such of those projects on which there are published evaluations is that they do, with relatively few exceptions, reach poor people (though not often the very poorest people); and they also show a high rate of return. (In other words there is no conflict between 'poverty-orientation' and economic efficiency.)

Since the proportion of aid devoted to such projects is not large, however, one must ask about the contribution of aid in general to growth and poverty reduction. Here one is let down by the absence of recent research. But it can certainly be said for a large number of developing countries that aid has considerably raised the level of investment: in sub-Saharan Africa, aid constitutes 8 per cent of GNP, 40 per cent of imports, and 54 per cent of investment. For all least developed countries those figures are 10 per cent of GNP, 50 per cent of imports and 81 per cent of investment. While poverty has certainly not been abolished in these countries, and will not be for many years, it is not pleasant to contemplate what their prospects would be without aid.

'Development should be left to the private sector.' There is much that the private sector can and should do to promote development. In recent years much of the heat has gone out of the controversy about the role of multinational corporations. Developing countries have acquired, or can borrow from international agencies, the technical expertise to bargain for better contracts with the companies; and the companies, or some of them, have learned from experience that more desirable relationships can be built if malpractices or exploitative behaviour are avoided. The relationships are still far from perfect, and the countries still have some good reasons for being wary, just as the companies have reasons, at times justified, for being dissatisfied with the treatment they receive.

All that said, the notion that the private sector can replace government in most developmental activities is absurd. The private sector will not finance large infrastructure investments such as dams, hydroelectric stations, roads and the like; nor will it take on welfare activities in education or rural health; or carry out agricultural extension or ... the list is long. Nor can private finance cope with the kind of balance of payments problems countries are currently experiencing.

In the poorest countries the role of private capital is likely to be limited for a long time. They find it difficult to attract foreign private investors; and in the domestic economy the problem often is that a commercial sector simply does not exist and can take years to foster into being. Thus in India, for example, if you want to get a road built, many private construction firms will tender for the job. In several African countries there may not be any firms at all. It is partly for reasons of this kind that governments have taken on activities which elsewhere are left to the private sector.

If genuine Third World development is in our interest, why do we do so little to secure it? It is very commonly a question of the victory of short-run expediency over long-run desirability; of sectional over broader interests. But often it is a question of ignorance.

The standard of public debate on these issues is deplorably low; the media give little attention to the profounder issues, indeed to any development issues save disasters and conflicts. When they occasionally do debate the important questions, they like to present battles between extremists. Hence the prominence given to the passionate and wrong-headed opponents of cooperation, parts of whose case I have answered here.

From a lecture to the 1983 meeting of the British Association for the Advancement of Science.

The economic squeeze that promises to end in catastrophe

Charles William Maynes
Published 30 September 1983

The world is on the verge of a human catastrophe and a political disaster that America seems determined to ignore, notwithstanding the great damage it will do to her security and welfare.

While Washington's attention is riveted on whether the debt crisis in the Third World will weaken or seriously harm the banking structure in the West, developing countries are being put through an economic wringer that is undoing the achievements of several decades. Countries that achieved independence in the early 1960s and began the process of modernisation in the early 1970s are now being demodernised. Investment projects are lying idle, children are not being taught, disease is spreading, beggars are filling streets from which they have been absent for decades, people are looting food shops, and the middle class is being destroyed by bankruptcy and high interest rates.

Increasingly, the economic strains that Third World governments are experiencing are proving too great for existing political structures to sustain. We seem to be entering a period like the 1930s, when economic distress triggered violent revolutions from Vietnam to Nicaragua. If this economic crisis is not solved there will be political upheavals that can pose grave dangers to the United States.

Perhaps we no longer fear the nexus between economic crisis and political change because in recent years the industrialised North has shown remarkable political stability in the face of economic adversity. Governments have fallen in every major industrialised democracy in the last few years, but, unlike the 1930s, there has been no major challenge to the system itself.

This stability, however, may be a tribute to the safety net of the welfare state that even developed countries are finding very expensive to maintain. Most developing countries do not have such a net; they are faced with the anger of disadvantaged populations, and there is good reason why these populations should be angry.

In the last 30 years, local governments, aid donors and international organisations have uprooted traditional ways of life of Third World people and urged them to pursue the path of 'economic progress'. Pushed by economic conditions from the farms and villages and lured into the cities as development economists emphasised industrialisation over agriculture, these people turned cities like Jakarta, Mexico City and Lagos into wretched megalopolises. In only three years, for example, the population of the Lagos area has risen from 100,000 to 1.5 million, and by some estimates, to 3 million. It is as if all the pain and misery that people in the West experienced over more than 100 years of movement from country to city has been compressed into a period of three decades.

After many years of effort, citizens of Third World nations were beginning to make the adjustment from one way of life to the other, only to be told now that mistakes were made, that the future is no longer bright, and that they should return to a way of life they have abandoned. But the agricultural skills have been lost – the land has been taken – and the family unit is no longer organised to sustain the previous existence.

Even without taking China into account, the last count of the International Labour Organisation put the number of unemployed or underemployed in the developing countries at half a billion. Unemployment rates have been increasing faster than in the developed countries and may now be around 40 per cent.

Although the modest recovery in the developed North will have some positive impact on the developing countries' export markets, overall the situation looks bleak. Receipts from commodity exports have dropped perhaps 25 per cent in the last two years.

Whole continents have seen their hopes for the future disappear. According to the World Bank's 1981 report on Africa, the net flow of outside aid into Africa will have to double by 1990 if average per capita incomes are to stop eroding and begin to increase again significantly. On the other hand, if the established patterns continue, the overall per capita growth rate will be zero or negative, and there are alarming possibilities for even steeper downward spirals in some, as populations continue to grow.

Developing countries, to maintain their growth, need a regular flow of commercial loans and government grants from abroad. Yet, according to Morgan Guaranty, if the 20 per cent increase in net new bank lending to Third World countries that occurred in 1981 did not take place in subsequent years, the developing countries would lose about $50 billion in investment funds from abroad. The consequence would be a drop of three percentage points in their real growth rate. Growth in Latin American countries perhaps would decline by more than 5 per cent. That is only a prediction, but, regrettably, reality seems to be supporting it. In the first quarter of 1983, private bank lending to the developing countries dropped to almost nothing.

The effects on the Third World of these reversals are extraordinary, real income for the average person in these countries has declined for three years in a row. Sacrifices that the industrialised world has not experienced since World War II are being imposed on helpless populations. In Chile the International Monetary Fund is demanding a 50 per cent cut in government spending, even though Chile's unemployment rate has risen from 4 per cent to 26 per cent in the last two years. In Argentina, following IMF guidelines, the government is attempting to cut its budget deficit by an astonishing two-thirds, even though the unemployment rate has tripled in the last two years.

It is no coincidence that there have been massive street demonstrations in those two countries in the past few weeks. The military governments in Santiago and Buenos Aires are in difficulty, with pressure for political change coming even from their own supporters.

Developing countries are already rebelling against IMF discipline. The main debtor countries of Latin America met in Caracas last month to discuss common action. Although the consensus at the meeting has reduced pressures for a time, many politicians in South America continue to talk about declaring a moratorium on debt payments.

In Africa, populations are actually returning to the bush. Thousands of Ghanaians expelled from Nigeria during the last year had no work to go back to in Ghana. They had to retire to their villages. Africa today has millions of people moving across borders and within countries in a search for survival.

Even the favoured are suffering. No country in the Third World has been as blessed by the arrival of Ronald Reagan to power as Jamaica. The President has repeatedly cited the victory of Edward Seaga over Michael Manley as a victory for democracy. Jamaica, which the administration would like to turn into a showcase, now is the fifth largest per capita recipient of US assistance. Nevertheless, unemployment is nearing 30 per cent and a major foundation of the Jamaican economy has become the illegal drug shipments to the United States.

There is a Potemkin village quality to the Jamaica seen by foreigners. Government officials urge potential foreign investors to visit the two 'model farms' run by Israeli investors. But these employ only a few hundred people. Meanwhile, Seaga's free market policies, which are operating in a harsh international environment, have proven to be a catastrophe for the thousands of small farmers whose products cannot compete with cheap foreign food, and who cannot find jobs in the city.

Jamaica is a good example of the problems Third World governments are facing today.

Seaga has not misgoverned Jamaica. In his first year in office
he curbed the rate of inflation, increased tourism and attracted
the interest of foreign investors.

But any effort to float one boat in the fleet higher in the
water than the others will fail. Jamaica has found that its
economy floats at the same level as its neighbours, notwithstanding a favoured place in US aid disbursements. Investors
cannot be attracted to Jamaica when the world economy is in
such difficulty.

Will the Third World accept its economic fate without major
political protest? Here the lessons of the 1930s are instructive
and chilling. In Latin America the collapse of commodity prices
in the great depression helped stimulate 50 revolutions by
1943. In El Salvador, a rebellion and the brutal repression that
followed claimed tens of thousands of lives. The anger and the
mythology that help fuel Salvador's civil war today date from
that conflict.

In Asia, too, the collapse of sugar, rubber and other commodity prices encouraged vast political changes. The sugar
issue set off the first American attempts (sponsored by sugar-
state senators) to grant independence to the Philippines.
Gandhi began his civil disobedience campaign by seizing on an
economic issue when he led a march to the sea to make salt
illegally. The collapse of Vietnam's colonial economy led to the
first serious challenge to French authority there since the turn
of the century. Although put down, it fuelled hatreds against
the West that blazed again in the '50s, '60s and '70s.

In the 1980s the predictable consequences of economic depression will be reinforced by a powerful new factor: the large
number of young people in the Third World. Social scientists
have long identified a correlation between youth and violence.
The 1980s may be a new age of disorder.

A world away from women's liberation

Soon Young Yoon   *Published 7 September 1984*

An international feminist movement united, embracing all
races, raising a single voice of protest against world hunger
and political oppression—is still a dream. Many Western feminists are impatient to make this dream come true. As they see

it, the world is on the frontiers of a feminist revolution, and it
desperately needs their help.

**Consciousness raising in the school of life: girls pumping
water in Andra Pradesh, India**

At international conferences, these women bring their own
gospel of how to liberate women. They pound the platforms to
defend the Third World women's rights to end female circumcision, domestic violence and rape. They are trying to build the
foundations for a movement they know can change human
history.

But in Mexico City and Copenhagen, many Third World
women rejected this leadership of the West. At the forthcoming
UN Conference on the Decade for Women in Nairobi they will
probably do the same. They accuse American and European
feminists of being obsessed with sexual issues and of paying
too little attention to poverty and national liberation. They see

the Western initiatives as another example of high-handed missionary zeal among the supposedly unknowing, and they resent what they see as feminist imperialism.

They do not appreciate international attention when it sensationalises patriarchal violence among Asians and Africans and ignores the greater violence of infant deaths due to hunger and wars. Third World women do understand internationalism, but only when it is based on a principle of equality. That is a lesson which has been difficult for many in the US and other Western countries.

The controversy concerning female circumcision in Africa illustrates the point. Female circumcision and infibulation are forms of sexual mutilation which vary from minor cuts near the clitoris to complete removal of all external sexual parts. They are recognised as major contributors to infections, infertility and diseases such as fistula in adult women, and may account for a high percentage of infant deaths in Africa.

However, female circumcision is not a 'barbaric practice' of Third World countries alone. Until the end of the 19th century, it was also reported in Russia, England, France and the United States. In all cases the aims are similar—to 'control female sexuality' and enforce patriarchal custom. But the degree of mutilation as well as its meaning varies widely: in some African countries circumcision is reduced to a tiny ritual scar, and many women may believe that it will ensure their fertility and sexual power.

In the last few years, female circumcision suddenly made headlines in the Western media. American and European feminists rallied around the cause demanding that governments enforce anti-circumcision laws. Pictures of operations were widely circulated, petitions were signed, and UNICEF speedily passed a resolution of protest. African women were not pleased.

As Belkis Giorgis, a leading African expert in public health, wrote, 'the debate being waged between certain Western women and African women has arisen because of the conflict between certain Western women's desire to perform a civilising mission and African women's desires to define their own ways and means of struggling against oppressive structures . . .'

In a similar tone, Alasebu Gebre-Selassie of Ethiopia, speaking in Geneva at a work group on female circumcision, said, 'I am not enthusiastic about the problem being talked about in the West. Sensationalising the subject is an insult, and it doesn't help to change the situation for women in the countryside of Ethiopia.'

The furore created in the West also gave little credit to the African women's own efforts against female circumcision; yet much is being done. The Association of African Women for

Research and Development has actively condemned the practice of female circumcision. In 1979, at the second regional conference on the Integration of Women in Development in Lusaka, participants passed a resolution appealing for the solidarity among all African women to combat harmful female circumcision while recognising the value of African tradition.

Projects are underway in countries such as Egypt and Ethiopia which emphasise local and national action, and participation of women's non-governmental organisations. As many African women see it, the problem must be tackled by the women in each country because they alone understand the complexities of the problem and its cultural context.

The lessons learned from this experience can also be applied to other issues. One of these is birth control. In an effort to give Third World women reproductive freedom, many feminist groups supported international programmes on family planning. Although they never actively supported coercive population control programmes, they often did not fight against them.

In some cases, working through the International Planned Parenthood Association, Western feminists promoted introduction of oral contraceptives and intra-uterine devices into developing countries where there were no health facilities. Not only were the priorities wrong, the pills caused severe side effects and IUDs introduced new iatrogenic diseases among malnourished rural women. Many died of complications.

Again, development resources were placed in the hands of feminists who did not understand the Third World women's experiences.

Whether the issue is birth control, rape or circumcision, Western feminists do not seem to understand the reluctance of Third World women to 'go into the streets' to protest or even to confront the problems openly in public debates. The absence of aggressive campaigns involving masses of women is interpreted as a problem of consciousness-raising. With that comes a feeling that they should support Third World women who appear to be isolated advocates of feminism in their own countries.

The truth is that Third World feminists are often isolated, but this has little to do with states of consciousness; it has to do with survival. In Egypt, Nawal El-Sadaawi was imprisoned for her writings advocating feminism. In India, girls may be impoverished and disinherited for open protests against dowry and arranged marriages. The consequences of confrontation must be borne by those who struggle, and these are the realities which so often escape outsiders.

The histories of women's struggles and their socio-political contexts are different, and when Third World women say that they do not want to carry on their movement like 'Western feminists', they are expressing this simple truth.

Where, then, is the role of international sisterhood? Many Third World women have been radicalised to such a point that they no longer believe it is possible. They are also wrong. Just as Third World women are not a single, homogeneous group, neither is there such a thing as a Western feminism—it is a false target. There are many sisters to be allied with among progressive groups in the West and minority women of colour living in the advanced industrial countries.

But some things will also have to change. A lead has been taken by Danish feminists working within international development agencies. For example, Kirsten Jorgenson, a consultant for DANIDA, has acted on behalf of Third World women by ensuring that the development aid money is channelled into women's programmes and that policies encourage Third World women's participation and self-reliance.

As for an ideological unity, Western feminists must acknowledge that 'political issues' like the racism in South Africa and human rights in South Korea are feminist issues and that they have priority over others such as lesbian rights. An international list of feminist issues would show many common interests among women in all countries such as the struggle against domestic violence. And, disadvantaged women in the West rightfully see themselves as members of a Third World.

The problem is the unequal distribution of power and resources, for this has allowed a few to set the feminist agenda for the many. Third World women have recognised this, and demand a more equal share of both so that they can fight for their own cases, as they experience them, and as they wish to have them known. In their own movement, American and European feminists would surely ask for nothing less.

A debt bomb primed for the next recession

Andre Gunder Frank
Published 12 October 1984

Henry Kissinger said in the 1970s he did not give a damn about the Third World, but has now joined the chorus of those who express serious concern about its debts. Last year he wrote that 'the current rescue effort to "solve" the debt problem is insoluble in the immediate future.'

He went on to criticise IMF conditionality for 'contracting the economy, increasing unemployment and reducing consumption' in Third World countries, and then turned to his main concern: 'At risk here is the internal political evolution of several developing countries, including many important friends of the US. If the debt crisis winds up spawning radical anti-Western governments, financial issues will be overwhelmed by the political consequences.'

Kissinger returned to the problem in a recent article in which he observes that 'there is no chance of any principal being repaid for a decade or more. Even interest payments will become politically unbearable unless handled as a political and not a technical economic problem. Continued refusal to accept these facts will provoke a political confrontation between the US and principal Latin American debtors.'

What Kissinger neglects to mention is that the same mechanism which turns the economics of debt into a political problem also makes it increasingly difficult if not impossible to reach political agreement on reconciling the conflicting economic interests. His faith in statesmanship is insufficiently modest and realistic in the face of the 'technical economic problem' that policy makers will face through the cumulation of debt, rise of interest rates, bunching of debt maturities—and the next recession, which threaten to explode the debt bomb.

There have been more than 40 recessions since industrial capitalism began around 1800 and four since the beginning of the present world economic crisis in the mid-1960s. None has been essentially modified – let alone prevented – by economic policy, and all have significantly affected, if not determined, economic policy formation instead. No responsible or informed business, government or academic economic analyst or observer now doubts that another recession will come. The question is when, and with what consequences.

There has been debate about whether the next recession will or will not precede the presidential elections of next month, and how it would affect the outcome of the election. But it would be more realistic to consider how it will affect the policy of the next US administration. The last two recessions, after all, have vitally affected, even changed, the policies of American, other industrial, Third World, and socialist countries' governments.

Not only will the Third World debt bomb be detonated by the next recession, but consumer credit, corporate debt, and various level government debts, now receiving much less attention than their dangers merit, may also explode and the detonation of any one of them can explode any or all of the others and accelerate the development of the next recession. There also is a massive bunching of debt maturities in the mid-1980s.

Thus, these debts constitute a time-bomb whose fuse is about as long as the present recovery, which started in 1983 and may well not end until next year or the year after. The next recession must explode the debt bomb if it is not defused before.

If the pile-up of debt permitted the 1973–75 recession, but then aggravated that of 1979–82 through the resultant liquidity crisis as we have seen, it will become clear that any failure to resolve this problem of the transition from liquidity crisis to insolvency will inevitably mean that the next recession and its renewed strain on Third World balance of payments, will make one country after another completely insolvent. They will simply not be able to continue servicing their debts, no matter what policy is pursued in the North or the Third World itself.

The most authoritative analysis of the debt crisis remains *International Debt and the Stability of the World Economy*, by William R. Cline, published by the Institute for International Economy in Washington last year.

Cline asks whether the debt crisis is one of liquidity or of insolvency. By way of answer, he constructs economic model simulations for the period 1983 to 1986.

Under the most favourable projections, the crisis is only one of liquidity, which can be managed and which will be only temporary. But this conclusion is based on projections of economic growth rates for the OECD industrial countries in the world economy of 3 per cent a year up to 1986 and other assumptions about oil prices and other variables.

But Cline does not contemplate another recession until 1986, and beyond that he makes no more projections. But any realistic analysis of world capitalist development during the present crisis should project the coming of the next recession, most probably before 1986, and very possibly with growth rates of far less than 1.4 per cent if not negative growth rates as in the two recessions already past, as well as other variables.

Cline himself recommends contingency planning in case his optimistic projections are not borne out by facts, and he considers a further decline in the price of oil as the most likely factor leading to a possible default. This is because it would hurt each of a few oil exporting countries more than it would help the many oil importing countries.

But the question remains: if these dangers and those that Kissinger, Robert Muldoon and others see are so serious and so imminent, why does not somebody do something about them? But who and what?

In the world financial poker game it is quite rational to

continue to bargain while the money keeps rolling in. The US retains relative financial dominance based partly on the lack of a realistic alternative to the US dollar as a major world currency, and the US is able to continue to operate with other people's money. A large portion of the US armaments programme is being paid for, not by the American tax-payers, but by others in the world who are financing the US deficit. While American banks and industry expect the present situation to continue into the indefinite future, it is rational for them to play this financial blackmail against the Third World and indeed against their European and Japanese partners or competitors. It is also rational for the others to go along with this game and to play by the same rules.

But what is rational for each player in the short run, is irrational in the medium or longer run for all the players. The resulting arms race and the now continuing debt pile-up aggravate the situation through each round and make an accidental explosion of the debt bomb increasingly likely.

The debt bomb could bring on a financial crash that would make the present system of international trade and payments no longer workable. Moreover such a breakdown of the financial and economic system would generate further pressures for a financial and economic war among economic blocks – a dollar zone, a mark zone, a yen zone, maybe a rouble zone – and the increased economic and political conflict could also erupt into military conflict with war as a result.

The situation in the Third World is analogous. Competing interest groups there also try to live in the present. As long as the system continues to operate at all – as long as finance and trade keep flowing, albeit with difficulties – the cost of trying to introduce any radical change is very high, especially if attempted in isolation, and particularly if it is a small country.

In this case, any default, for instance, could be 'covered' and the defaulting country could simply be excluded from international finance and would have to pay cash for all further imports. If Brazil or Mexico were to default or even to declare a unilateral moratorium on debt finance, its apparent power would be greater, precisely because debts of these countries are so great and any payment stops would be threatening to the banks.

The other alternative, of course, is a debtors' cartel. There have been many proposals to form such groups, or to negotiate or even to declare moratoria as a group. Even so, at the Latin American finance ministers' meetings with the Americans, held in Caracas last year and at the Latin American Presidents' meeting in Quito earlier this year, such debtor cartel proposals were rejected. The principal objections came precisely from the largest debtors, those who are most concerned about keeping up their credit ratings to get large new loans they need and who have little interest in making common cause with their smaller and weaker neighbours.

In spite of all this, a part of the Kissinger concern is realistic in that more radical measures – and, as he fears, by more Left radical governments – may still be adopted, not so much as a mattter of policy but as a matter of fact, once there is no alternative.

When, as a result of the next recession or before, it has become physically impossible to continue to service debts then there simply has to be a moratorium or default. When that happens it will not be a matter of policy but a matter of fact.

US aid strings tighten

Alex Brummer   *Published 1 February 1985*

When the White House budget director, Mr David Stockman, sent his ideas for budget cuts to Congress in December it caused the inevitable anguish just down the road at the development banks. Having failed in a first Reagan term to cut off the flow of funds to the multilateral banks, Mr Stockman, who appears to enjoy taking swipes at the poor (at home and overseas), took aim again.

His confidential paper sent to the Republican-controlled Senate budget committee argued against any new funding for the multilateral banks beyond current commitments. The proposal, which at best would have saved a few million dollars at a time of horrendous economic decline and famine in Africa, so angered one Congressional aide that he wrote a steaming memo back suggesting the real targets of his attack ought to be the billions of dollars of grants made each year to Israel and Egypt.

The importance of Mr Stockman's proposals is his belief that he could get away with it. The complexities of the World Bank and IMF are generally not understood on Capitol Hill where populist resentment of banking and multilateralism run high. Moreover, Mr Stockman believed this was one bureaucratic battle within the administration that he could win.

For the last four years the Reagan Administration, cheered on by ideologues within the treasury, has been conducting an undeclared guerrilla war against the Bretton Woods Institutions. Ironically the US is the largest shareholder in the

IMF and World Bank and one of the founding fathers of the International Development Association (IDA), the bank off-shoot which makes no-interest loans to the poorest of the poor.

On virtually every major issue to come before the Bretton Woods Institutions since President Reagan was sworn in, the Reaganauts have been on the wrong side. Indeed, the US has been so extreme on issues such as new funds for the IDA that other conservative governments, notably Mrs Thatcher's, have appeared at times to be on the side of the angels. The statistics provide a record of their own. In the four years of President Reagan's tenure the Administration has voted down some 50 routine loans made by the World Bank—the largest record of disagreement with lending policies in the bank's 40-year history.

The current effort by Mr A. W. Clausen, the president of the World Bank, to establish a special fund for sub-Saharan Africa provides a useful case in point. The success of such a fund inevitably rests on American support. Without US partici-pation, other large donors, notably West Germany and Japan, are unlikely to go along. But while the US publicly supports the project it is refusing to tip in any money.

Its reasons are largely ideological and political. President Reagan, who watches TV a great deal, has been personally stunned by the African famine. As a result the response of the Agency for International Development, America's aid arm, has been exceptional—one billion dollars.

But Mr Peter McPherson, the director of AID, has made it clear there is nothing in the kitty for the bank's sub-Saharan African scheme, which is for longer term economic reform. This Administration likes bilateral aid which can be dished out with political strings attached. It views the aid budget as a geopolitical tool.

As a result of this do-it-yourself approach the sub-Saharan African initiative is in some trouble, in spite of considerable efforts by Mr Clausen to get it to fly. Representatives from donor countries are meeting in Paris, but the US is not offering money and the three-year Africa fund, instead of being $2 billion, as envisaged in last August's report by the bank, will be lucky to make $1 billion. This in spite of public American praise for the scheme.

Cash flow turns into a torrent

Michael Simmons   *Published 22 March 1985*

THE FIVE LEADING AID AGENCIES					
Agency	Director	Full-time saff	Supporters or helpers	Voluntary income This year (est'd)	last year
Oxfam	Guy Stringer	about 700	20,000	£40m plus	£23.9m
*Save the Children	Nicholas Hinton	860 (incl. part-time)	818 branches	£38m	£16.5m
Christian Aid	Martin Bax	about 160	3,000 cttees	£20m	£11.2m
Cafod	Julian Filochowski	36	700 support groups	£12m	£6m
War on Want	George Galloway	16	6,000	£6m plus	£1.7m

* Roughly two-thirds of Save the Children's income is devoted to work overseas

Against the rumblings of a distant war against famine, Britain's aid and development agencies compete strenuously – and very successfully – for funds. In the five months since last October they have collected as much as they did in the whole of the last financial year—much of it to feed the children of an Ethiopian regime which many Western Governments have anathematised.

The influx of funds on an unprecedented scale has led to new and unquantifiable strains on the agencies, as well as a certain genteel cut-throat competition in the market-place for the paying British conscience. The three biggest have recently changed, or are in the process of changing, their director, and Oxfam, the biggest, has created alarm among its staff by appointing an ex-regular officer as deputy director.

Thousands of pounds have been spent on advertising, not simply to bring in funds but also applicants for newly created posts in accountancy and computer use. Organisations which until now thrived on mainly middle-class preoccupations with aid and Third World problems, now find they are appealing to all social classes. They also find they are looking for skills pre-

Ethiopian appeal at Oxfam headquarters, Oxford

viously unsought in an essentially charitable and voluntary-run context.

It has led to the Oxfam fraternity competing with dozens of lesser known, even unrecognised, agencies for funds and to organisations like Help the Aged, apparently with energy and resources to spare beyond what it does at home, joining in. In its campaign the sweet old dear with a stick and wearing a woolly cardigan has been replaced by a wretched and emaciated elderly African or Asian.

With so much more money to spend, and with more 'clout' to argue how aid and development money should be spent, the agencies inevitably find themselves rubbing the Charity Commissioners and governments – and occasionally international organisations – the wrong way when it comes to the grey and thorny area of politics and political activity.

Last week, as Mrs Thatcher and her entourage flew to Moscow and the Chernenko funeral, she will have had little time to study the petition – supported by 760,000 signatures – handed in at Downing Street on Tuesday morning. Given the anodyne statements from successive aid Ministers, she will probably have had little inclination to accept the message in the accompanying letter.

This accused her government of an 'inadequate' response to the African famine, of misdirecting aid resources, failing to take a lead when one was desperately needed, giving less than Norway or Holland – or even Nigeria – to such a worthwhile organisation as the International Fund for Agriculture Development. In a rare public act of collaboration, the letter was signed by the directors of the country's seven leading aid and development agencies.

Politics, of course, means all things to all bureaucrats. Even the Charity Commissioners can be momentarily blind or deaf. Clearly, as almost all agency people agree, giving a hungry child something to eat is just as political as withholding something to eat. Building a well for one village means not only upsetting the local power structure; it can also mean not building one for the equally needy village farther on.

Last week in Geneva, a peculiarly UN event took place. Ministers, and a sprinkling of statesmen, came together under the benign eye of their host, the Secretary-General himself, to discuss the Africa famine. One by one, they delivered formal speeches, sometimes offering money, and then caught the next plane home. The agencies' reaction included anger as well as cynicism. 'It was,' said one representative, with long experience, 'a political charade.'

Away from the rostrum, the same conference gave delegates and officials scope to express their views of the agencies—or Non-Governmental Organisations as they call them. At one level, a UN official could say that while 'too many people were going round Africa with solutions to problems they do not understand', it was also true that the NGOs were playing a most important part. 'They are great,' he said, 'because they are small. They can get through to the villages, where it matters, and be effective.'

At another level, the Ethiopian Commissioner for Relief and Rehabilitation, Dawit Wolde-Giorgis, seized his opportunity to argue about priorities with the US Vice-President Bush, who had dropped into Ethiopia to see how things were before making his contribution to the debate, and Mr Dawit suggested that War on Want, which is operating in Tigre, was 'a war on Ethiopia organisation, helping bandits and terrorists.'

While that argument was going on, and as War on Want

marshalled its by now well-rehearsed responses, Oxfam's chairman, Chris Barber, until recently financial director of Associated Biscuits, was at the House of Commons addressing the All-Party Group on Development.

Starting from the (controversial) premise that probably no one in Britain was better qualified than Oxfam to speak for the world's poor, and buttressing his arguments with references to over 30 field officers at work in 76 countries, helped at home by more than 20,000 volunteers, he argued through case studies and factually backed debating points, that Britain should do more and should urge the Americans to do more in Central America, South Africa, Kampuchea, and elsewhere.

'If the children of people now in extreme poverty are to live in peace with our children and grand-children,' he told the MPs, 'We have to bestir ourselves. It's getting late.'

Unloading EEC grain

The MPs, predictably, were mixed in their response, not without agitation and some discomfort at the government's record. But civil servants who had burned the midnight oil at the Overseas Development Administration down the road to prepare the minister's speech for delivery in Geneva, did not even know Mr Barber was in town.

British agency impatience is not directed solely at British government efforts. The EEC bureaucracy, which can take months to solve a problem that should have been solved yesterday, is a regular target. So, too, increasingly, is the bureaucracy – especially 'in the field' – of the United Nations itself.

Seasoned agency officials are appalled, for instance, that the Food and Agriculture Organisation in Rome is barely on speaking terms with the World Food Programme, which is literally next door. They are angry that the UN, which has the machinery and the people, was so late in appointing an emergency co-ordinator for Ethiopia, that it has yet to name one for Sudan, that is has given no (published) thought to appointing one for Chad or Mozambique.

Running beneath the anger and the arguments is the philosophy, touched on by Djibril Diallo, of the UN Emergency Office for Africa, when he was in London last week, that 'one of the prime functions of aid is to get rid of aid'. In ten years' time, said a War on Want man not long ago, War on Want should cease to exist. To which another agency person replies that 'enough is never enough. We only pick at the problems which won't go away.'

But such rarefied arguments, say Christian Aid and others, are a luxury. The television cameras have now returned to base, the public's will to give has marginally slowed down, and what the Americans have called 'compassion fatigue' may be setting in. In Ethiopia and parts of the Sudan, the grain is finally getting through, while elsewhere, where infrastructural facilities are minimal or non-existent, the relief effort has yet to take off.

In parts of the Sahel where crops and battered morale would have been lifted by seasonal 'small' rains, no rains have come. The drought persists and what Oxfam has called the 'silent holocaust' goes on. Even though they are only working on a relatively small scale, the agencies derive an increasingly professional pleasure at the flexibility they can bring to bear, which governments and international organisations cannot.

There have been literally hundreds of applicants to fill the vacant post of director for Christian Aid, and Voluntary Service Overseas (VSO) is no longer astonished when it has about 30,000 inquiries a year, to fill about 500 posts.

Creating a helpful climate

Michael Simmons meets Sir Crispin Tickell of the Overseas Development Administration
Published 21 June 1985

Permanent secretaries of government departments are 'mandarins' who dispense wisdom with inscrutability, advise ministers with pugnacious impartiality, and speak to the outside world only 'unattributably'. Given the sometimes controversial, not to say niggardly, record of the present Government towards the Third World, this off-the-record posture suits Sir Crispin Tickell, chief mandarin at the Overseas Development Administration, very well.

'You can quote me,' he said after an hour's sophisticated but neutral conversation, 'on anything except Nicaragua.'

Since the Government has been highly ambivalent about Reagan's attitudes to Nicaragua, this hesitation is understandable. Tickell is happier to talk – at length – about the growing carbon dioxide content of the upper atmosphere. Climatology is one of his absorbing interests, and an early priority when he joined the ODA last October, was to commission from East Anglia University an assessment of climatic trends in sub-Saharan Africa.

His own thoughts are distilled in a little book he wrote as a fellow at Harvard University a few years ago. It has a sobering conclusion: 'The most precious thing we have is the tiny, damp, curved space which is our living room. The pleasantly warm moment we enjoy in it will not last forever. The room itself is changing, partly as a result of our actions, and we face intimidating responsibilities for it. We have no option but to meet them.'

From the cosmos to the windswept corner of Victoria which houses the ODA is quite a leap, but Tickell has had a distinguished career to date and could yet finish up running the Foreign Office.

Asked just how committed he is to the Third World, he answers precisely: 'It is a term about which I am very sceptical. Like "North–South dialogue", "developing countries", and the rest of the jargon, it is profoundly misleading. But I do feel a great commitment. The problem, after all, is as fundamental as nuclear war or world recession.'

By the same token, he rejects the word – or, as he says himself, 'challenges the concept' – aid. Help is the one he prefers. 'Aid,' he suggests, 'smells of Western experts, of making

people worse off at a cost of several billion pounds . . .' Help,
on the other hand, can be given, and is given, in various forms:
developmental, commercial, short-term, or political.

Political? 'Yes,' he says emphatically, 'but we are not in the
business of changing systems. We are responding to appeals
for help. We do, however, make judgments, and we are more
likely to help our "friends".'

Smiling quizzically he seeks to bring the conversation back
to 'the biggest problems' which he sees as 'over-population
and environmental degradation'. In other words, the effect of
climate on a country's past and its present. 'I don't have a bee
in my bonnet about it,' he adds, still smiling, 'but it is a
dimension which needs consideration. After all, there are cave
paintings in the Sahara depicting the hippopotamus . . .'

Quitters' folly

Basil Davidson   *Published 16 August 1985*

In the grand all-star scenario of the Reagan–Thatcher circus
there may be nothing as impressive as its claim to purity of
views and comment. They and their agencies do not and could
not tell a lie. Suppression or distortion of the facts is what the
public will never have to suffer from them. They simply tell it
as it is. They are defending democracy in Nicaragua. Their
hearts bleed for the victims of apartheid. They care most
warmly for the unemployed. If in Thatcher's case the governors
of the BBC decide to ban a programme, this is because the
governors have done it entirely on their own. But of course.

Another view will have it that the Reagan–Thatcher dispensation has produced, among other disasters, a notable lowering
in the standard of government attitudes to the honesty of
news and comment. An older fashion held that newspapers, for
example, ought to be measured for their virtue by the vigour
of their independent opinion, which is why, of course, *The Times*
of long ago was celebrated as 'The Thunderer'. Lately, judging
by the antics of the aforesaid scenario, the measure has got
itself turned upside down.

Now this may not be so. But the thought that it really is
so occurs to me with growing force when contemplating the
Reagan–Thatcher onslaught on Unesco and its director-
general, the sturdily contentious Amadou Mahtar M'Bow. As

it happens, I shall not be the first to sing the praises of Unesco. Its merits have not always shone, while a small-minded feeling of unease, whenever I pay my income tax, enters to prejudice the view of comfortable beneficiaries who pay no tax at all.

With due allowance for the frailties of tax-exempt human nature, it remains that Unesco has accomplished, and continues to accomplish, many good things attempted by no other organisation of its scope. One of these is the promotion of literacy in ex-colonial countries. Another is the encouragement of better schools and teaching in the same area. And the effort to secure wider and clearer channels of public information, free or less unfree from Big Brotherly (or Sisterly) bias, is undoubtedly a third.

It seems to me, rising above the income tax question, that Unesco has been and is, on balance, a thoroughly useful institution in spite of rotundities of staff, and the latter's occasional tendency to occupy salaries instead of jobs.

If criticism is needful, sometimes greatly so, this is no more the case than with other 'supra-national' organisations, not least the EEC. But Reagan and Thatcher have told us that their patience is exhausted. Ronnie has decided to pull out the USA, and Maggie follows suit.

I shall leave Reagan to his electors. But in the case of Thatcher, withdrawal will deprive Britain of any further say in the affairs of Unesco. Beyond that, seen from a national standpoint, it will be as large a blunder as the laming of the overseas services of the BBC and the British Council. Let the world get on without us, Maggie says; but if this may be an arguable position it is surely not a position that a prime minister could be expected to take. And the immediate reason for withdrawal, presented as deriving from the person and policies of M'Bow, is perfectly inadequate as well as perverse.

No one will be able to contest M'Bow's intelligence or probity, while his administrative and pedagogical records are in no way inferior to those of any of his predecessors in the job. It is M'Bow's political record and convictions which are really under fire. This is not because Reagan–Thatcher allege bias towards Moscow; and not even Caspar Weinberger in his wilder flights of oratorical intervention, I believe, would level any such accusation.

M'Bow's offence lies in his intellectual independence. Against a long personal record of anti-colonial agitation in his own country of Senegal, M'Bow persists in asking for more liberation of Third World thought and understanding.

His great crime is to have backed the enormously wide Third World demand for independent Third World news dissemination.

To this the Reagan-Thatcher axis replies that the Third World cannot be trusted with any such thing. Suppression and distortion, unknown in the free world of the West, would infallibly follow. This may indicate a controversy of some value. But quitting Unesco on any such grounds as those now used is merely stupid. To seek to excuse this by making a scapegoat of M'Bow is worse than stupid.

Why Britain should keep faith with the Unesco dream

Arthur Gavshon   *Published 4 October 1985*

Britain is under attack at home and abroad for its copycat threat to follow the US out of Unesco unless the institution quickly mends its ways. The Heritage Foundation, a wealthy, far-right Washington group, claims it master-minded the American–British offensive, and behind the scenes Washington and London have been urging the Japanese, among other conservative-minded governments, to consider walking out too.

The position of the Thatcher government is being assailed not only by Labour, Liberal and Social Democratic opponents in Parliament, but also by the Tory-led Foreign Affairs Committee of the House of Commons; member-states of the European Community; the Commonwealth and the entire Non-aligned Movement. No one disputes Britain's right to seek reforms. All recognise the validity of some British complaints. In fact, Unesco's 160 members have prepared a package of more than 100 improvements to be considered and probably approved at the coming regular biennial General Conference in Bulgaria. Britain's delegate, William A. Dodd, participated in negotiating reforms and only the other day expressed appreciation for progress so far registered. But he also stressed Mrs Thatcher's ministers still stand firm on their threat to leave unless and until they get their way.

While all this had been going on, Britain has been augmenting US attempts to convince Japan it too should serve notice of withdrawal. President Reagan first raised the idea with the Japanese Prime Minister, Yasuhiro Nakasone, last January. Since then there have been regular British–Japanese exchanges on the subject.

Britain's attitude has alienated friends and angered adversaries. In a still-secret report the Foreign Affairs Committee has concluded that coupling demands for reform with the threat to withdraw was tantamount to political blackmail. A British pullout, the Committee says, would be a greater danger to Unesco than the US walkout.

Gough Whitlam, former Australian Prime Minister, puts the view of Britain's overseas critics differently: 'There must be a better way of changing an organisation than by seceding from it.' Whitlam, now Australia's Ambassador to Unesco, adds: 'Britain would never have given notice to withdraw if America had not already done so.'

Ambassador T. N. Kaul of India, which leads the Non-aligned Movement, reflects Third World opinion when he warns fellow-delegates in the agency, as he did last month: if the American–British plan goes through it 'will end all forms of international multilateral cooperation.' It also would damage 'the whole UN system'.

The reality of this threat has been taken seriously. For years Heritage has been lobbying in favour of American disengagement from the system. A 1984 anthology, published by the Foundation and called *A World without the UN: What Would Happen if the United Nations Shut Down*, left readers with the impression most Americans would be better off.

Inevitably, the Heritage role in the Unesco crisis has attracted international attention, intensified when Foundation leaders boasted that they had been responsible for the American and British decisions on withdrawal. Edwin J. Fuelner Jr, Heritage President, asserted in a fund-raising letter last October that Reagan's walkout 'was a direct result' of a Foundation paper listing what he called Unesco's 'shocking abuses'. One month later Owen Harries, former Australian Ambassador to Unesco who joined Heritage to campaign against the UN agency, was delegated to London to influence British ministers and media.

Harries argued the Heritage case for American–British solidarity on the issue in meetings with three ministers—Education Secretary Sir Keith Joseph and Overseas Development Ministers Timothy Raison and Timothy Renton. He and the incumbent US Ambassador to Unesco, Mrs Jean Gerard, also had a series of private meetings with influential British columnists, editors and broadcasters.

In the weeks that followed a rash of anti-Unesco articles and editorials appeared. In that way a political climate was created which made it easy for Sir Geoffrey Howe to announce Britain's intention to quit Unesco at the end of this year unless major reforms were introduced. Harries last June told an interviewer he had been 'amazed' at the impact his lobbying had made on

British newspapers. Whitlam saw the episode differently: 'Few would have thought that a British government was so vulnerable and the British press so manipulable.'

The Heritage Foundation, formed in 1973, functions as a think tank and worries most about the whole world going Communist. With funds from Colorado brewer Joseph Coors, Pittsburgh multi-millionaire Richard Mellon Scaife and industrialist John Olin among others, it aspires to spread the values of 'responsible conservatism' and American socio-cultural exceptionalism around the globe.

It stood foursquare behind Ian Smith before Rhodesia became Zimbabwe; it services as a protagonist for President P. W. Botha's concept of preserving South Africa as a white supremacist state.

In a world polarised between east and west there could be no place on the Heritage agenda – which President Reagan has always respected – for the internationalism of the United Nations except as a target to attack. But the demands of strategy required the Foundation to focus first on easier, more immediate goals.

This brought the specialised agencies of the United Nations into Heritage's line of fire. Unesco, with its built-in intellectualism, its dissemination of knowledge rather than goods, thus became the obvious candidate for a campaign which Ambassador Kaul characterised last week variously as 'malicious', 'false', 'inhuman and medieval' in fact and in purpose.

- Unesco came into being in November, 1946, following a conference held in London, convened by the British Government.
- Headquarters: Paris. Director-General: Amadou M'Bow (Senegal).
- Budget 1984–85: $374.4m.
- Objective: to promote peace and security through international collaboration in education, science, culture and communications.
- Membership: 160 countries; Non-member: One (US); Uncertains: Two (Britain, Singapore).

Unesco was conceived by the wartime allies in London to promote world peace and understanding which, as the founders put it, 'begin in the minds of men'. It began life in Paris with 20 member-states and with the Soviets and their friends remaining aloof. Thus the Western powers were able to run the shop their own way until the countries of the awakened Third World moved into the arenas of international diplomacy in the late 1960s.

Since then Washington, London, Paris no longer can count on asserting their will or their wishes. A new word crept into the diplomatic lexicon: 'Politicisation'. It is a fancy way of saying the West does not have enough votes to keep unwelcome issues off Unesco's agenda.

So the battle for the survival of Unesco was joined and with it the concept of universality in an international system committed to the preservation of world peace.

The family of nations' poor relations

Eqbal Ahmad writes on the fortieth anniversary of the United Nations
Published 15 November 1985

The contributions of the United Nations organisation to keeping the peace in the world have been less than satisfactory. It legitimised for the United States and its allies in Korea, the internationalisation of the first large scale conflict after World War II and it remained paralysed for a decade during the historic and inhuman escalation of war in Indochina.

It has demonstrated scarce capacity to protest, much less prevent superpower military interventions in small countries, it has been unable to dislodge South Africa from its illegal 'trusteeship' of Namibia, and it has even failed to stop Israel from acquiring territories by force. More examples can be cited.

On its fortieth anniversary, the organisation in which the world had invested so much hope deserves a critical, even harsh appraisal. Yet, one fears giving comfort to anti-UN propagandists who would like it to be more an instrument of imperial purpose.

UN-bashing comes a close second to Arab-bashing in America's conservative political discourse these days. The fashion arose in the early 1970s as a reaction to the perceived decline of American power symbolised by the defeat in Indochina, and the loss of unquestioned US control over the United Nations and its subsidiaries. But the propaganda assault on the UN had a remarkably swift effect on official US policy.

The appointments, by Richard Nixon and Ronald Reagan respectively, of Daniel Moynihan and Jean Kirkpatrick as Ambassador to the UN, were obviously based on their reputation for polemics and their antipathy to Third World aspirations. Both have moved on but the image, which they helped consolidate – of the UN as a vehicle of Third World radicals – survives. Yet the perception of the UN as a Third World-dominated body lacks substance. To be sure, decolonisation has more than tripled its membership from 51 to 159 since 1945, and in the General Assembly the one member–one vote rule accords them considerable collective strength. The 'quota system' has also assured the Third World bourgeoisie a presence in the burgeoning UN bureaucracy.

But the focus of power in the UN remains the Security Council whose resolutions alone are mandatory. With the power of veto, the Council's permanent members – the big five (the US, USSR, UK, France, and China) – retain the decisive voice over the UN's primary role concerning questions of war and peace. Their veto all but cancels out the possibility of an effective UN contribution in situations involving one of the great powers or its ally. The US and Soviet Union are understandably the most frequent users of the veto. In the hierarchical structure of the UN system, the Third World is relegated to a subaltern rank.

The arena of Third World activism is the General Assembly. Here, the majority's voice is heard, heated debates are held, controversial resolutions are passed. Those ringing appeals for justice and peace, condemnations of apartheid, calls for an end to pioneer settlements in the nuclear age, demands for a New International Economic Order and a New International Information Order, are largely ineffectual. The General Assembly's resolutions are not mandatory; it has no legislative powers.

In some areas independent organisations frequently do better. Amnesty International, for example, is a more authoritative defender of human rights than the UN Commission on Human Rights.

Observers who have witnessed the misuses and sclerosis to which the great powers have subjected the UN, expect the Third World members to reform the organisation or at least put it to better use. The expectation suffers from the false assumptions that Third World governments are sovereign enough to perceive their interests independently of the dominant power; that they represent the aspirations and seek to defend the rights and welfare of citizens; and that they have the values and motivation to act collectively to attain a common goal.

In fact, dependence on a foreign power, poverty of politics, and illegitimacy of government are the characteristics common to all but a few states of the Third World. The modern state, served by centralised bureaucracies and well-equipped armies, and controlled by consumerist minority elites, is imperialism's gift to the Third World.

However, in one respect, the UN has increasingly served a Third World interest since the early 1970s.

Commanding a clear majority, the Third World delegations have frequently been using the UN, especially the General Assembly, to articulate their 'demands', and announce their political positions on important issues. When asked what was the UN's greatest contribution to the Third World, representatives of three countries had the same answer: 'It is the most important international forum for the airing of Third World viewpoints.' All three cited its role in popularising the notions of New International Economic and Information Order. Two, from Muslim countries, also mentioned the importance of the UN's 'contribution' to the 'question of Palestine'.

The least acknowledged contributions of the organisation have been those of its subsidiary agencies. For example, no agency has done more for the world's children than Unicef and few, if any, have administered famine and flood relief more judiciously than Undro (United Nations Disaster and Relief Organisation).

Also, no international organisation has done more than Unesco to preserve the ill-protected architectural and artistic heritage of the Third World, and when IMF and the World Bank decide to accord greater weight to the needs of Third World nations than to the preferences of American policy, they would do well to learn from the UNDP (United Nations Development Programme).

These and other agencies serve important world, especially Third World, interests. Yet, they are the ones most under attack by the United States. Ironically, they are also the more ignored and neglected by the Third World bureaucrats who stalk the corridors of the United Nations.

Can the UN be more responsive to Third World aspirations for development and democracy? The answer is a stark no, as long as the UN remains subject to the will of nation states. Recent press reports say that cholera has returned to Africa; at least 12 countries are believed affected by it. Thousands, mostly children, have been its victims. But because the governments concerned do not wish to acknowledge it – presumably fearing that the publicity might adversely affect their image, exports, and international travel of the elites – the state-controlled media describe it euphemistically. In self-styled Ethiopia, the authorised term is 'acute diarrohea'; in the Sudan, it is 'severe gasto-enteritis'.

The World Health Organisation, a UN agency, is bound by a charter which requires that unless a government formally reports an outbreak, WHO do not acknowledge its existence. Similarly, WHO and Unicef field officials were aware for months of the famine gathering in Ethiopia and the Sudan, but were prevented by UN rules and callous local governments from preparing world opinion and relief organisations to deal with the catastrophe.

The United Nations bureaucracy is undoubtedly larger than it ought to be; it is often wasteful, and always slow. The pay scales are more inequitable than an international organisation with pretences to social justice should allow.

The UN's record on employment of women is scandalous. Yet the UN bureaucracy is one of the few in the world that is engaged in peaceable, non-oppressive endeavours.

Meanwhile, many of the invaluable services sorely needed by Third World countries and provided by the UN go largely unused. For example, ECOSOC (Economic and Social Council) produces excellent research and advisory material, and few if any, Third World countries have the resources or the inclination to conduct this sort of necessary research.

In so far as it mirrors the world's ills, the UN performs a primary function. It works to the best of its limited ability for progress and relief of the needy. When occasionally the international power brokers and parties to a conflict agree on making peace, or ceasing fire, the United Nations comes in quite handy, providing the know-how, mechanism, and forces to keep the peace or enforce the ceasefire. In the process, its employees occasionally get shot at, run over, and kidnapped as they have been these last few years in Lebanon. When a state wishes to defy its authority it can do so with impunity, but to its own discredit and ultimate disadvantage.

The failures of the UN are not its own. An organisation of states, the UN can only be as good as its members at their best. That it is, for it does not engage in war, or torture or repression.

Creative force at the UN

Michael Simmons gives an appreciation of the work of Hans Singer
Published 29 November 1985

'It becomes increasingly evident,' wrote Hans Singer recently, 'that the type of proposals put forward by John Maynard Keynes at Bretton Woods more than 40 years ago, are of vital importance again today.' Keynes, according to an earlier Singer treatise, was the 'real creator' of development economics, having made the important break with the view that economics was 'a universal truth applicable in all countries and in all conditions.'

Singer, who is emeritus professor of economics at Sussex University's Institute of Development Studies, belongs to that small band of practical thinkers who have made that break through their work. One consequence, says Sir Alec Cairncross, who has known him well for half a century or more, is that 'Singer is better known in the developing countries than any other economist.' He is 75 today.

Singer's concern with the Keynes legacy is total and personal; he was Keynes's student at Cambridge in the early 1930s. Where Keynes had underlined the need to create a 'soft' aid mechanism within a United Nations-type framework, Singer has seen the Brandt Commission and its supporters come up with the same idea.

The idea of the need for soft financing for development was born and developed, says Singer, at the same time that studies intensified on global terms of trade, and particularly on how the terms of trade for Third World primary products has steadily deteriorated in relation to First World manufactured exports. If such thinking seems unexceptional today, Singer will say that when he was first promoting its cause, not so long after Bretton Woods, it was branded 'revolutionary and even subversive'. And that was at a time in the US when 'Communist sympathies' could kill a promising career, even in the United Nations.

Singer was for a brief moment accused of just such sympathies, but survived without too much difficulty. He arrived in Britain in 1933, a newly-married Jewish refugee from the first wave of the holocaust, with very little English, ten marks to his name, but a postgraduate scholarship for Cambridge. He came from Bonn University, where Schumpeter, a seminal name in thinking about trade cycles, market forces, and the role of interest, had been his teacher. Cairncross says: 'I took him under my wing.' So, when Cairncross got the second PhD ever to be awarded by Cambridge in economics, Singer got the third. Later, in a street market in Addis Ababa, Singer helped Cairncross. He knew better than the Scotsman how to haggle over prices—and win.

On leaving Cambridge, a contemporary recalls, Singer soaked himself in unemployment. Sponsored by the then Archbishop of York, he went to live, and to study joblessness at first hand, in the depressed areas of Wales, Scotland, Merseyside and Durham. The book, *Men Without Work*, was the result.

The war brought a brief hiccup. Singer, because he was German, was 'locked up' for a month near Liverpool. But it also brought academic distinction; six years at Manchester University and a spell at Glasgow, followed by a period as a Government economist when he helped to draft the 1949 Town and Country Planning Act.

But it was in 1947 that Singer, the pioneer, took off. Finding joblessness was not the issue he expected in postwar Britain, he turned to development, joining the then pocket-sized Economics Department of the new United Nations Organisation. The Third World section employed just two people at the time—but the poverty Singer was now to see, opened his eyes.

'Singer stayed with the UN for 22 years,' says a current Unocrat. 'He played a leading and intellectually creative role at the initiating point of virtually every UN agency. Nobody did it quite like he did. Ideas which are now accepted are ones that he argued and fought for . . .'

He was in at the birth, for instance, of the Special Fund, which led to the UNDP; the World Food Programme; the African Development Bank, and he held senior posts with UNIDO, the UN Institute for Social Development, the Economic Commission for Africa, the UNDP, the ILO . . . Today, says a Sussex colleague, he believes in the UN because he has to; he is one of the few who influenced the way it is today.

On the wider stage, Singer's interests embraced international finance, trade, and associated institutions, almost always with the objective of improving the situation of the poorest. In early UN days, he forecast – when such projections were not fashionable – the coming fall in Third World commodity prices and likely repercussions. Many Third World governments listened to him and respected his advice.

But Singer has grown used to formidable opposition in the UN, in governments, or government departments, and either winning the argument, or quietly and carefully redirecting his energies to a profitable position. He is an adviser to the Labour Party, admits to being Left of centre—though he is certainly no Marxist.

Africa's real need

Djibril Diallo *Published 10 January 1986*

The international community can rightly feel deep satisfaction over having helped Africa avert what threatened to be the worst peacetime tragedy of recent history. The media played a catalytic role in the worldwide mobilisation of concern, graphically portraying not only the agony of the drought-stricken areas but providing extensive coverage of the complexities of underdevelopment and poverty, the underlying causes of famine.

As an African who has frequently visited the affected nations, I can attest to the tremendous sense of gratitude that is felt in even the most isolated African villages whose plight put many of them in contact with Westerners for the first time.

But among the many international accomplishments in alleviating the emergency situation, there has been one lapse which has deeply disappointed Africa. In the millions of words that have been written and thousands of feet of film shot about the crisis, very little can be gleaned regarding the African role and perspective in dealing with the crisis. By focusing on external relief efforts, news stories have incorrectly portrayed Africans as passive bystanders in the midst of a mess of their own making.

Similarly, innumerable Western experts have been quoted on what Africa needs to do if famine is not going to be a permanent part of its landscape. But rarely, if ever, have the media sought the views of African planners, leaders, scholars or public officials, not to mention our agronomists or peasant farmers, in the intense, ongoing debate over the continent's future.

Opinions are thus being formed and the stage being set for the implementation of new plans of action in which Africans themselves have contributed only their assent—the assent, at best, of an unequal partner. This course will result in a new round of policies out of harmony with primary African needs which are likely, once again, to fail.

This lapse in media coverage reflects the long-standing tendency in development and investment circles to treat Africa as a continent unable to formulate effective policies on its own. This perception has, not surprisingly, proliferated in the wake of the inability of Sub-Sahara Africa to feed so many of its people. I have on more than one occasion heard the comment that it is really up to 'us', the outsiders, to go in and 'save' Africa.

Unfortunately, the view that outside experts – some of whom arrive in African capitals with briefcases bulging with solutions for problems they do not fully understand – know what is best has carried considerable weight even in Africa itself. This has led to a readiness to accept guidance from those who do not take into consideration the needs and complexities of our diverse societies and fragile ecologies.

Unlike the early days of independence, many, though not all, African countries possess highly skilled professionals in the major disciplines. Rarely are these experts given the opportunity to play their rightful role in the formulation and execution of national policies in the relief and development arenas.

To say all this is not in any way to minimise the international role in the famine relief effort, which helped save the lives of at least three million Africans last year and which must continue well into 1986 for many countries. Even less is this a call for the international community to offer blind and uncritical support, or indeed to let Africa fend for itself. But, it must be underlined that the only effective solutions to the problems facing the continent are those to which Africans themselves are committed.

Fortunately, there is now a palpable spirit of self-criticism on the continent. Africans are taking a hard look at where we have gone wrong. Many African leaders have resolved to make far-reaching structural changes in their economies, including the introduction of policies designed to rapidly increase food production. To do this they must reach out to their people at the village level as well as the international community.

What Africa needs now is a commitment from the international community to stick by us through the several years needed to recover momentum for development and begin to restore a severely deteriorated environment. It is critical that you consider our needs and let us make these needs our priorities.

Djibril Diallo, a Senegalese national, has been chief of information of the UN Office for Emergency Operations in Africa.

A Final Word on Human Rights . . .

Michael Simmons

This cartoon is taken from a collection of drawings done by prisoners in Turkey. An Exhibition of their work was organised in 1985 by the Istanbul satirical magazine editor, Oguz Aral (see the interview on p. 210). The exhibition proved so extraordinarily popular that Aral organised a book of the work shown, *From Israel With Love*. Proceeds were invested in drawing materials which were sent to the prisons for distribution. But the post-martial law regime in Turkey, concerned that its security services might be shown up in a bad light, pounced on the book in September 1985, and launched an official investigation into its suitability for public consumption.